Lewes at War 1939-1945

by

R A Elliston

By the same author: *Eastbourne's Great War 1914-1918*

Lewes at War 1939-1945
First published by Alma Cott Publications May 1995

This revised edition published 1999

S.B. Publications, 19 Grove Road, Seaford, East Sussex BN25 1TP

© R A Elliston 1995

All rights reserved, no part of this publication may be reproduced, stored in a retrieval system, or transmitted in any form or by any means (electronic, mechanical, photocopying, recording or otherwise) without prior permission of the publisher and copyright owner.

ISBN 1 85770 185 2

Printed by Biddles Ltd, Guildford and King's Lynn

Contents

	Illustrations	4 & 5
	Acknowledgements	5 & 6
	About the book and the author	7
	Dedication	8

Chapters			
	1	Uneasy Peace	9
	2	Forging the Shield	15
	3	Stand To	25
	4	The Young Ones	30
	5	The Air War	43
	6	Enemy Action	52
	7	Law and Order	65
	8	The Fire Services	74
	9	Civil Defence	88
	10	The 16th Sussex Home Guard	100
	11	Fortress Lewes	111
	12	Garrison Town	122
	13	The Military	131
	14	Misadventure	142
	15	The War Effort	154
	16	Victory	177
	17	The Aftermath	188
	18	The Roll of Honour	195
		Bibliography	216
		Appendix	217

Indices		
	Persons	221
	Subjects and Places	224
	Military	227

Cover Design   *David and Heather Elliston*
Front Cover   *Remembrance 1994*   *RA Elliston*
Back Cover   *Lewes at Peace 1994*   *R A Elliston*

Illustrations

Bomb damage in North Street	6
Canadian Honour Guard	8
Armistice Service 1938	10
Six inch gun Naval prison	12
ARP Demonstration room	13
Gas Mask Assembly	15
Nevill Green trenches	16
Mayor's ARP appeal	18
Avro Anson crash	19
ARP Practice	20
ARP advertisement	21
"Evacuees" Mountfield Road	22
ARP Control Room	25
Cinema advertisement	26
Lewes Ration book	27
Glyndebourne evacuees	31
Evacuees Christmas party	34
Shelters Mountfield Road	36
Lewes Army Cadets	38
Victory diggers County School	40
464 Sqd Air Training Corps	41
3200 Sqd Girl's Training Corps	42
Gotha at the Gallops	44
Gotha Pilot	44
Me 109 at Houndean	46
Halifax "K for Kitty Melbourne	48
Halifax "K" for Kitty Landport	49
Dakota at Newmarket	50
Air Raid Alert notice	52
Upended car Dunsford's Garage	53
West Street after raid	56
North Street Salving furniture	57
The Stag after the bombing	58
Remains of 28 New Road	59
Jackson's window before raid	60
Jackson's window after raid	61
Bomb damaged Savings Centre	62
Constable in air raid order	65
Special Constables on parade	66
Observer Corps at Caslte	67
Trailer pump at *Shelleys*	76
AFS wet pump drill at the Pells	77
NFS with Heavy pump	79
Static water tank High Street	80
Fireman's pumping diagram	81
Wheelbarrow pump Town Hall	82
Water cans Sun Street	83
Stirrup pump sign Thomas Street	84
Firemen laying steel pipelines	85
Map of Fire Services	87
St Anne's First Aid post	88
Wardens at Post No 4	90
St John and Red Cross on parade	91
Gas training certificate	92
Stirrup pump practice Southover	94
Surface shelter Pelham Terrace	95
Interior of BCF shelter	96
ARP advertisement (Ruggs)	98
Map of Civil defence services	99
LDV Volunteers Pelham House	100
Lt Col Styles' insignia	102
Lewes "Cossacks"	103
Kingston First Aid team	104
Cup grenade launchers	105
Women's Auxiliary Home Guard	108
Vicker's guns Convent field	109
Home Guard certificate	110
Falmer Hill road block	111
Snowdrop Inn Anti-tank block	112
Rise Farm Pill Box 1940	113
Rise Farm Pillbox 1994	113
School Hill Pill Box	114
Cliffe Bridge anti-tank block	115
Hamilton Bridge Southease	116
Type 22 Pillbox at Prison	118
Map of Fortress Lewes	121
Dispatch riders Albion House	122
Headline Cinemas	123
Albion House canteen staff	124
Ald Crisp at Westgate St canteen	125
WVS mobile canteens Southover	126
Canteen Licence	128
War Wedding at St Thomas à Becket	130
Tank road construction	133
Balsdean Farm Evacuation	134
Kenyon kerbstone memorial	135
US army lorry and NFS parade	139
Blackout shutters at Woolmores	141
Tank accident headline	144
Matilda tanks at Seaford Head	145

War workers Culverwell's	154	"VE" party Waterloo place	179
Servicemen in Forces	155	"VJ" dance Town Hall	181
Lewes prisoner of war	158	"VJ" party Toronto Terrace	182
Women painting Station	161	Victory Day programme	185
Womens Land Army at Plumpton	162	Servicemens scroll	187
Womens Land Army on Parade	163	Demolition of shelters	188
National savings leaflet	165	Shelter into garages	189
HMS *Lewes* off East coast	166	Anderson shelters at Haredean	190
Headline British Restaurant	171	Fireguard watchtower Town Hall	192
Burgess family at War	174	Wardens Post No 8	194
Morrish's Drapers shop	176	Unveiling War Memorial plaques	215
Grange and prisoners of war	178		

Acknowledgements

This book could not have been written without the help of the following, so readily given

The County Archivist and his staff at the Maltings Lewes especially in the search room and the muniments store.
The Editors of the Sussex Express and Evening Argus for permission to publish extracts and photographs from wartime newspapers
The staff of the Maritime Information Centre Greenwich
The staff of the Fleet Air Arm Museum Yeovilton
The staff of the Royal Air Force Museum Hendon
The librarians at the Imperial War Museum London
The librarians at the Fire Service College Morton in Marsh
The searchers at the Commonwealth War Graves Commission Maidenhead.
The Trustees of the Imperial War Museum (IWM) for permission to reproduce photographs
The British Library for permission to use photographs
The Royal Commission on the Historical Monuments of England (RCHME) for use of photographs
The curators of the Royal Engineers Museum Chatham, Royal Corps of Signals Museum Blandford, the South Lancashire Regimental Museum Warrington, the Welch Regimental Museum Cardiff.
U.S. Air Force Historical Research Agency, Maxwell Air Force Base Alabama
East Sussex Library Service Lewes Library and the County Council Estates and Highways Departments
the Archivist Glyndebourne Opera House
Peter Bailey Newhaven Local and Maritime Museum
Pat Burgess Tangmere Aeronautical Museum
Mrs R Hedger for help with Home Guard photographs and information from Lt Col Styles' diaries.
Mr Cayton Bannister and Colonel M Foster for help with Military Bridges

Residents of Lewes past and present for information and photographs:-

George Baxter, Mr B G Beck, Rowena Bingham, Maurice Breese, Richard Brickell, Geoff Bridger, Hilary Bristoll, Fred Burgess, Rex Carter, Joy Carvill, Mr E J Cosham, Les and Cath Davey, Mr T J Dumbrell, Brenda Fletcher, Lucy Fuller, Marion Fuller, Brian Funnell, Ken Funnell, Mike Green, Ray Hallett, Ron Hoad, Mr and Mrs P Horrocks, Mary Hurst, Frank Jacobs, Miss Kidgell, Peter Longstaffe-Tyrrell, Michel Lorec, Miss J Petrie, Richard Philcox, Mrs Edna Piper, Daphne Robinson, Sidney Staffel, Phyllis Stegall, Ian Sutherland, Bob and Jean Thomas, Colin Thompsett, Bob Towner, Graham White, Fran Whittle, continued

Bill Williams, Rendall Williams, Ruth Woakes, Ivor Wycherley. My sincere apologies to anyone who has helped in any way and is not mentioned.

Appreciation is recorded for the specialised help given by Keith Fuller, Roy Fuller, John and Shirley Geering, John Tillstone, Tony Whittington and for the cartography of Susan Rowland. To Edward Reeves for permission to reproduce photographs, to Dr Alfred Price for consent to the use of an extract from "Battle of Britain 18th August 1940 The Hardest Day". To Mr R V Kyrke for permission to quote from his "History of the Sussex Police Force", and Les Davey for encouragement along the way, for reference to his "History of the Lewes Fire Service" and for veryifying some of the Lewes detail.

Special acknowledgement is due to my daughter Jane Armstrong for the foundation work on the Roll of Honour, for coaching in word processing and proof reading, to her husband Nick for second proof reading and preventing my worst electronic misdemeanours, to my daughter Ruth Rowland for continuing encouragement and proof reading, to her husband Nick , for rescuing me from computer "crashes" and tidying up floppy disks, to my son David for help with aircraft, to my eldest son John and his wife Donna, for newspaper references, also to my wife, Doreen for her researches especially with the Roll of Honour and the rest of my family who have "lived" the book for the past three years.

Bob Elliston   Eastbourne

Mathematical Tiles fall to the bomb blast in North Street 20-1-43 *RCHME*

About the Book

On the occasion of the 50th anniversary of "VE" Day what could be more appropriate than the publication of a book to remind today's Lewesian of the way things were during the dark days of the Second World War. Painstaking research has enabled Bob Elliston to compile a comprehensive record of Lewes during 1939-1945. His work is chronicled in a series of narratives each recorded with meticulous care.

Memories are merged with military, civil defence and civilian facts and activities. Whatever this uncannily detailed account may have achieved, its significance cannot be denied. Can any other small county town claim to possess such a comprehensive and authoritative record of its history during those turbulent years. For some of his readers the book will revive memories that may have faded with the passing of time. Those called for service overseas can now learn for the first time what actually happened back home.

Had Hitler not been forced to abandon his invasion plans the town would have found itself in the front line of warfare. Lewes never suffered a sustained attack although it was under the flight path of planes heading inland. "Hit and Run" raids and jettisoned bombs from retreating aircraft, did, alas cause casualties and much damage.

The Roll of Honour gives the circumstances of each individual's sacrifice, which is now recorded for posterity in a spirit of remembrance, adding to the inscriptions on the Lewes War Memorials.

L S Davey

About the Author

R A (Bob) Elliston is a Brightonian who attended Pells and Mountfield Road Senior Boys' Schools followed by Brighton Technical College. He spent his younger days in wartime Lewes. After a lifetime in hospital pathology he took early retirement from the Eastbourne Health District Laboratories as Chief Medical Laboratory Scientific Officer in 1982. Since then his interests have centred on local history and in particular the recent history of Lewes.

DEDICATION

This record has been prepared for the fiftieth anniversary of the ending of the Second World War, in Europe on 8th May and in the Far East on 14th August 1945. It is dedicated to all those Lewesians, men and women, who served their country in the town and away from it both in England and abroad. Also remembered will be the many servicemen and women who came to the town from elsewhere especially those from Canada, and all those who, through the supreme sacrifice, did not return to their homes.

Edward Reeves
Canadian Infantry form the honour guard to the Assize Judge, St Michael's Church 1941

1. An Uneasy Peace

Lewesians paid homage to those who had given their lives in service of the country in The Great War on Wednesday 6th September 1922, when General Sir Henry Sclater unveiled the War Memorial at the top of School Hill. The Memorial lists 236 members of the armed services who had fallen in the war. In common with most inscriptions on Memorials the list of names is not definitive. Names were included by public invitation. Some names were not notified to the memorial committee, while it was acknowledged that other names arrived too late to be included. Those who mourned and those who paid tribute at this service could not have comprehended that in just under 21 years time similar sacrifices would again be called for.

The Great War of 1914-1918 was one that had produced casualties on a scale never before suffered by the nation in war. It was therefore acknowledged to be "The War to End Wars" these feelings reflected the interest in setting up the League of Nations in 1920 following the ratification of the Versailles Peace Treaty in the same year. These two events may be recognised by historians as essential ingredients for World War Two (WW2) which followed from 1939-1945. The League of Nations excluded the vanquished countries, Germany, Austria, and Turkey. Italy and Japan were among the victorious allies but were to be on the side of Germany in WW2. Russia having embarked on a revolutionary course was also left out and the United States of America isolated itself from Europe's problems and opted out of the League. The authority of the League was flouted first in 1922 when Greece declared war on Turkey ending the next year with defeat for Greece.

From 1919 Lewes strove to bring about improvements, the progress of which had been halted by the war. Gas and electric street lights were restored after wartime restrictions. The first twenty Council houses were built on the Nevill Estate. The Pells was given to the town, while some roads in Lewes still awaited tarmac surfaces for the first time. In the mid-thirties plans for a combined Senior Boys' and Girls' School at Malling were turned down at a Public Enquiry. The school relocated in Mountfield Road. Slum clearance programmes started. Electric train services from London and along the coast commenced in 1934. Escape from reality was provided by the enlarged Cinema de Luxe now with a balcony and by the new arena type Odeon Cinema in the Cliffe.

Lewes accurately mirrored the mood of the nation during the inter-war years. From 1920 there had been a rapid demobilization of the armed forces and a run down of the defences of the country. It was appreciated that England was vulnerable to air attack, demonstrated effectively by Zeppelin and aircraft attacks on London and East Coast Towns in 1916. In 1924 a secret subcommittee of the Imperial Defence Committee was established to plan air raid precautions. The following year an Observer Corps was created with the observers being enrolled as Special Constables. Control of the Observers Corps was vested in the Chief Constable. The Lewes post Numbered M1 was located on Brack Mount and reported to a control centre at Horsham.

Timetable of Aggression 1

1926	Allied occupation armies leave the Rhineland
1932	Japan annexes Manchuria
1935	Germany reoccupies the Saar
1935	Italy conquers Abyssinia despite League of Nations sanctions
1936	Germany remilitarises the Rhineland contrary to the Versailles Treaty
1936	Spanish Civil War a proving ground for German, Italian and Russian forces
1937	"China Incident" Japan invades China
1938	Germany annexes Austria
1938	September, Munich agreement gives Hitler Sudeten Czechoslovakia
1939	March, Germany occupies rest of Czechoslovakia breaking Munich agreement
1939	April, Italy occupies Albania
1939	May, Anglo-French guarantee to Poland
1939	23rd August, Russo-German non aggression pact
1939	1st September, Germany invades Poland
1939	3rd September, Britain and France declare war on Germany
1939	16th September, Russia invades Eastern Poland

The last pre-war Armistice Service Friday 11th November 1938   *Sussex Daily News*

The Peace Movement

Against this darkening background, England continued a pathway of arms limitation but later, reluctantly started to rearm, ever hopeful that sense and diplomacy would prevail. In November 1934 at the Lewes Branch of the League of Nations meeting in the Corn Exchange a verbal confrontation occurred between the Rev Kenneth Rawlings of St Michael's who took a pacifist viewpoint and the Rev C Ensell of St Anne's, who took an opposing stance. The meeting eventually being called to order by the Mayor Councillor (Clr) Kenward. Such was the interest in the meeting that many would be attenders could not get in.

One of the protagonists, the Rev Ensell, had served in the Boer War and in France from 1914-17 where he had taken up a post in the Chaplaincy. Those who knew the Rev Rawlings well understood his sincerity borne of World War 1 experiences in the RAMC in 1914-15. Afterwards he served as a Lieutenant in the Lancs and Yorks Regiment during 1916-17. This finally led to his being invalided out of the army. He and a friend were curates in the Birmingham Diocese in 1914 and were refused permission by their bishop to become chaplains. Both curates resigned Holy Orders and enlisted in the army. Kenneth Rawlings survived but his friend did not.

A genuine and positive "Peace Movement" had now appeared in Lewes. The Rev Rawlings refused a request to allow St Michael's Parish Room to be used for Anti-Gas Training in April 1936. The Rev Rawlings was unswerving in his devotion to peace. As the war progressed he admitted that his congregations and offertories had decreased, yet he continued to organise petitions against the area bombing of Germany. When in February 1944 Bishop Bell of Chichester spoke in the House of Lords about the air offensive against Germany a member of the House of Commons Mr P Purbrook, member for Walton Liverpool, asked the Home Secretary if he would detain the Rev Rawlings, under Defence Regulation 18b, for subversive activities.

Three months later a Peace Rally took place in Railway Field, Mountfield Road, addressed by the Rev Dick Shepherd of St Martins-in-the-Fields London and Mr George Lansbury, Labour politician and devout Christian, who, in 1937 made a fruitless peace mission to Hitler. Also in October 1936 Clr Miss Fowler-Tutt a former Central School teacher is reported to have expressed admiration for Hitler's Nazism at a meeting of the Lewes Society for the Study of Religions while, on 13th November, the Fellowship for Reconciliation was addressed on the subject "Soldiers Cannot be Christians". An alternate view was provided by the Bonfire Societies who burnt effigies of Hitler in 1933 and Mussolini in 1935!

Re-Armament

The portents of war appeared more clearly as the thirties progressed. Nationally in 1931 only 27% of the available anti-aircraft guns and 22% of searchlights could be manned. Of the 52 Fighter Squadrons deemed necessary to give a creditable air defence, by 1932 only 17 were in being. Fighter Squadrons became a resignation issue during the 1940 Battle of France. Air Chief Marshal Sir Hugh Dowding protested over sending more fighters to France. Out of 36 squadrons left in England in late May, Dowding was asked to send 10 more to France. Of the 261 planes sent only 66 returned. Such was our unpreparedness for what was to follow.

In Lewes the Observer Corps post was now moved from Brack Mount to the Castle Keep. RAF activities aroused the public interest with flying displays at Hendon Aerodrome. Air exercises took place over southern England that brought about a spate of accidents. In January 1938 a mid-air collision at 4,000 feet took place over Ridgewood between two planes flying from Hornchurch. Sgt Pilot G Gaskell lost his life but Pilot Officer Roland Stanford Tuck, later a decorated Battle of Britain pilot, was able to parachute to safety. The next month Ringmer was the site of an upside down landing of a training biplane flown by Pilot Officer Saunders who escaped unhurt. In February 1938 an RAF Hawker Fury of No 1 Squadron on a flight from Tangmere hit power cables at Brakey Bottom, Blackcap, Pilot Officer M V Baxter being killed. On 17th January 1939 an Avro Anson flying from Thorney Island on a naval co-operation exercise crashed in mist on Kingston Hill, the injured crew being taken to the Royal Sussex County Hospital Brighton. Pilot Officer Mills of No 3 Fighter Squadron Kenley crashed his Gloucester Gladiator biplane at Alfriston and was killed in February 1939. Two months later one of a flight of three RAFVR planes en route for Shoreham from Gravesend crashed at Streat killing Sgt William Read of Tunbridge Wells.

Six inch gun for the TA arriving at the old Naval Prison 4th March 1938 *Sussex Express*

Lewes had always supported the Territorial Army with a Company of the 5th Cinque Ports Battalion of the Royal Sussex Regiment meeting in the corrugated iron Drill Hall in Mountfield Road now appropriately the site of Royal Sussex Court. The old Naval Prison in Lancaster Street gave a home to the 159th Battery (Sussex) Royal Artillery and to the 210th Field Company Royal Engineers. During the interwar years pre-service youth organisations did not have units in the town although there were a number of Scout Troops and Cub Packs, Guides and Brownies. The 1st Lewes Scouts and Cubs met in the Naval Prison. In March 1931 it was proposed to build a rifle range at the Cement Works to supplement the rifle butts at Oxteddle Bottom, Southerham. In March 1938 a team of regular soldiers from Woolwich installed a six inch gun weighing seven and a half tons in the Naval Prison for 159th Battery RA to practise on. The installation took eight and a half-hours to complete. No record exists of the date or man hours taken to remove it after the fall of France and install it at Newhaven in the summer of 1940 but the invasion threat injected urgency into the move.

Air Raid Precautions

July 1935 saw the arrival of the first Home Office Circular in Lewes on air raid precautions (ARP) but the town like the nation was preoccupied with National events. May 1935 was the occasion of the Silver Jubilee of King George V, sadly followed by his death in January 1936. Edward VIII abdicated in December 1936 and in May 1937 King George VI was crowned. Times for sadness and rejoicing, anodynes for the threatening international scene.

By 1936 the Government had accepted that war was inevitable, the time for disarmament was over, and while pursuing a policy of negotiation to avoid war some preparations were essential. The first circular on the air raid precautions had been issued to local authorities on 24th July 1935. In April 1936 the St John Ambulance Brigade in Lewes started anti-gas training with three members gaining ARP Instructor's Certificates in October. The following month Major Sutton addressed the Rotary Club on the subject of ARP. The East Sussex County Council, on 16th December 1936, took over the empty Watford's Butcher shop, vacated along with Shaw's shop at Cliffe Corner for road improvements, and set up an ARP demonstration room fitted out to show residents how to improvise a splinter and gas proof refuge room.

ARP Demonstration Rooms Cliffe Corner 1st September 1938　　　　　　　　　　*RCHME*

A Home Office Inspection carried out in Lewes on 2nd November 1937 reported that nothing much had been done in the town to implement the department's circular on Civil Defence. In May 1937 proposals were made to accommodate 500 persons in the cellars under the Corn Exchange. This could have been a popular venue as Findlater's Wine and Spirits stores were also housed there. In June a permanent ARP sub-committee of the Town Council was formed. Two months later in August 1937 it was reported that the County Council was taking an interest in ARP. Lewes turned down the idea of appointing a full time ARP Officer at £5 per week in October. In November Col Fooks ARP Officer for the County Council said that two "Air Raid Stations" would be needed for the town one in the Cliffe and one on the Race Hill. The exact nature of the "Stations" was not specified. Lt Col P O Stewart Hon ARP Organiser for Chailey Rural District Council stated that a big hospital for Lewes would be a mistake as Lewes being a railway hub would be bound to be bombed. The reason behind this observation is unclear, bombing which produced casualties would make adequate hospital facilities essential. Was it perhaps a defeatist acceptance of the obliteration of the town?

On 25th March 1938 the MP for Lewes, Admiral Tufton Beamish, in a speech defended our (England's) interest over "The Rape of Austria". On 20th May it was announced that Baxter's the Printers would be the first firm to install bomb and gasproof shelters for its staff. A week later the Lewes Co-operative Society reported that a bombproof food store had been constructed in their cellars. Small boys in those pre-war years would collect and exchange cigarette cards. Players produced a set in 1938 entitled "Aircraft of The RAF" while the Wills company sought to capture the interest of adults with a fifty-card series on "Air Raid Precautions". In 1939 Players kept patriotism up with sets of cards of "Uniforms of the Territorial Army" and "Modern Naval Craft".

In September 1938 the "Munich Crisis" developed. Hitler looked at his next conquest Czechoslovakia. A hastily convened conference arranged by the Italian dictator Mussolini attended by M Daladier of France and Mr Neville Chamberlain resulted in the "Peace in Our Time" agreement by which Hitler was given Czech Sudetenland, the German speaking border regions that contained an impressive series of fixed defences. The country was now emasculated and an easy prey for complete occupation the following March, which gave Hitler a significant stock of tanks and a heavy armaments industry. Another war was now inevitable.

****

2. Forging the Shield

Much Council thinking like that of the National Government was dominated by an ingrained habit of frugality. This was particularly evident in all the preparations for Civil Defence, a more positive name eventually given to ARP activities. Such local habits were untempered by the knowledge that these expenditures were extensively grant aided and little cost would accrue directly to the town.

In January 1938 it was reported to the Town Council that Mr W Barsby, a former member of the Royal Army Medical Corps, had been appointed Air Raid Precautions Officer at a salary of £5 per week. Later, in July, it was decided to purchase a second hand car to enable him to discharge his duties more effectively. £20 was voted for this purpose, a further £3:12:3 pence (£3.60) was agreed for the purchase of 12 maps of the Borough for ARP purposes, one of which survives today at the East Sussex Record Office (ESRO).

The Gas Masks

During April a team of lady volunteers had been assembling the first batch of civilian gas masks and sewing on name tapes of the residents who had been visited by ARP Wardens to take fitting details. There were three sizes of respirator or gas mask, large, medium or small for adults and older children. Younger children had a Mickey Mouse pattern in red and blue while infants were almost wholly enclosed in a bellows operated respirator.

Marion Fuller Sussex Express
Chief Fire Officer George Carter and Borough Treasurer Mr C T Brown assemble gas masks 30.9.38

Up to the beginning of September 1938, the time of the Munich crisis, the assembly team had completed 700 gas masks! The masks once labelled with the residents' names were to be stored centrally until needed. With 12,000 people living in the town, the impracticality of such an arrangement defies comprehension. Two plain green vans bearing Home Office markings were reported outside the Fitzroy Library on the 9th September unloading cartons each containing 50 gas mask kits. These were shelved on the top floor of the library, in all 11,000 being received.

At the height of the Munich Crisis a team of Council employees and volunteers had assembled 11,000 Gas Masks and 90% of these were delivered in one evening. A loudspeaker van toured the town asking residents to stay indoors from 6.00 pm to receive the masks. The task was completed within seven and a half hours. Once the war started, masks were supposed to be carried always when out of doors. To carry them 5,000 individual cardboard boxes with a sling had been ordered in October at a total cost of £81. The boxes very quickly disintegrated and commercially available carriers were soon in demand.

Munich Before and After

Digging air raid shelter trenches Nevill Green September 1938   *Sussex Daily News*

In March 1938 there were 45 volunteers signed up for various ARP duties, by May the number had reached 309. Mrs Cheale offered the Cliffe Rectory at 21 Malling Street as a shelter for 50 persons. Two first aid posts had been set up, one at Cliffe Church Hall, and the other at St Anne's Parish Rooms using the Scout Hall, together costing £583. An approach from Chailey Rural District Council regarding help for rural areas from Lewes ARP received a negative response. Consideration was given to using the Boys' and Girls' County Secondary Schools as first aid posts. In June Mr Barsby ARP Officer was offered a better post elsewhere and 28 applications were received for the post. Gas protection demonstrations at the Cliffe had cost £19 and the total cost of ARP so far had been £134. Application to the Home Office was made in October for a clerical assistant at 25/- per week, five trailer pumps, extra hoses, and 50 pairs of Wellington boots.

The Munich Crisis at the end of September 1938 was undoubtedly a watershed. Much more needed to be done in the town to protect the inhabitants. The Mayor, Alderman (Ald) E T Hall, convened a Public Meeting in the Town Hall on 21st October when over 800 people tried to get in, the overflow being accommodated in the Corn Exchange. The Munich Crisis had concentrated the minds of the townspeople on the need for action.

Mr W R S Johnston the Chief Air Raid Precautions Officer reported to the meeting that after three years of preparation they had not got very far with the arrangements. The main perceived danger was not from gas attack but from high explosive blast and incendiary bombs starting multiple fires. The town was only one quarter prepared for a war. An air raid siren had been ordered and until it was installed, Every's Phoenix Ironwork's hooter would sound a wailing note in case of an air raid. This would have been impossible with the single pitched note of the Ironwork's steam hooter. This warning would be supplemented with rattles and handbells these were reserved for "Poison Gas Attack" and "All Clear of Gas" signals.

Two gas decontamination stations had been planned, one at the Corporation Yard in North Street, the other to be at the Old Brewery in Malling Street. North Street was to be ninety by thirty feet and could be capable of decontaminating 150 persons in two hours. These stations were essentially shower baths with changing rooms on each side of the showers, contaminated clothing being retained on the inward side for reissue after treatment at Mann's Dry Cleaning works in Lansdown Place. On the outgoing side casualties would be issued with spare clean clothing. There were separate facilities for both sexes.

Two trailer pumps were on their way, which meant that like the siren, an order had been placed and delivery was awaited. Trenches had been dug at Nevill Green, Bell Lane Recreation Ground, the old Southdown Brewery in Malling Street, the Castle Green and at the Wallands. The meeting was also presented with the latest ARP recruiting position. Figures in brackets show the required strength. Auxiliary fireman 20 (60) first aiders 100 (150) wardens 250 (400) vehicles/drivers 70 (120) messengers 20 (150). It was expected that the messengers would come from youth organisations. Also 35 gas mask fitters were still needed.

Lewes was considered a safe area and designated to receive evacuees from London. These would be school children, children under school age accompanied by mothers, expectant mothers and registered blind persons. The Council were given few details of these proposals in advance except that on the first day of an emergency evacuation fourteen trains would arrive at Lewes. There would be a further five on the second day bringing in all 14,000 evacuees, 6,500 for the town the rest for the rural areas. Quite rightly the Council protested to the Home Office about the lack of time for preparation and information about the scheme.

On the 6th October the Mayor Ald E T Hall expressed his thanks in Council for the support that had been forthcoming in the recent National Emergency (Munich Crisis) and said he would be sending a letter to every home in the town calling for more volunteers for ARP. By December the number of ARP volunteers had reached 705 men and women. An electrical siren had been installed on the Town Hall chimney stack at a cost of £18.

LEWES
Inspected 23.10.39.

BOROUGH OF LEWES

Town Hall,
Lewes.

Dear Sir or Madam,

AIR RAID PRECAUTIONS.

The Home Office has issued instructions for the preparation of schemes for safeguarding the Civil Population against attacks from the air. The need for them does not arise from the belief that war is imminent, but because the risk, however remote it may be, cannot be ignored. Preparations to minimise the consequences of such an attack cannot be improvised on the spur of the moment; if they are to be effective, they must be made before the emergency occurs.

Accordingly, provision must be made for the treatment of casualties, rescue work, demolition of unsafe buildings, gas decontamination, repair of damaged roads, air raid wardens, fire fighting organisations, etc.

The first essential step is to obtain a large number of voluntary helpers for the following services :—

MEN.—Air raid wardens; demolition works; rescue services; auxiliary firemen; first-aid duties; gas decontamination duties; ambulance duties; messengers.

WOMEN.—First-aid duties; gas decontamination duties; ambulance duties.

The duties of air raid wardens when manning their posts may be summarised as follows :—

Where local A.R.P. services are to be found.

Advise persons in streets where to find nearest shelter.

Report fall of bombs, fires, presence of gas, and damage done.

Distribution of respirators.

Enlighten police, fire brigade, first-aid parties, etc., on arrival.

Nerve, be an example of coolness and steadiness thus reducing the risk of panic and loss of morale.

Local classes of instruction in anti-gas and first-aid have been arranged for any person undertaking any duty which makes such knowledge desirable or essential.

The Air Raid Precautions Committee appeal for your co-operation and assistance, and to enable them to verify and revise previous lists, also to obtain further names, they ask you to complete this " business reply card " within the next SEVEN DAYS.

The Secretary of State has instituted a badge for distribution to persons who volunteer for air raid precautions services and who undergo the necessary training.

Yours faithfully,

Ernest T. Hall

MAYOR.

The Mayor Ald E T Hall's appeal for ARP Volunteers 1938   **ESRO A3/65**

Avro Anson crash at Kingston Ridge 17th January 1939   *Edward Reeves*

The air raid trenches dug at the time of Munich were now filled in. It was stated however that it would take but a few days to reopen them. The old British National School in Lancaster Street, latterly the Practical Instruction Centre for woodwork and domestic subjects for elementary schoolboys and girls, and now due for demolition, was given a reprieve as a possible gas decontamination centre but eventually became a Civil Defence store. In the early part of the war the building was used as a store for the NAAFI (Navy, Army and Air Force Institutes) a worldwide government sponsored canteen for service men and women. Other measures considered were the possible use of Cliffe Cut and sewers as emergency fire fighting water supplies. Stretcher fittings were purchased for Council and contractors lorries and fire hydrants were to be edged with luminous paint. Telephone lines were to be laid to both the first aid posts but telephones were not to be installed at present. The nine cast iron red painted fire alarm posts in various parts of the town, the most remembered one being on the west side of the Town Hall entrance, were to be fitted to take plug in telephones.

Countdown to War 1939

January

In January 1939, The Mayor Ald E T Hall made an appeal for families to register to take in evacuees. This was reinforced by an appeal in the local schools. Approval was given for the floodlighting of the Fire Brigade practice tower at the North Street Fire Station. The newly fitted siren on the Town Hall was tested and found to have an effective range of one mile but in prevailing westerly winds could not be heard at St Anne's nor on the Nevill Estate. Later in the month Captain R B Newson was appointed Billeting Officer for evacuees with Miss E W Foster as Honorary Assistant. A survey of homes for the reception of evacuees would start on the 8th February after a Public Meeting called for the previous evening by the Mayor at the Town Hall.

February

It was reported that Mr W Johnston the ARP Officer had constructed a gas and splinter proof shelter in his garden at his home in South Way at a cost of £8. An ARP test was planned for the town on the 20th of February. During the test three RAF biplanes flew over the town at 300 mph! Siren tests of the "Alert" and "All Clear" were carried out. The Town Hall Sub-Control room was staffed. All components of the ARP services turned out, messengers, first aid parties, decontamination teams, rescue and demolition squads, fire and ambulance services. The Assembly Room at the Town Hall was fitted up as a hospital with twelve beds. Houses under demolition in Morris Road provided a realistic site for the rescue of casualties.

Nevill Crescent had "six casualties" caused by AA shrapnel, "three cases" of gas burns were dealt with at the Bastion, Kingsley Road and "three people were hurt" by "high explosive bombs" (HE) at the Railway Station. A sign outside County Hall proclaimed that it had been "bombed." The mock up casualties

ARP Practice February 1939 *Sussex Express*

caused some conflict when a burns case was presented to the first aiders who claimed they had not been trained for this. They were then told to get on and treat a broken arm by the supervising Medical Officer. Further consternation was caused when wardens were reproached for not telling the Railway Station and Gasworks that bombs had fallen there. The wardens concluded that if it was a real raid the staff at those places would have certainly been aware of what had happened!

Protests were made by some members of the local clergy that not only had the test taken place on a Sunday but it had occurred during the hours of worship. The peace lobby persisted with the Rev Kenneth Rawlings drawing attention to the need to have an all nations peace conference. The retiring President at the Lewes and District Teachers' Association said that any state money available was being spent on armaments rather than education.

March

In March the Council agreed to let the Women's Voluntary Service (WVS) have the use of a room in the Town Hall and the same month authorised the purchase of £500 worth of curved corrugated iron for use in constructing Anderson pattern domestic garden air raid shelters.

Sir George Courthope in a speech entitled "By Jingo if we Fight" dealt with National Service and problems with recruiting and the apathy towards preparedness created by reserved occupations. Agricultural workers were often exempted from the pre-war conscription of men for the army.

An additional siren was fitted at the civil prison during the month. Seven extra trailer pumps had been ordered, with 36,000 sandbags and fifty cubic yards of sand. A further thirteen stirrup pumps, for dealing with incendiary bombs, based on the "Mysto" hand operated garden spray, along with rattles, whistles and notebooks had been purchased. Concern was expressed at the number of withdrawals of volunteers from the ARP service attributed to a lack of equipment.

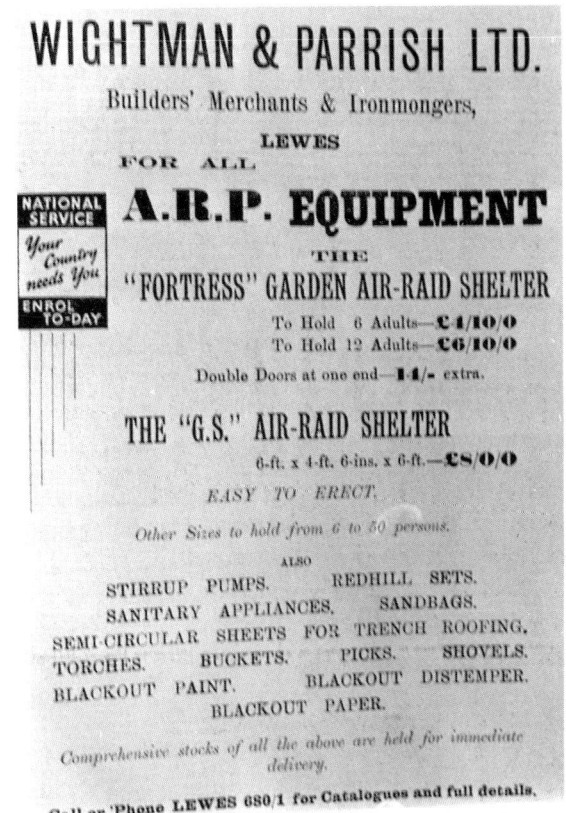

ARP Advertisement 1939 *East Sussex News*

April

The East Sussex Constabulary on the 4th of the month increased its establishment by five Sergeants and one Inspector to cover duties in connection with the issue of air raid warnings and control of ARP services. A proposal by the Borough Surveyor to excavate a tunnel under Cliffe Hill as an air raid shelter was turned down by the Home Office.

Two owners of premises had refused permission for them to be used for wardens' posts and consideration was given to requisitioning them. Meanwhile the Military Service Act had come into force which permitted conscription of young men for compulsory military service with the first call up taking place on the 3rd June 1939. The conscripts or militiamen registering in Sussex totalled 2,641. It was reported that there were few objectors on conscientious grounds.

May

In May opposition came from Lewes Town Council to the proposal that the Police should control the ARP services of the town.

June

On the 11th June Lewes had a trial blackout from 10.00 pm until 2.00 am,* street lights were turned off and all vehicle lights screened. The Home Office would be asked if the few steel helmets in stock could be issued. Four incendiary bombs were to be obtained for demonstration purposes but would have to be collected from Woolwich Arsenal by the ARP officer. A lunch time demonstration of how to use a stirrup pump on an incendiary bomb, supervised by a Police Sergeant, took place later that month in the yard of the Fisher Street Forge. A meeting of Chief Fire Officers at Brighton reaffirmed that the Auxiliary Fire Service (AFS) was under the respective Chief Fire Officers' control and not under the Warden Service. June also saw the establishment of an evacuation committee, under the chairmanship of the Mayor Ald C D Crisp. It included Dr Dunstan, Medical Officer of Health. Church workers and the Women's Voluntary Service (WVS) completed the team to make the necessary arrangements to enable Lewes to function as a reception area for 2,400 evacuees from London.

Pupils of Mountfield Road School welcome "evacuees" June 1939   *By permission of The British Library*

* In the book the 12 hour clock is used for civilian times, the 24 hour clock for service times.

On Saturday 17th June the London Daily Sketch as part of a patriotic series ran a centre spread on what the evacuees would experience. Lewes was chosen as the town for thirteen pictures that included Council Officials making arrangements, and a typical home in the country where they would be billeted - Ashcombe Manor! A staged welcome for evacuees was provided for the photographer by boys and girls at Mountfield Road School with Miss Flight and Mr Bowley, head teachers, in centre stage.

The government had decentralised its most important departments to 12 Regional Headquarters. That for the South East which included Lewes was located at *"Ledbury"* Mount Ephraim Tunbridge Wells with Sir Auckland Geddes as Regional Commissioner. In June he urged better education of the public in ARP and commended a series of leaflets, 1.What to do if War Comes, 2. Your Gas Mask & Masking your Windows, 3. Evacuation Why and How, 4. Your Food in Wartime.

The Rural Dean Canon Griffiths used the Aubers Ridge memorial service commemorating the sacrifice of the Royal Sussex Regiment in the Great War to urge support for National Service. On the 10th June the Rev K Rawlings attended a mass meeting of clergymen organised by the Peace Pledge Union at Kingsway Hall London. A resolution was passed calling for a conference of all nations on disarmament.

July

Recruiting for the Territorial Army continued apace with the aim to increase the units in East Sussex by 5,000 men. Colonel Powell Edwards, who later was to found the Local Defence Volunteers (LDV), suggested that professional and amateur cricketers should form a unit, an idea popular in the Great War. By July the TA strength had risen threefold in the past twelve months. The increase since May 1938 being 2,283. The County National Service Committee called for a further 1,200 "Terriers" (Territorials), the goal was to increase the enlistment target from 3,900 to 7,000 in East Sussex.

On Sunday 9th July another ARP exercise was staged with a "Plane Crash" on the roof of the Town Hall. HE bombs fell at St Mary's Hall Highdown Road, St Anne's Crescent, Middle Way, Rotten Row, Westgate Street, Abinger Place, Prince Edward's Road and Southover Road. First Aid Posts were set up at Landport and Winterborne Hollow. Gas decontamination of casualties was carried out at St Nicholas Lane and Western Road. The ARP services had no prior warning of the incidents.

A blackout test followed that evening with traffic signals screened. Lewes had just two sets at Fisher Street and at Library Corner at the foot of School Hill. Homes were to be blacked out so that no glimmer of light showed. Shop display window lights and neon signs were extinguished. Lewes and District Electrical Supply Company assured residents that power would not be cut off during the blackout.

Just five weeks before the outbreak of war the full Council Meeting refused to sanction the Education subcommittee's decision to spend £2,700 on air raid shelters for the Junior and Senior Elementary schools. Instead it decided to allow £1,500 to be spent stockpiling the materials. The outcome of this decision was that the restart of schools after the August holidays was delayed, because shelters were not ready, with other reasons contributing as well. The shelters were constructed in haste and as a result they leaked like sieves especially those at Mountfield Road Senior School and in the following years extra funds were required to try to waterproof them.

August

Two captured field guns from the Great War that had originally been displayed chained to the lamp standard at the top of School Hill where the War Memorial now stands, and had subsequently languished in the Corporation Yard at North Street, were disposed of and the space reserved for a shed to hold the two new AFS trailer pumps that had arrived in February. These had stood in the open for six months.

Another trial blackout for two nights was enforced from 8.00 pm on the 9th August to 7.00 am on the 11th. By this time 51 AFS men had completed their training. Wet drills often took place on St John's Hill with the suction hose of a trailer pump drawing water from the Pells and a branch jet of water arcing up the hill wetting many of the youthful crowds of sightseers.

Amid all the international gloom a diversion was in store for the residents of the town. The "Sussex Express" together with local traders organised a "Spot It" competition open to those over 16 years of age, this much to the annoyance of those under age who formed themselves into groups of observers for older members of the family. The participating traders placed an object in their window display that was not normally sold by the shop. Competitors filled in an entry form from the newspaper with the most correct answers gaining a £5 voucher, about two weeks pay for the average man, to spend in the shop of their choice. The competition ran from the 19th August to the 2nd September. War did not stop the award for on the 8th September it was announced that there were two joint winners to share 1st and 2nd prizes, Mrs E Hancock of Market Street and Miss Biddlesden of the High Street.

On the 25th August mobilisation notices arrived for key service reservists. The muniments room in the basement of Pelham House had been cleared for use as a County Control Room for ARP purposes and fully manned from that date. Ald Crisp was designated sub-controller of the Lewes ARP Services and the Observer Corps manned the post on the Castle Keep. Traffic signals were permanently masked and neon signs switched off. During the week piles of sand had been delivered to strategic sites in the town - Cliffe Corner, County Hall, St Anne's Crescent and Edward Street for the Police Station. Volunteers of all ages filled sandbags to protect vital points. On Friday 1st September the territorial army units mustered at Mountfield Road Drill Hall and the Old Naval Prison. The Lancaster Street entrance to the prison sported a line of army transport, most of it early vintage 6 x 4 Albions and by the next day they had gone to war.

September

On Friday the 1st at 9.50 am the first trainload of evacuees arrived. Voluntary workers including local teachers met the trains. Air raid trench digging started on Saturday the 2nd at the schools. They would reopen as soon as work on the trenches was well advanced. The next day Lewes would be at war.

3. Stand To

"Stand To" is a military term used to describe the readiness of defenders of a position to repel an attack in the hour before dawn. It might describe the period of the war between the 3rd September 1939 and the German invasion of Denmark and Norway on the 9th April 1940. The term "Phoney War" is often used but to the RAF men making bombing raids on German naval ports and to men of the Royal and Merchant Navies facing death at sea, war was all too real. The first Lewes casualty of the war was suffered when Boy Seaman William Dunk was lost in the torpedoing of the battleship HMS *Royal Oak* on the 14th October. Two Lewes women had fianceés among the 175 men on HMS *Exmouth*, a 1,450-ton Destroyer flotilla leader lost in the North Sea in January 1940 due to mining. On Sunday the 3rd September 1939 Churches in the town had arranged for worshippers to be informed of the Prime Minister, Mr Neville Chamberlain's 11.00 am speech on the radio. Few will forget those fateful words delivered in a voice of a man wearied by his efforts to avert war and in failing health. An ultimatum had been given to Germany to give an undertaking to cease warlike actions against Poland by 11.00 am but, quoting the end of the Prime Minister's speech, "I regret to tell you that no such undertaking has been received and we are therefore now at war with Germany".

ARP Control room 1939 Lt to Rt W R S Johnston, Ald Crisp and F C Russell   *L Davey*

At St John-sub-Castro, the Parish Clerk Miss H Sandles who had listened to her radio, at home 2 Church Row, hurried into the church to give the Rev H E Langhorne the news, which he announced from the pulpit. As he spoke the first air raid warning was sounding, sending ARP services hastening to their war stations. One of Burchett's contractors lorries passed the church at speed carrying men wearing steel helmets, waterproofs and with gas masks on, they were AFS men on their way to the Wallands action station. This alert at 11.20 am lasting 20 minutes proved to be a false alarm. Another three days later also false was to be the last alert until the eve of the Battle of Britain the 7th June 1940. On the BBC 9.00 pm news the first night of the war a mobilisation order was broadcast putting all AFS personnel on full time duty.

The Lewes Town Council elected a "War Cabinet" to conduct its affairs, some of the formal committees' business being amalgamated for the duration of the war. The "Cabinet" consisted of Ald C D Crisp Mayor, Ald A N Innes, Ald Sutton, Clrs Baker, Channon and Witcher. One of the first acts of the local war cabinet was to commandeer four petrol pumps in the town on Regional instructions for the supply of ARP vehicles. The pumps were at Lewes Motors Western Road, Caffyn's Malling Street, Rugg's Garage Station Street, and J C H Martin Cliffe Bridge. A further pump was taken over at the Central Garage Ringmer.

The Cinema de Luxe and The Odeon Cinemas in common with all places of entertainment where large numbers gathered were closed on Government order. The last film showing at the Odeon was the "Mikado". The order was relaxed after two weeks much to everyone's relief. The Cinema de Luxe re-opened with "Blackwells Island". Kerb painting commenced with alternate stones painted white to assist blackout driving. By the 13th October thirteen trench shelters, dug at the time of the "Munich" crisis and then filled in, had been reopened. These wood lined trenches would provide shelter for 975 persons. They were intended for people caught in the street when a raid started. By the end of the month concern was expressed at the amount of water penetration in the trench shelters. Two other steel shelters covered with sandbags were erected, one at the Pells and the other at Cliffe Corner.

The Presbyterian Church Hall in Market Street was offered as a rest centre for evacuee mothers with young children. The Christian Alliance for Women and Girls organised a rota at other church halls in different parts of the town so that each weekday there was somewhere for the mothers to go. Clr Harry Stacey offered the Grange Gardens for recreational purposes for the evacuees and the Scouts and Guides volunteered to help with this. During the first wartime Christmas many parties were arranged for the evacuee children and later servicemen, especially the Canadians, would help in this way. In September it was reported that Southover Manor School would be evacuated to Firle Place. The change of home would be short-lived. After the fall of France in June 1940 the school moved further away from the invasion coast. The army then moved into both Firle Place and the Southover Manor School. For the duration of the war the Manor School's home was to be at Holt Castle three miles north of Worcester. The school returned to Lewes in 1946.

On the outbreak of war 120 prisoners at Lewes Prison, near the end of their sentence, were released early. A party of 130 prisoners evacuated from London by coach stopped at Chailey where two escaped through a window. One was recaptured immediately the other got clean away. In the prison it was reported that the men carried their gas masks all the time, a first aid post had been set up and vital points protected with sandbags. In October prisoners who had been evacuated from Wandsworth Gaol after two weeks of unrest attacked one of the warders. It appeared that they hated a small country prison. The trouble was defused by an allowance of money to buy tobacco or sweets, the average weekly earnings being sixpence. Other corporate evacuees settled into their new quarters. Billingsgate Fish Market had been accommodated at Caffyn's Garage in Malling Street and the Beard's Maltings in Castle Ditch Lane had become a home for wholesale Provision and Bacon Merchants I G Beer Ltd, also from London.

Friday 29th September 1939 was National Registration Day. Householders were asked to provide a flat surface for the enumerator to write on. The questions asked were similar to those of a Census - names, dates of birth, marital status, and forces status. The author was allocated the Registration Number EJJD:70:3 the letters referred to the Registration District Lewes being EJJ the last letter "D" being the subdistrict, 70 was the house number in the Register, 3 being third in the household. Billeted servicemen were excluded. Buff coloured National Identity cards were issued. The primary purpose of the Register was to establish the food rationing system. After registration anyone moving home must, within three days, re-register at the nearest Registration Office, which for Lewes was in the Corn Exchange. If a card was lost the loser had to pay one shilling for a replacement, a similar sum was paid to any finder of a card on return to the Registration Office. In 1943 a blue security printed Identity Card was issued in an attempt to counteract forgery and ration book fraud. The new card had five spaces for authorised change of address alterations, which, on the old cards, had been made by the use of stick-on labels.

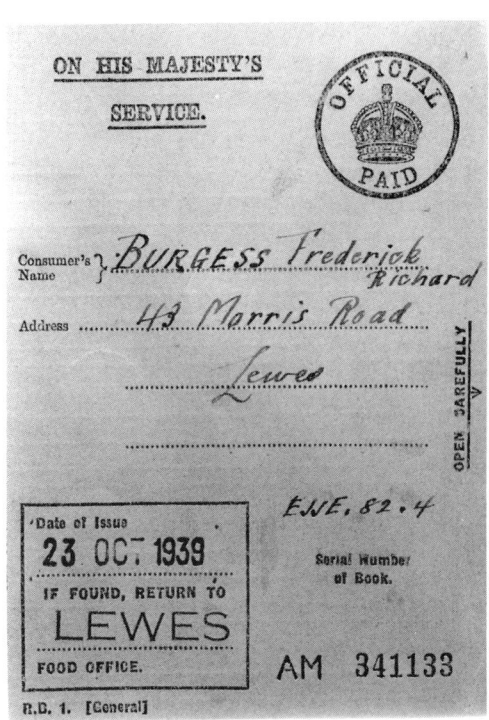

Lewes Ration book first issue   *F Burgess*

In October 264 food retailers had obtained licences from the Food Control Office in the Corn Exchange. By November the first issue of 12,800 ration books had been made to the public. The Chamber of Commerce proposed that all shops should close at 6.00 pm on weekdays except Wednesdays 1.00 pm and Saturdays 7.00 pm. Later closing times on Fridays and Saturdays were common before the war. Residents registered with their butchers for meat which went on ration on the 8th January 1940.

In December 1939 the International Friendship League recommended that aid should be given to conscientious objectors to compulsory military service. Clr Miss Fowler-Tutt resigned from the League in protest. In May 1940 patriotism triumphed when two lady clerks in the Food Office, one with four years' service with the Council the other with just one day in post were found to be members of the Peace Pledge Union. The Town Clerk Mr C W Stephenson sought advice by telephone from the Ministry of Food in London. Following which it was felt inadvisable that the clerks should continue to be employed. Further outrage occurred when the air raid wardens at post number 9 discovered that one of their members was a pacifist, and refused to go on duty with him. There is no record of how the matter was resolved.

The first prosecutions for blackout offences took place in December 1939. A chain store and a local library were among the first offenders for allowing lights to shine after dark from premises. Housewives were also fined the amounts ranged from 2/6 (12p) to £1. A motorist was summoned for failing to have the car bumper painted white. Government advertising in newspapers started. For each group of three ships importing goods one was for munitions one was for food and one was for luxuries, consumers were urged to use less of the latter. The Ministry of Food advised of the reasons for rationing, 1 Prevent waste, 2 Help the war effort, 3 Divide supplies equally, 4 Prevent uncertainty. Commercial advertising continued. The Sussex Express advertised a new Ford Anglia car, a two-door eight horse power saloon, at £125. Wightman and Parrish offered an Anderson type air raid shelter of corrugated steel for £8:8:0 (£8.40).

Timetable of Aggression 2

1939 November 30th	Russia invades Finland
1940 April 19th	Germany invades Denmark and Norway
1940 May 10th	Germany invades The Low Countries and France
1940 June 15th	Russia occupies The Baltic States
1940 June 22nd	Italy invades France
1940 June 27th	Russia occupies Bessarabia (Eastern Rumania)
1940 October 7th	Rumania becomes a German Satellite
1940 October 28th	Italy invades Greece
1940 November 11th	Hungary becomes a German Satellite
1941 March 1st	Bulgaria becomes a German Satellite
1941 April 6th	Germany invades Yugoslavia and Greece
1941 May 19th	Germany invades Crete
1941 June 22nd	Germany invades Russia
1941 December 7th	Japan attacks Pearl Harbour, Hong Kong and Malaya

Matters of finance continued to exercise both the Town Council and the County Council. The latter agreed to make up the pay of their employees who had been called up for military service but the Town Council would not follow suit until later in the war. A volunteer typist for the town's ARP Service was replaced by a paid employee. This resulted in heated exchanges in Council. They did however agree to increase the wages of manual workers by 3/- (15p) per week to 50/- (£2.50). It also noted that ARP uniform denim overalls were to cost 11/- each (55p) less 60% Government grants. It was reported that the East Sussex County Council (ESSC) had lost 400 roadmen to the services in the "Call Up". Road maintenance was to be reduced and a further 300 would be made redundant. Hours of work for the remainder were to be reduced from 50 per week to 48. The Town Council were pleased to record a saving of £1,135 on the street lighting bill. Only one of the shops on the Landport Estate had been let, the other three might be converted to housing. For the duration of the war chickens and rabbits could now be kept on Council estates.

A list was published detailing some of the 18 wardens' posts which had been established and the names of the Head Wardens were given. No 1 Mr H Pennington at Malling Laundry, No 3 Mr B Sanger Cliffe Corner Shelter, No 4 Mr S V North Mansfield's Garage, No 5 Mr L Smith Market Tower, No 6 Mr C Frank *The Elephant and Castle,* No 7 Mr J T Mellers *New Station Inn,* No 9 Mr A W Appleby Dusarts 58 High Street, No 10 Mr E C Rundle H L Smiths 58 Southover High Street. Other posts were located at *The Swan Hotel, Rhynie* Houndean Rise, Fitton's Stables Winterbourne, Witcher's Garage Western Road, *Black Horse Hotel* and *Shelleys Hotel.* These arrangements were modified later.

Hospital arrangements in the town were adapted to meet the needs of war. The Victoria Hospital had relied on voluntary support now received government funding which required that some of the beds were kept empty to treat air raid and other war casualties. The Isolation Hospital in Nevill Road with 25 beds unused since October 1938 was prepared for emergency use. *Elmdene* at 52 Grange Road was fitted out as an Evacuation Hostel in March 1940 for patients moved from London hospitals but had minimal use. It was kept staffed and operational until February 1944. Southover Old Rectory in Rotten Row near Antioch Street was loaned to the town free of charge by Mr John Every for use as a nursing home but following his death in 1942 the executors were obliged to raise charges on its use.

Children at Mountfield Road schools, when on the playing fields facing the railway, had an occasional reminder of the war in France when they saw the ambulance train passing. White panels on the side and roof of each malachite green car carried a red cross. The Southern Railway had provided an eleven coach train of five ward cars, four administration cars including pharmacy, kitchen, stores and pantry. One sitting case car, an officer's car, with medical officer's sleeping compartment and a brake van completed the train. The train which met hospital ships at Newhaven could take 180 cases in cots. This service ceased after the fall of France and later in the war the train could be seen parked at Hassocks South sidings.

Bureaucracy continued despite the needs of war. In February 1940 the Town Council received a demand from the Home Office that the new £70,000 Police Headquarters planned for Mountfield Road should be proceeded with, although the Council had abandoned plans for a new sewer to serve it in response to a request from the Ministry of Health for wartime economies. A further letter on the 17th May from the Home Office insisted that building work must start. The reason advanced was that "The Superintendent of Police did not have a room suitable for conducting business in with persons of high standing". Hitler's Panzer tanks had been rampaging through France and Belgium for over a week when this instruction arrived. Both the Superintendent and those of high standing would now have to wait until after the war for a suitable room.

4. The Young Ones

The Evacuees Arrive

Friday 1st September 1939 saw the arrival at 9.50 am of the first trainload of evacuees. Guides (adult helpers including local teachers) went to the station to meet the trains and shepherd the children and their teachers to the control centres. The control centres and the marshalls in charge were The Odeon Cinema: Clr Newling, Cinema de Luxe: Clr Tappenden, All Saints Parish Room: Clr Hamilton Dicker, Southover Church Hall: Captain M Morris, St Anne's Infants School: Clr D Whittington, Methodist Church Hall: Clr Markham, St Mary's Hall Highdown Road: Clr W Penfold.

The entrance to the station on the approach bridge was converted into an office for Captain Newson the Evacuation Organiser for the town. The local Scout and Guide Troops helped with shepherding the children on foot or by bus to the more distant control centres. They were also accompanied by their teachers who had travelled with them from Croydon and London. At the control centres the children were given sweets, biscuits and fruit and then divided into small groups. These groups set out again on foot each child carrying the permitted single piece of hand luggage and the obligatory gas mask in its cardboard box. Again they were accompanied by their own teachers and an adult volunteer from Lewes armed with a list of prospective families willing to take in the evacuees.

There were a few unhappy doorstep scenes where either the hostess did not like the look of the offered child or perhaps the child realised that the new home was not all he or she imagined it would be. It would be a long time until Monday before they saw friends and teachers again. Mostly the arrangements went well and after a period of adjustment on both sides many lasting friendships were made. Social differences were keenly felt when children of the poorer areas of Croydon and Bermondsey were placed in the modern homes on the Nevill and Landport Estates. Conversely some boys from better off Tooting would have their education advanced after experiencing some of the more modest homes in the town, many without electricity and often one cold tap in the kitchen or scullery, no bath and just an outside toilet. One family of a mother and three schoolgirls were fortunate enough to be placed with Sir Frank and Lady Sanderson in Malling Deanery, a very pleasant contrast to their London home. When rationing came they were doubly fortunate as the farm kept the house plentifully supplied with butter, cheese, cream, eggs, with an occasional hen and rabbit for the table as well. One of these schoolgirls remained in the town after the war and married a Lewesian.

The first batch of children allocated to the town totalled 1,219, a further 1,700 had been sent to the surrounding villages in the Chailey Rural District. These children were taken to the Dripping Pan and then to their village homes by bus. On Friday 1st September Lewes received 511 scholars and 60 teachers. In addition 233 mothers came with 360 children under school age. Another batch of 160 adult blind evacuees arrived from Croydon accompanied by sighted attendants. These were housed in St Wilfrid's Youth Hostel. On Saturday 2nd September 90 mothers arrived with young children and a further batch of 143 mothers with 211 children all under school age came on Sunday 3rd September. Another contingent of 158 school children and 30 teachers arrived on the next day. Belatedly air raid shelter construction had commenced at the schools on Saturday 2nd September and it was then announced that the schools would not reopen until the shelters were nearly ready. The schools opened two weeks later for the Autumn term.

Every evacuee had brought with them only one small piece of hand luggage so an immediate demand arose for beds, bedding, cots, pushchairs and prams. An appeal was made for 1,000 blankets. The boarding allowance was 10/6 (52 pence) a week, sufficient to board an extra person but inadequate to fund quantities of bedding.

Placings of children and adults in the Chailey area were 360 to Ringmer, 77 to Beddingham, 53 to Firle. Chailey took 363, Newick 190, Rodmell 73, Barcombe 114 and Hamsey 114. In Lewes the schools struggled to adapt to extra classes of evacuee children besides their own. All the Junior schools had to run a two-shift system. The Council rented most of the Church halls in the town for educational use. Some were released after the first month. Others, namely St John's, the Tabernacle Sunday School Hall until recently the Riverside Centre, Southover Church Hall and the Young Men's Christian Association (YMCA) premises in Westgate Street were kept on, in some cases until 1943 when the drift back to London of the evacuated children removed the need for their use.

Glyndebourne Nursery Evacuees

LCC infant evacuees at Glyndebourne 1940   *Glyndebourne Archives*

In the Chailey Rural District 372 children "In Care" with 84 staff from LCC residential nurseries were sent to Glyndebourne. Some were to remain until January 1946. At the time of the Munich Crisis, September 1938, the Home Office had telephoned Mr John Christie's London Office asking for a number of children to be accommodated at Glyndebourne. No previous planning or provision had been made for this in advance so when the crisis faded there was much relief all round.

In the intervening year arrangements were set in hand so that a proper reception for them was possible. Red London Transport buses brought the infants and their nurses to Glyndebourne. The children and staff came from two day nurseries, a private nursery and Peckham Union poor law institution, totalling 456 in all. They brought with them some equipment including cooking utensils, cots, bedding and baths. The estate workers were kept busy stuffing mattress covers with straw and erecting cots. Some vital equipment had been left behind. It is recorded that Mr Rudolf Bing, General Manager of Glyndebourne, journeyed into Lewes and managed to buy a large number of enamel chamber pots. This must have caused the first wartime shortage! After the first few weeks the numbers of children were reduced to 100 and it remained at this level throughout the war until the nurseries returned to London.

The Tooting Bec School

The London County Council (LCC) Tooting Bec Boys' Secondary School had prepared well for their evacuation. Staff were recalled from holiday on 24th August by announcements on the radio. From the 26th a daily assembly of masters and boys took place with practices of the order of march. On Thursday 31st August the order was given for the evacuation to take place the following day Friday 1st September. The journey went with military precision. The school assembled with hand luggage and gas masks and marched off from the school in columns of fives to Balham Station. Crossing the busy Balham High Street had been planned. The boys halted in columns turned right and the traffic was held up so they crossed in a matter of moments. On the platform they were marshalled in groups of ten younger ones with an older boy in charge of each group and entrained for Lewes.

On arrival in Lewes they were marched to the Secondary School in Mountfield Road where they were each given a pack of biscuits and a tin of corned beef as emergency food for their host family. They were then taken by Southdown coaches to Chailey where the masters accompanied them to billets that stretched over a wide area. The County Chief Education Officer, Mr J H Baines, realised the unsatisfactory nature of the arrangements and tried to get the school moved into Lewes but the Ministry of Health, the responsible department for the evacuation scheme, would not allow any change. The only building large enough to hold the whole school was the Church. To begin with a roll call was held there each day and the pupils dispersed to other buildings in the village including the Village Hall, *Five Bells* and *Kings Head* for lessons aided by blackboards transported from Tooting strapped to the cars of some of the masters. Much time was spent helping on the land, grubbing thistles, "Dodging Docks" lifting potatoes and sugar beet.

This unsatisfactory state could not continue. After repeated representations, and with the influence of the Mayor Ald Crisp, the whole school of 300 boys under their Headmaster Mr S R Gibson was brought into Lewes in October 1939. Initially lessons were held in St Wilfrid's YMCA and its gymnasium. The Conservative Club was also pressed into service. Later they were transferred to the County School for Boys, where again a two-shift system operated, with some boys of both schools being accommodated in the County School for Girls' thereby anticipating co-education that was to follow in the years to come. The Tooting Bec influx placed a considerable strain on the town's accommodation and at one stage 20 boys were faced with having to return to Tooting, but homes were found for them just in time. After 1940 when Lewes became a defence area further evacuation was discouraged. Later the respite from air attacks enjoyed by London led to a starvation of the pupil intake and a decision was taken to return to Tooting. The Bec School remained in Lewes until 3rd December 1943 when they returned to London unfortunately to experience the German V1 pilotless plane attacks and rockets from June 1944. The Bec school roll of honour for the period 1939-45 amounted to 75 boys who gave their lives, six of whom would have been Lewes evacuees. One scholar A A Green is commemorated on the Lewes Rugby Club memorial.

After the first six weeks of the war there was a noticeable drift back to London of the evacuees. In the Lewes and Chailey areas this was estimated to be 400 children and adults. 1940 would see another influx when the raids on London started when another 450 came to Lewes. A number asked to go home for Christmas 1939. This request raised the question whether the billeting allowance would be paid to the householders during the absence. The total expended by the Council on billeting allowances in the first twelve months of the war amounted to £20,840. This was reimbursed by central government. Another source of friction arose when some of the parents from London visited their children by car thus emphasising the gap in living standards between some of the families. From 1941 special eight-day rail vouchers for cheap travel were made available for parents to visit evacuated children in the summer holidays. The Bec School Parents' Association also chartered coaches so that visits to their children in Lewes could be made.

Lewes had been asked in 1939 to take another 350 girls from the Haberdasher's Aske Hampstead School but vigorous protests from the billeting officers were supported by the plea that the Lewes Outfall works were already overloaded! This convinced a visiting Inspector from Regional HQ that Bournemouth would be a more acceptable destination. The Raines Foundation School also found a wartime home for its pupils at Hurstpierpoint. For the remainder of the war the billeting office aided by the Women's Voluntary Service was hard pressed to maintain an adequate register of homes willing to take evacuees. Some children remained with the same family throughout the war. Other children were moved frequently for good reasons on both sides. Out of 246 Bec placements 84 had one home, 67 moved twice, 59 three times, 26 four times 7 five times 2 six times and one managed to get through seven families during his stay.

In 1938 education in the town had been reorganised with the closing of the Central School and the opening of the Senior Boys' and Girls' Elementary Schools in Mountfield Road. Western Road School, Council managed, the Church of England St. Anne's, Southover, Pells and Malling schools provided Infants and Junior Schools. St. Pancras was the Roman Catholic School. Despite organisational changes all the pre-war school buildings save Malling have survived. A Boys' County Secondary school was located in Mountfield Road and a Girls' County Secondary School was situated in Potters Lane Southover. This latter site is now shared by Southover and Western Road Schools. In recent years the Boys' and Girls' County schools with the former Elementary (Secondary Modern School) have formed the Priory School.

Evacuated Children Placed in Lewes Schools

School	Number	Evacuated From
St Anne's School	68	St Joseph's RC School Bermondsey
St Pancras School	38	St Mary's RC School Tooley Street Bermondsey
Southover School	62	All Saints RC School Bermondsey
Pells School	108	Croydon Junior Parish Church School
Western Road School	73	All Saints RC Boys School Bermondsey
Mountfield Road Boys'	98	St Joseph's RC School Bermondsey
Lewes County Boys' School	300	Tooting Bec LCC School
Lewes County Girls' School		Raines Foundation School Bethnal Green * Haberdasher's Aske Hampstead School *

* Small numbers of Pupils

LEWES EVACUEES' CHRISTMAS TREAT

St Pancras Church Hall 22nd December 1939   *Sussex Express*

Trenches and Teachers

The Town Council was the Education Authority for all schools except for the two county schools controlled by the County Council. The Town Council provided pre-cast concrete slab air raid shelters constructed partially below ground at St Anne's (Baxter's Field), Western Road playground and Mountfield Road playing field, where 10 were installed labelled A to J. These shelter foundations were discovered when the Leisure Centre was built in 1991. The headmaster, Mr J H Bowley, drilled the boys so that they cleared the school in 94 seconds when the alert sounded. The earth covering the "Trenches" (as the shelters were known) was used to extend the school allotment to a total of half an acre under cultivation supervised by Mr P G Barton. The shelters had wood slatted seats, an escape hatch at the opposite end to the entrance and a chemical toilet. Sometimes the shelters were so wet that pupils remained in the school and lay on the inner corridor floors during alerts.

Curved steel sandbagged shelters were provided for Malling School in the Coombe. The Southover School shelters were sited in the County Girls' school playground. Pells School also had the same type of shelter opposite in Pelham Terrace. These were under the trees, and additional shelter accommodation was dug into the bank by the railway cutting near Cabbage Path. Brick surface shelters followed later at the Pells and were also used for other schools. By 1940 the sandbags had rotted and were replaced with a layer of concrete. Remedial work was also required at Mountfield Road with £350 expended on bitumastic waterproofing and the installation of slow combustion stoves.

The East Sussex County Council was responsible for the Boys' and Girls' County Schools. The Boys' School in Mountfield Road had shelters made from large diameter spun concrete pipes sunk below ground level. The Girls' school in Potters Lane had brick surface shelters which, much to the irritation of pupils and staff, were placed on the school gardens lovingly constructed the previous year after the opening of the 1938 extension.

War changed much. The Town Council had ruled in the thirties that women teachers on marriage would be required to resign. They were however warmly welcomed back during the war as supply teachers. Mrs Beeforth and Mrs Bentley among the first to return were posted to Mountfield Road Boys' where from the staff, Mr A H Bristow, Mr D S Griffiths, Mr L A Turner and Mr H Valentine had been mobilised as Territorials. One teacher from St Pancras school was also called up. Help came from three teachers lent from the LCC and two from the Croydon Education committee. Mr D E Cotter, Headmaster of St Joseph's Bermondsey, came with his school. In total 40 London and Croydon teachers, including 20 nuns, came to Lewes. Mr Valentine returned in 1943 from war service, Mr Bristow and Mr Griffiths came back at the end of 1945. Mr Turner became Headmaster at Pells on his return from war service.

The County School for Boys' lost teachers to the armed services. Mr Pett and Mr Smith, Mathematics masters, joined the Navy. Mr Courteney served in the Pay Corps, Mr Dolden, Physical Training became a Staff Captain, Mr Stripe went to the RAF as a Pilot Officer, Mr Page and Mr Stevens both became Officers in the Army.

Air raid shelters Mountfield Road School 1939   ESRO

School Welfare

For the first wartime term Schools reopened two weeks late on 18th September giving time for preliminary timetables to be arranged, allocation of rooms for the evacuees, and provision of teachers, many of whom had to teach unaccustomed subjects. Rugg's Garage in Station Street had been contracted to bring children in a 20-seater bus from the outlying villages of Iford, Rodmell, Kingston and eventually Falmer. Other changes were accelerated by the war. Between the Boys' and Girls' assembly halls at Mountfield Road School a central kitchen had been installed. In February 1940 a meals' service commenced with five meals for 1/6d (7p) a week per child. It was planned to start with 150 meals per day. Children from other schools in the town would walk to Mountfield for their meals. Later there was an outcry when the price increased to 2/1d per week (10p). Ultimately a delivery service to the other schools and church halls, pressed into service to accommodate the evacuees, was arranged. In September free and assisted school meals became available to those according to need. The daily morning one third of a pint of milk per school child continued to be available. This was not without difficulty, the Brighton Co-Op had for years supplied pasteurised milk for this scheme but there had never been a contract. Wartime distribution economies dictated to the Education Committee that they must use Southdown Dairies who could only supply Tuberculin Tested at increased cost. To quote the committee "We are no longer our own masters in our own house".

Health and Safety

1940 saw the introduction of the mass immunisation campaign against Diphtheria with very high take up rates among Lewes children. Other infectious conditions prevailed. In March 1940 one of the worst outbreaks of German Measles since 1926 occurred and the following May classes were decimated through an epidemic of "Yellow Jaundice" (Acute Infective Hepatitis) a viral condition for which fluids and bed rest were the prescribed treatment and no school until one resumed a normal colour.

Everyone was required to carry their gas mask with them at all times, the regulation cardboard boxes did not survive this treatment well so shops sold canvas covers for the boxes, and purpose made canisters were produced by The Metal Box Co. These were at least durable but awkward to carry. School children achieved high rates of attendance with their masks. Ald Crisp the Mayor made inspection trips to the schools to verify this in his capacity as ARP sub-controller. On 8th October 1940 it was reported that 5,000 pairs of soft rubber earplugs, to protect against the effects of blast, had been issued, children received theirs at school. At this time a supplementary filter had to be added to everyone's gas mask. This green lacquered Conex filter was secured with adhesive tape. School children fitted their own in the classroom. Adults went to fitting centres at St Mary's Hall, Highdown Road, the *Tally Ho*, the Town Hall, St Anne's and Cliffe First Aid Posts Blackout curtains had been fitted to some school windows but a thirty minute earlier finish at 4.00 pm with a shorter lunch hour enabled schools to avoid blacking out. Normal finishing was reverted to in February 1940. Windows also received a coating of adhesive lined gauze to reduce the risk of flying glass splinters.

The Council expressed concern at the projected cost of dental treatment of £4,810 for the evacuees and intended to recover the cost from the sending authorities. With the fall of France in 1940 Lewes became a neutral area for evacuation purposes, no longer a reception area yet not dangerous enough to become an evacuation area. Despite this, 120 children had their names registered for the Overseas Evacuation Scheme with destinations in the Dominions and the United States.

School in Wartime

Mr P Barton, Woodwork Master at Mountfield Road, formed a Model Aeroplane Club, the boys building some impressive elastic motored flying models. All too soon these interests and Mr Barton's were to be channelled into the Air Training Corps. School holidays were curtailed for various reasons, the 1939 autumn half-term was cancelled due to the late start in September while in 1940 the invasion threat reduced the summer holidays to a fortnight.

Despite all the anxieties there were some compensations. On 29th January 1940 there was a very heavy fall of snow of about 18 inches. Attendance was affected both by the snow and illness and most of that morning was spent in officially approved snow fights at the schools. In the afternoon the Local Education Authority (LEA) closed the town's schools. About this time the Bec School started a school magazine and a club, and St Joseph's followed suit with their *Worth* Club being held in St John's Parish Room in Talbot Terrace.

School log books continued to record normal activities, Ascension Day services were attended at All Saints Church, and preparations continued for competition in the Brighton Musical Festival. Scholarship Examination day came in April when the pupils of eleven years of age attempted the earlier equivalent of the 11 plus exam. The 1940 Whitsun holidays were subject to a national recall to schools broadcast on Whit Monday. The war situation had deteriorated with the German Blitzkrieg on The Low Countries and France. The customary half-day holiday for Sunday School outings fell victim to the war. At Mountfield Road an open day in July was attended by 200 parents who watched a physical training display. The start of the August 1940 holidays was delayed until 15th with explanations about the lost fortnight the previous September. School log books tell a different story that children were being kept together in case of a German invasion and that the teachers would require permission to be absent from the town for the holidays.

Lewes Platoon Army Cadets Royal Sussex Regiment November 1943   *H Windless Sussex Express*

The prolonged air raid alerts in the closing stages of the Battle of Britain resulted in schools being closed on 1st, 25th and 31st October 1940, with parents being informed that they may decide whether to send children to school during an alert. The evacuated school children brought some compensations. A concert by professional musicians was provided by the LCC. This was followed by a gift of sweets and biscuits to each child. The music was classical with explanations of its character, but an afternoon free of lessons plus the gifts was sufficient reward for the pupils.

Schools were mobilized to help in the National Savings campaigns and again Mr Bowley's enthusiasm in promoting savings, which took the form of books in which penny savings stamps could be fixed, earned the Boys' School top place with a picture of Polegate Mill to display in the hall for a year. A Savings Certificate costing 15/- (75p) was a large investment for a child. That meant a dedicated saver with 3d a week to invest would take over a year to get one Savings Certificate. In September 1941, Police Sergeant Simms visited the schools to talk about "Dangerous Objects". With the surrounding downland under military occupation and the amount of material resulting from air activity the warning of the dangers was timely. The County School for Girls' had a similar visit a year later and again in 1943 school children were warned of the dangers of "Butterfly" anti-personnel bombs. The police also made visits to lecture the children on the importance of securing bicycles against theft.

Youthful Observers

Despite the dangers involved the interest of small boys in the military activities of the time could not be curbed. Young Richard Brickell of Iford was a keen observer of all the army units that he saw on his travels from home to the County School in Mountfield Road. He maintained a diary of unit identities and insignia, but alas for the historian it disappeared taking with it a treasure trove of information. John Tillstone of Valence Road displayed a great interest in vehicles especially armoured cars and tanks. He was to have plenty of opportunities to observe them passing the busy Prison crossroads and driving on to the Gallops to carry out exercises. His extensive knowledge on the subject is now referred to on occasions by The Royal Armoured Corps Museum at Bovington, Dorset.

Tony Whittington of Toronto Terrace made friends with a Bren gun carrier driver of the 1st/4th battalion of the South Lancashire Regiment which kept their vehicles under the chestnut trees by the Pells. One summer day Private Clifford Kenyon, for the amusement of young master Whittington, marked a kerbstone with his initials using steel dies. It was fated to be a permanent memorial to him in Lewes. The marked kerbstone opposite 5 Pelham Terrace survived the upheavals at the Pells during the 1987 hurricane. Private Kenyon was posted abroad as a reinforcement to the front line battalion. The 1st South Lancs were in action on 24th July 1944 at Sannerville in Normandy during operation "Goodwood" to capture Caen. He was a radio operator, maintaining a link with Brigade HQ, in a M14 half-track, a lightly armoured vehicle of Canadian origin. The orchard in which they were located was under enemy observation and eventually a torrent of shell and mortar fire rained down on the position setting fire to the radio half-track and mortally wounding Private Kenyon. He was buried in Banneville-la-Campagne War Cemetery.

Roy Fuller who lived at Landport was a keen wartime observer and had a first hand view of the Halifax bomber which crashlanded above Meridian Road. He also visited the two German planes which came down outside the town during the Battle of Britain, the Messerschmitt shot down at Houndean and the Gotha which landed near the Gallops. He was not alone in this interest at the time but in the years that followed he has researched the details of the planes and makes regular visits to the surviving crews in Germany.

The East Sussex County Council organised Junior Service Squads in schools to promote National Savings, gardening and knitting comforts for the Services. The Lewes Council provided money for evacuees' Christmas parties. In 1943 they spent £25 of which they managed to recover £13 from the London County Council. Older school children were encouraged in practical ways of helping the war effort. Boys and girls from the County Schools formed parties to help local farms with tasks such as weeding, singling mangolds, potato harvesting and haymaking.

The County Girls' school was sent to a farm camp, under canvas with board provided, during the August Holidays, at Plumpton and Buxted, for which they were paid the hourly rates of 5d (2p) under 16 years, over 16 years 7d (3p). Visits of the girls were made to Glyndebourne to see the work of the evacuated LCC nursery school. Knitting was another wartime contribution of comforts for the searchlight units stationed on the Race Hill and at Ringmer. Books were also collected for dispatch to a merchant ship adopted by the school.

"Victory Diggers" County School for Boys' *Betty Turner*

A new note was struck with the opening of the school grounds on Saturday mornings for tennis. The County School for Boys' maintained a large colony of rabbits in the east quadrangle. A piece of land at the rear of the school was taken over for allotment gardening and later they extended their gardening to land at the rear of the Mountfield Road Drill Hall. Each year impressive amounts of vegetables were grown. In 1942 the "Barbican" reports the harvesting of three and half tons of potatoes, eight hundredweights of carrots, three hundredweights of onions and four and a half hundredweights of peas and beans collectively valued at £44:10 shillings.

The Youth Services

No 464 Squadron of the Air Training Corps (ATC) was formed in April 1941 under Squadron Leader N R J Bradshaw, County School Headmaster. The squadron was organised in three flights, No 1 for County Grammar School boys with 60 enrolled, No 2 for the Bec boys that had 40 enrolled and No 3 for 90 boys from outside the two schools who needed extra mathematics tuition. The unit was based at the County School in Mountfield Road. Besides providing pre-service training for the RAF the boys helped as messengers for the ARP service and it was a severe blow to this service when the Bec School went home in December 1943. In January 1943 an appeal for band instruments was successful in equipping a capable bugle band. A notable feature of ATC activities was the summer camps with flying opportunities, some of which were spent at RAF Halton. As much as 30 hours' flying training was undertaken by the cadets when they camped at RAF Wratting Common and on Beaufighters at Thorney Island.

No 464 Squadron Air Training Corps May 1943   *T J Dumbrell Sussex Express*

The County School for Girls' was home to the Girls' Training Corps Squadron No 260. Forty-two girls formed the first intake of recruits with ages from 16 to 18 in May 1942. The Junior Training Corps Squadron No 3200 ages 13 to 16 was also based there. Both units ran courses to prepare girls for entry into the women's services giving opportunities for physical training, sporting and social events. In July 1942 a Lewes No 2 Platoon of the second company of the Royal Sussex Army Cadets was formed at Mountfield Road School. This unit also sported a fine bugle band. The Company was commanded by Lt J Green a prison officer. Lt Worman filled the role of adjutant, with Second Lts Cooke, Baker and Kelley assisting. The company was part of the Brighton Battalion. Another company had its headquarters at the Boys' County Secondary School. A lance corporal's stripe was a much desired achievement as was the War Certificate"A" which signified a level of proficiency that advanced one's service career when called up. Training included firearms' practice at the Old Naval Prison indoor range. Exercises were undertaken with the Lewes Home Guard and Canadian Army units stationed in the town.

In July 1942 young persons of 16 years of age and over had to register for youth service. The registrants in the town totalled 71 boys and 68 girls. In April 1943 Lewes Youth House was opened in the Tabernacle Church Hall. It was run by the Council and was a meeting place for table games, dances and non-alcoholic refreshments. The building, until recently called the Riverside Centre, now has an uncertain future.

A proposal to add sex education to the school syllabus in the last year at school was considered in May 1943 but amid misgivings the proposal was deferred.   However, by November 1943 the idea was approved. In 1945, the Sussex Express, in reporting the return of a party of evacuees from the station, noted that Mrs King of Priory Street had, during the war, looked after ten in her home. This return signalled the end of a chapter in the wartime history of the town.

Women's Junior Air Corps at The County School Southover June 1946   *Marion Fuller Sussex Express*

It was not completely the end of of the town's hospitality towards children. The Lewes Rotary Club sponsored and arranged a visit of 60 Dutch Children from war torn Holland for eight weeks from 1st February 1946.

****

5. The Air War

East Sussex, unlike its western counterpart, at the commencement of the war, did not possess any regular airfields, service or civilian. Flying clubs had been established at Wilmington and Friston and a gliding club at Firle. This airfield situation changed very little during the war. The nearest landing ground to Lewes was at Chailey between Godleys Green and Plumpton Station. The site was surveyed in 1942, construction commenced in January 1943 with two metal track runways being ready by the summer of that year. It was used for grazing until the spring of 1944 when four blister hangars and hardstandings were installed for D-day use. The landing ground had a short life, from April until 28th June 1944. During this time three squadrons of fighters operated from the field.

Described as six miles east of Lewes, Deanland Advanced Landing Ground at Golden Cross, operated nine squadrons at various times from 1st April 1944 to October 1944. The field was intended for single engine fighter operation but some four engined disabled strays managed to set down there. Friston, four miles west of Eastbourne, became an emergency landing ground in 1940. In 1942 it became a satellite for Kenley and remained busy with fighter aircraft and army co-operation planes, except for the occasional landing of distressed four engined American Air Force planes, until it was closed in 1946.

Despite its relative unimportance, Wilmington was shot up by a lone enemy raider on 14th August 1940. Two years later, on 9th July 1942 at 0650 hours, Friston was attacked by two Messerschmit 109s. An aircraft on the ground, two army huts, a Nissen hut and a hangar under construction were damaged. There were minor injuries to personnel. On 6th September 1943 25 Flying Fortresses landed at Friston, all low in fuel and some suffering flak (German anti aircraft fire) damage sustained during a raid on Stuttgart.

Vapour or contrails marked the passage of aircraft at high altitudes. During the Battle of Britain the tracery showed the twists and turns of dog fights over the town in the Autumn of 1940. A photograph by Edward Reeves captured the skies above Lewes and if proof were needed a battlement of the Castle is framed in the picture. Four years later, in 1944, the townspeople would see them again. Unlike 1940, when the single engined fighters each left one sinuous trail, this time each four engined bomber left four trails as they headed in straight lines for Northern France and Germany as the American Air Force daylight bombing missions prepared the way for "The Second Front".

Air activity on this scale inevitably led to crashes of damaged planes or those out of control due to crew injury. Shortage of fuel was a frequent cause of forced landings. The Downs and countryside around the town became the last resting place for 30 distressed British and 10 German aircraft. The Police incident records show the totals for East Sussex.

Police Record of Aircraft Incidents

1940	74	1941	35
1942	32	1943	103
1944	103	1945	8

The Lost Gotha Biplane

An unusual arrival by air took place on 28th August 1940 when at 1740 hours a German Gotha 145 biplane from StabJG27 (HQ Flight) landed intact on the Racecourse above the Prison. The pilot jumped down from the cockpit to find a reception party waiting for him consisting of Mr Jack Palmer, of the County Surveyor's Department, in his Home Guard capacity complete with denim battledress blouse, rifle and his entire stock of ammunition, just ten rounds. Accompanying him, from his Houndean Rise home, was his evacuee, Mr George Bennett, a modern languages master from the Tooting Bec School who managed the translations. The pilot, Leonard Buikle has recounted in later years his fear at having the rifle put to his nose by his captor. The apprehension was shared by Mr Palmer who expected the pilot to draw a revolver at any moment and start shooting.

Gotha down at the Gallops 28th August 1940 *Pat Saunders*

The pilot admitted to being lost, having set out earlier from Cherbourg in France with mail for the German troops occupying Jersey. Various accounts have been offered for this episode. They range from the plane being forced down by Hurricanes, to the mail being a cover for the landing of an agent from the second cockpit. Both suggestions were subsequently denied by the pilot. The most likely explanation lies in the pilot's statement that he was lost. An examination of a map will show that a course from Cherbourg to St Helier on Jersey would take a southwesterly bearing, a reciprocal course would have taken the plane northeastwards making a landfall between Brighton and Newhaven. It would not be the first occasion when reciprocal compass error has led someone astray.

Gotha Pilot Lenard Buikle *R Fuller*

The official surrender was taken by Capt. J C Wilson, Adjutant of the 16th Sussex Home Guard, who was the County Librarian. The prisoner was escorted to Lewes Police Station to await interrogation and a military escort. After a spell in English prisoner of war camps the pilot was transferred to Camp 133 in Lethbridge Alberta Canada, returning after the war to Mannheim to serve his country again in the Police service. The Gotha plane which still had the engine turning over when the pilot surrendered, was soon surrounded by a horde of curious spectators of all ages. After being protected by armed sentries, it was, on 31st August, moved to the Gallops and flown off by Sqd Leader H J Wilson to Farnborough. It was repainted with British markings and issued to Maintenance Command.

The Battle of Britain

The events of the Battle of Britain have by now been classified into five main phases with two critical dates for the German offensive against England. "Eagle Day", 13th August, the commencement of the offensive to eliminate Fighter Command of the RAF and "Operation Sea Lion" the seaborne invasion. Hitler announced on 11th September that the countdown would start on 14th September for the invasion to begin on 24th September. On 14th September the decision was postponed for three days and on 17th September it was postponed again, this time indefinitely. The RAF had yet to be defeated.

Air Raid Alerts in Lewes during the five Phases of the battle

1st	1/7-7/8	Attacks on coastal convoys	5
2nd	8/8-23/8	Shipping, airfields and radar installation targeted	11
3rd	24/8-6/9	Major attacks on airfields and night raids on northern cities	12
4th	7/9-30/9	Attacks switched from airfields to London and large centres	67
5th	1/10-31/10	Widespread attacks on London and industrial centres	83

The Houndean Bottom Me109

During phase four of the Battle of Britain Wednesday 11th September 1940 was a day of raids on London, airfields of the south east, and the cities of Portsmouth and Southampton. A Messerschmitt 109 fighter plane was chased over the town by a Hurricane at low level in a southerly direction. The Hurricane's eight machine guns had dealt the German plane a mortal blow causing it to crash in flames at Houndean Bottom 100 yards north of the Brighton Road. The Queen's Own Regiment provided a guard and took possession of several unexploded cannon shells at the scene. The plane came down in flames at 1600 hours attracting a crowd of onlookers, mainly youthful, who made their way to the site immediately school finished hopefully looking for souvenirs, the collection of which was both dangerous and illegal. The German pilot Hauptmann Wiggers was killed. He was buried, unidentified, in Lewes Cemetery but later his identity was established and he was re-buried in Cannock Chase German War Cemetery, Staffordshire. Fire consumed almost all of the plane leaving a mass of charred and twisted metal. The Lewes section of the Chailey RDC's Fire Brigade dealt with the fire. Sergeant Higgins the victor died three days later in another action.

The scene at Houndean Bottom on Wednesday 11th September. The wreck of the Messerschmitt 109 smoulders away. Fire tenders from the Chailey brigade are in attendance. Just visible are the houses on the skyline of Juggs Lane.

Sussex Express

Police Record of crashed enemy aircraft

28-8-40	1740	Lewes Racecourse	Gotha	Navigational error
9-9-40	1755	Court House Farm Barcombe	Junkers 88*	AA fire, crew fired plane
11-9-40	1600	Houndean Bottom	Me 109 #*	Combat damage
15-9-40	1230	Lodge Wood Isfield	Me 109 #	Crashlanded intact
25-10-4	1330	Harvey Cross Farm Iford	Me 109#	Crashed
1-10-40	1430	Balmer Down Falmer	Me 109 #*	Crashed
28-10-40	1645	Towning Farm Chailey	Me 109#	Crashed
28-11-40	0145	South Heighton	Dornier 17*	Exploded on impact
31-1-41	1525	Plumpton Agricultural College	Heinkel 111 *	Hit overhead power lines
30-5-43		Longford Farm Barcombe	Junkers 88	Intact bomb load, one injured

* Thus marked indicates crew fatalities.
# Messerschmitt.
An unexploded bomb was found on 10-8-1993 at the Heinkel crash site of 31-1-1941.

Police record of crashed British and Allied aircraft

Date	Time	Location	Aircraft	Cause
4-7-40	1200	Southease	Hurricane	Engine failure
9-9-40	1800	Coomb Hill Falmer	Hurricane	Czech Pilot
27-9-40	0935	Lewes Racecourse	Spitfire	Hit railings overturned
12-10-40	1540	Iford Farm	Spitfire	Hit hedge, overturned
27-10-40	0935	Sewells Farm Barcombe	Hurricane	Engine failure
1-12-40	1035	1/4 Mile East of Falmer	Hurricane	Combat damage, Polish A/C
21-3-41	1830	Balmer Down	Lysander	Fuel shortage
16-7-41	0450	Beddingham Hill	Beaufort*	Crashed in fog
17-10-41	1530	North of Woodingdean	Boston Havoc	Engine failure
8-1-41	1400	Blackbrook Fm Westmestn	Spitfire	Flak damage
13-12-41	1445	Broyle Lane Ringmer	Spitfire*	Mid-air collision
25-2-42	1245	Mount Fm Isfield Lane Ringmer	Magister	Lost, fuel low
22-5-42	1710	Firle Stanford Building Union Workhouse	Spitfire	Collided with building. A fire followed
14-3-42	1725	Sedlow Wd Wesmestn	Spitfire	Crashed, pilot baled out
19-8-42	0550	Bevendean Farm Falmer	Spitfire	Crashlanded
13-8-42	1440	Lower Malling Farm	Spitfire	Hit cables, pilot to LVH#
19-8-42	0750	The Brooks Rodmell	Spitfire	Norwegian Pilot to LVH#
16-3-43	---?	Lewes Cliffe Hill	Thunderbolt	Crashed landed
16-3-43	1630	Bishopstone Farm	Spitfire	Crashed, pilot baled out
17-4-43	0525	Landport Allotments	Halifax	German flak damage
16-8-43	1200	Swanborough Farm Iford	Spitfire	Crash landed
20-10-43	1337	Furlongs Farm Beddingham	U.S. Flying Fortress	Engine failure, crew to Swanborough Manor
24-11-43	0030	Lewes Brighton Rd near Falmer	Mosquito *	Disintegrated caught fire
6-2-44	1320	Beddingham Hill	Mosquito	Flak damage
21-2-44	1730	S Heighton Cement Works	Auster	Engine failure
13-5-44	1700	Beddingham near Black Cap Farm	Typhoon	Engine Failure
8-6-44	1637	Beddingham Toy Farm	Lightning*	Crashed
30-6-44	1030	Bineham House Chailey	Thunderbolt*	Crashed
3-8-44	1810	Plumpton Race Course	Fortress	Caught fire, exploded
19-11-44	1504	Newmarket Plantation	U.S. Dakota*	Burnt out
6-2-45	1445	Celtic Fm S. Malling	Mustang	Fuel shortage
3-4-45	1055	Loose Bottom Falmer	Waco Glider	Adverse weather

LVH# Lewes Victoria Hospital

On Sunday 18th August 1940 at 1300 hours a patrol of the Brookside Platoon of the 16th Sussex Home Guard observed enemy aircraft at treetop height flying northwards at Rodmell. The planes, firing as they went, veered westerly and dropped a bomb near the railway line. Other members of the 16th Sussex coming from the Downs at Juggs Lane let fly at the planes with revolvers which drew return fire from one of the enemy aircraft. The planes were described as long and thin. Mr and Mrs Birch working in their garden in Houndean Rise also saw the planes passing southwards of the town.

Dornier 17s of the 9th Staffel (9 planes) of the 76th Bomber Geschwader (81 planes) had crossed the Channel from France making a landfall at Beachy Head, flying past The Seven Sisters and turning over Seaford to follow the railway to Lewes and thence to London turning off to make a devastating attack on Kenley airfield near Caterham.. Dramatic proof exists in a series of photographs taken from one of the planes, of landmarks on route, including Southease Station and the main street in Burgess Hill. This attack was part of three major air assaults that day when over 130 British and 100 German aircraft were destroyed or damaged.

Halifax "K" for Kitty

Friday 16th April 1943 Halifax DD791 Mark ll call sign "K for Kitty", not many months old with less than 70 flying hours logged, stood ready for another night raid on German targets. The crew at No 10 Squadron's Melbourne airfield in Yorkshire were briefed on the operation that was to be a long haul of ten hours on a round trip of 1500 miles to bomb Pilsen 60 miles South West of Prague. The loaded plane's take off weight was thirty tons. It took off with its crew of seven and an eighth observer at 2134 hours taking a route by Colne Point and Dungeness to Pilsen. The target was bombed from a height of 8,000 feet with one 500 lb and four 1,000 lb bombs. While over the target, the plane was hit by flak disabling the port outer engine. The plane managed to reach the French coast at St Valery where it was hit again by flak putting the port

Halifax "K" for Kitty and Crew Melbourne Yorks   *T Whittington*

inner engine out of action. A landfall was made at Newhaven, the crippled plane losing height all the time, followed the course of the Ouse up the valley looking for a clear space to set down. The pilot struggled to hold the plane to a course that would bring the plane to the Race Hill but the 100-foot contour line on the Offham Road was to be the final resting place of the plane just north of the Kingsley Road Bastion at 0523 hours on Saturday 17th April.

Canadian Soldiers of the 3rd Light Anti-aircraft Regiment Royal Canadian Artillery manning a Bofors light AA gun by the Bastion were first on the scene and got the crew clear of the plane. Nearby residents made tea for the rescued men and Mr Sains, ARP Officer, who lived at Landport arranged for ambulances to take the crew to the Victoria Hospital, the Police arrived to mount guard and protect the wreckage from the attention of souvenir hunters. The Fire Service attended, as there was a considerable fire risk from the fuel tanks and oil, a foam carpet was laid. At the Hospital the duty doctor had been called in, the police were asked to get other doctors and dispatched two officers to the hospital to help remove the heavy flying clothing. All the crew members suffered from shock and bruising, two remained in the hospital for some days with bone injuries.

The Captain, Flight Lieutenant J A Wood, visited the Town Hall and thanked the Mayor for the help given to his men and later a silver cigarette box, the gift of the crew was sent to the nurses at the hospital. The remains of the aircraft that was 70 feet long and had a wingspan of nearly 100 feet straddled the Offham Road just above the Meridian Obelisk. One of the four engines had rolled down onto the allotments. The plane was officially marked as Category "E" unsuitable for repair and was taken away some days later on a low loader. One youthful resident with a camera and some film snapped the wreckage, quite against the law, and must have had an accomplice who developed it. Such darkroom finds were required to be handed in to the Police.

Halifax "K" for Kittty Offham Road 16-4-43 *J Carvill*

Members of the crew after recovery from their injuries, returned to operational duty, two were lost on subsequent raids but six survived the war. A Lewes resident taking up employment after the war with a large retail Chemist's was interviewed by an area manager who on finding the new staff member came from Lewes identified himself as the Halifax Pilot who crashed at Landport.

The Dakota Crash at Newmarket

The events of Sunday 19th November 1944 make sad reading for this was the occasion of a tragic accident, when at 1504 hours an American Dakota Transport Aircraft No 315046 crashed south of the Plantation on Newmarket Hill with severe loss of life. The only sighting of the aircraft coming down was made by an artilleryman, Gunner Johnson, who had come on duty at an anti-aircraft gun site as an air sentry at 1500 hours. His report said that the aircraft flew from west to east disappearing behind a ridge and immediately afterwards a loud explosion followed by a sheet of flame was observed. He then asked a farm labourer as to the best way to get to the crash, borrowed a bicycle and reached the aircraft in twenty minutes accompanied by two other artillerymen. Several American soldiers were lying outside the wreck in no danger from the flames, they pulled one clear who was half out of the plane, and then in response to a plea from an American Sergeant went to get more help. Gunner Potter went to the telephone kiosk at Falmer to call for assistance. Meanwhile Sgt Keeble of the AA battery collected all available men along with first aid equipment and hurried to the scene at 1543 hours. On his way back to the crash, on the back of the unit's dispatch rider's motorcycle, Gunner Johnson overtook an NFS tender that had become bogged down in the mud. A REME (Royal Electrical and Mechanical Engineers) three ton lorry arrived from the top track and took the injured away. Afterwards only the dead remained to be collected.

The Police reports logged 25 killed and five seriously injured. Twenty-three of the dead were taken to the Lewes Mortuary. Six of the injured were taken to the Royal Sussex County Hospital where two were pronounced dead on arrival. One was taken to the Queen Victoria East Grinstead. Friston Airfield the nearest RAF station was notified. The first Police Officer on the scene was directed to the site by an ARP Warden through the Plantation but the car became bogged down 500 yards from the site. On arrival they did what they could to protect the injured outside the plane, nothing could be done for those still inside. Verey Lights and ammunition were exploding all the time and the first aid boxes from the plane were scattered and soaked by the driving rain. At 1430 hours a message was sent to Police HQ giving full details, from the nearest telephone at the *Newmarket Inn*, half a mile distant. Half way to the scene two Army ambulances became bogged down in the mud, neither reached the scene and they turned back. Four Lewes Civil Defence ambulances arrived and were told to go via Falmer Cross Roads. One managed to get to the scene.

Plane Tragedy Near Brighton

WRECKAGE OF THE DAKOTA PLANE which crashed on an isolated part of the South Downs, midway between Brighton and Lewes, on Sunday.

Sussex Daily News

Assistance at the crash was rendered by three members of the 16th Sussex Home Guard, Sgt R B Coote of Littledown Farm Lewes, Lance Corporal W Bishop and Private L Noel, all members of No 6 Platoon from A Company. Lance Corporal Bishop was walking on the Downs some distance from the crash and ran about a mile to Sgt Coote's house for assistance, he immediately sent Bishop to telephone the Police and the ARP to organise a rescue party with blankets and supplies. An approach by car was difficult owing to the state of the ground but on arrival at the scene they were able to help move the injured from the plane and render first aid.

As postscripts to this part of the story 12 members of the Borough Surveyor's staff received a special payment for the work involved in recovering the dead from the wrecked aircraft. The Council also had to meet a bill for a tractor used to tow out the mired-in NFS Tender. The dead airmen were buried in the American Military Cemetery at Madingley west of Cambridge.

The C47A was a twin engine plane built by the Douglas Aviation Co Inc of Long Beach, California, and accepted by the United States Air Force on 26th January 1944. It was allocated to the Ninety-second Troop Carrier Squadron, 439th Troop Carrier Group, 8th U S Air Force based at airstrip A 39 Chateaudun 70 miles south west of Paris. The unit's planes had been extensively engaged on glider towing operations, paratroop drops, and ferrying troops on leave to England.

Lieutenant Donald Reid, the pilot, with four other crew members took off from Station 486 Greenham Common near Newbury at 1430 hours on 19th November 1944 for Chateaudun. It was loaded with 600 gallons of aviation fuel and on board were twenty-five passengers, all but two being members of the Troop Carrier Group's administrative and transport staff returning to duty from leave. The other two were members of the Free French Air Force attached to RAF Ovington Yorkshire.

The pilot had 952 hours flying Dakotas to his credit. Due to the weather, instrument flight clearance was given. RAF Friston reported wind SSW 15 mph, ceiling 10/10 at 300 feet, visibility 2,500 feet varying lower during intermittent rain. It was assumed that the aircraft had lost ground contact and during a descent to re-establish contact was buffeted by turbulence and hit the Downs which at this point rise 645 feet above sea level.

The point of contact was sixty feet below the summit. Five successive propeller slashes marked the wreck's progress along a 300-foot trail of debris. Both engines had propeller damage indicating they were under power at the time of impact. The engines, right wing and rear section survived but were detached from each other. The remainder of the plane disintegrated in the fire. Four United States airmen and one French airman survived. None of the crew were among those saved. The Newmarket crash cost the unit more casualties than all the rest of its war operations.

The aircraft with fourteen others of its squadron had been on a search mission two days earlier for a British Avro York missing between St Lo and Marseilles carrying Air Marshall Sir Trafford Leigh Mallory to take up a command in the Far East. The search was unsuccessful, but the plane was eventually found by a farmer high in the Alps 30 miles east of Grenoble on 4th June 1945.

6. Enemy Action

The Air Raid Warning System

The rising and falling note of the air raid alert sirens sounding "The Alert" and the continuous note of "The Raiders Passed" signals sounded on 1,051 occasions in Lewes during the war. The public soon used the terms "Raid" and "All Clear" instead of the official terms. At least two residents in the town kept diaries of the sirens. Schoolboy Fred Burgess of Morris Road and his father who worked for the Council recorded date and duration of every alert. Special Police Constable SC233 W Wells, who was later to be bombed out of his home in West Street, also made a similar record. An analysis of the frequency of the alerts mirrors the progress of the war.

The National Warning System originated alerts as the result of information on the identification of enemy planes from Observer Corps posts and from Coastal Radar Plots. The reports from the Castle Observer Corps Post were telephoned by direct line first to Horsham Observer Control who relayed them to Fighter Command Control, where an Alarms' Controller correlated enemy air activity over a wide area. Warnings were communicated to telephone areas and subsequently to Main and Sub ARP Control Centres. The Lewes manual telephone exchange in Abinger Place received warnings from the Brighton exchange and passed them to Lewes Control under Pelham House for the County and to Lewes sub-Control under the Town Hall for the town. The messages were colour coded, YELLOW Information only raid expected, PURPLE Raiders Expected to pass overhead, RED Attack imminent, WHITE Raiders passed.

These arrangements were not always satisfactory, often alerts were sounded but no raiders approached the town. Inhabitants had taken cover in shelters, commerce and war production had come to a standstill.

Miss Walton Wardens' Post 7   *Brighton & Hove Herald*

Later in the war when "Hit and Run" raids of German planes coming in at roof top height bombed and machine gunned towns on and near the coast a raid would be over before the sirens sounded. The warning system evolved to meet the new threat with Operation "Rats" where Ground Control Interception Radar Stations informed Fighter Command control direct of the approach of raiders and main telephone exchanges in the threatened area so speeding up the sounding of sirens. Regional HQ gave approval for large coastal towns like Brighton to install a local warning system known as "The Pips". This was sounded after rooftop spotters had observed enemy planes coming. This was denied to Lewes by Regional HQ. The town bypassed this by resorting to the "Local Business Alarm System". Factories undertaking war work were encouraged to have rooftop spotters who would sound the factory alarm on the approach of hostile aircraft. Every's Phoenix Ironworks carried out war work and possessed a steam hooter. The hooter was used to sound the start and finish of work before the war but had been silenced by the Control of Noises Order (1940) which had also stopped the ringing of church bells. A simple bell push between the Castle Observers and the works supplemented by its own spotter (Mr Stan Oram) ensured that the town had an effective local warning system with repeated blasts of the hooter.

All the sirens were electrically powered and had vanes to modulate the tone for the two signals. The first siren was installed on the Town Hall chimney but often due to the prevailing wind could not be heard on the western side of the town. This was remedied by the installation of another siren on the Civil Prison, a third on Cliffe Church and eventually a fourth on the *Tally Ho* at Landport. To begin with the simultaneous sounding of the sirens was impossible owing to the older part of the town using direct current and the newer parts using alternating current. Ultimately with some reluctant expenditure, the problem was overcome.

Lewes like the rest of the country did not have to resort to warnings of gas attacks, wooden rattles being sounded to warn of the presence of gas and handbells to give the all clear. The threat of widespread incendiary attacks led to a local warning scheme with hunting horns. In August 1943, following the second attack with "Butterfly Anti-Personnel Bombs" it was decided that the sounding of hunting horns to warn of incendiary attacks should cease and in future three blasts on the horns would signify the dropping of butterfly bombs. Mr G Sains the Chief ARP Officer for the town secured a further fifteen hunting horns, some of them being described as antiques, from Horace Jackson's Music shop in the High Street.

Bomb Versus Motor Car

This car was thrown up against a wall when a bomb exploded

Sussex Express
Dunford's Garage Railway Lane 5-10-1940

Ald Crisp ARP Sub-Controller scored a "First" for Lewes when he originated the idea of placing sign boards at the Railway Station exit and on all the roads into the town bearing the words "This Town is Under Air Raid Warning". The idea was taken up widely. A tailpiece to this is a plaintive note recorded in the Civil Defence Committee minutes in 1941 that the board at the Station had disappeared, believed stolen!

Quarterly Record of Siren Soundings in Lewes

	1st	2nd	3rd	4th
1939	-	-	-	2
1940	0	3	139	204
1941	79	119	8	204
1942	12	45	81	31
1943	40	63	30	41
1944	41	50	69	3
1945	0	0	0	-

The third and fourth quarters of 1940 reflect the onslaught of the Battle of Britain. This level of raiding continued into the first and second quarters of 1941 with the Blitz on London and the large cities and industrial centres in the midlands and the north. The German invasion of Russia at the end of June 1941 diverted air attacks away from this country. They were resumed in 1942 with The "Baedeker Raids" on cathedral cities such as Canterbury and Coventry. The following year 1943 saw an increase in the "Hit and Run" low level attacks and German reprisal raids on London following the RAF offensive against German cities including Berlin. Many airfields in northern France from which the German planes flew had grass runways that restricted flying in the winter if the weather was bad. Despite the D-day Normandy landings on 6th June 1944 air raid alerts continued and peaked in the third quarter due to the Flying Bomb campaign. The number of alerts dropped in the last quarter to three and the sirens sounded in anger for the last time at 2230 hours on Monday 11th December 1944.

On Sunday 27th October 1940 there were seven separate periods of alert in 24 hours. On the 8th December 1940 there was a continuous period of alert for 13 hours 10 minutes and three days later another of 13 hours 13 minutes. It was during these long night alerts that Lewes residents might be kept awake by the drone of German aircraft on their way to bomb London and cities in the north. German planes had a distinctive asynchronous resonating engine note whereas the RAF planes always had a steady note. During the Dieppe Raid, 19th August, 1942 there were three periods of alert 0552 to 0608, 0640 to 0657 and 1659 to 2012 hours

Where the Bombs Fell

The first to fall was on Friday 23rd August 1940 when a bomb that failed to explode on impact, designated an unexploded bomb (UXB), landed on the Golf Course but detonated later from a delayed action fuse. On Saturday 31st August 1940 the war came closer to Lewes with a bomb falling on the railway line to London near Beechwood Bridge at Offham cutting power and telephone lines. The first high explosive bombs to be heard in the town fell on Monday 29th September 1940 at Beddingham, damaging the river bank and causing some flooding. The next day a bomb fell 100 yards southeast of Blackcap.

On Friday 4th October 1940 at 0951 hours a bomb landed 20 yards west of the river on farmland at West Rise Farm, the blast damaged windows at Elphick's shop in The Cliffe and Browne and Crosskey's shop at the corner of School Hill and Eastgate Street. The records state the bomb fell near the schools in Mountfield Road. The first fatality occurred on Sunday 13th October at 2251 hours when two high explosive (HE) bombs fell, seriously damaging Ashcombe Farmhouse, killing one person. An oil bomb landed close to the Chailey Rural District Council (RDC) pumping station at Hamsey on Saturday 19th October. Oil bombs contained a mixture of 86% Benzene, 10% Rubber and 4% Oil and Phosphorous, with an explosive charge they represented a dangerous fire hazard when hitting a built-up area.

On Monday 4th November two bombs, which failed to explode, fell on the east side of the river 300 yards south of Southerham Bridge with a third falling in the river. Monday 2nd December 1940 a UXB was found 150 yards southwest of the Racecourse grandstand on Houndean Farm. Again on Friday 12th December cottages at Houndean were damaged by a bomb.

The Cliffe and Southover Raid 5th October 1940

The first significant attack on Lewes took place on Saturday the 5th October 1940 at 0936 hours when a stick of ten bombs fell in a line across the southern part of the town from Cliffe Hill to the Cockshut in Southover. Damage and disturbance followed but there were no significant casualties. Bomb number one fell 20 yards east of the Martyr's Memorial and exploded. Bomb number two crashed into the kitchen of Horne Lodge, Chapel Hill and failed to explode. Bomb number three exploded in Railway Lane by Dunford's Garage with spectacular results leaving a customer's car standing vertically on its boot. Number four exploded in the Cattle Market destroying a corrugated iron shed near the Winterbourne stream. Number five fell in The Grange Gardens 50 yards from Eastport Lane. Numbers six and seven fell in Southover churchyard disturbing gravestones and damaging a wall. Number eight fell close to the Cockshut level crossing and failed to explode. There were two other UXBs, one south west of the Waterworks at the Brooks and the other at Spring Barn Farm, both were blown up by the army.

An Army bomb disposal team defused the Chapel Hill bomb, the local residents having been evacuated for a few days while the disposal team worked. The Grange Gardens bomb was in waterlogged ground close to the Winterbourne stream. An Auxiliary Fire Service (AFS) pump was used to clear water from the shaft while excavations were carried out. Despite all efforts the bomb slipped deeper into the mud and ultimately a decision was taken on 22nd October 1940 to abandon the dig and plug the hole with concrete. Over the years the spectre of the bomb has almost become part of folklore as it grows in size with the telling. It was probably a 50 Kg bomb and its presence haunts any would-be developer of the adjacent empty Cattle Market site. While the Bomb Disposal teams worked, the nearby residents were evacuated. Like those from Chapel Hill, they were housed by relatives, friends or neighbours until the crisis had passed. These bombing incidents from August to December 1940 were unlikely to be targeted attacks on the town but more likely strays from major raids elsewhere or crippled planes unloading their bombs before returning to base in France. They may have been attracted by stray light from the Railway Marshalling Yard that was exempt from total compliance with the blackout. Clear cold winter nights with a full moon made the blackout more bearable but for good reason they earned the name "Bomber's Moon" with the countryside and towns lit almost like day.

The Lewes "Blitz" 20th January 1943

The town enjoyed a respite from bombs although not from air raid alerts, from January 1941 for two years, during this period the sirens would sound nearly 400 times without a bomb dropping. This lack of enemy activity had brought about an air of complacency. The sirens sounded the alert at 1224 hours on Wednesday 20th January 1943. Calmly everyone went about their business as usual. Shops were preparing to close at 1.00 pm for the customary half-day early closing. The County School Boys' and Girls' together with the Bec boys had been to a special showing of "The Young Mr Pitt" at The Odeon Cinema. Elsewhere people in their homes were preparing the midday meals. The Civil Defence Control Room now housed in a surface bunker behind Barclays Bank came to a state of readiness as it had done so on many previous occasions. Wardens' posts around the town were manned. Ambulances and fire engines, if they had not had their daily test, were warmed up. Policemen on street patrol donned their blue painted steel helmets.

West Street minutes after the raid of 20-1-1943 *RCHME*

The Royal Observer Corps on the Castle Keep, the spotters on the Town Hall roof lookout and those on Every's Ironworks scanned the skies as they had on so many fruitless occasions before. A boy, nine years old, had been sent from his home in Brook Street to Stevenson's shop at the top of North Street on a shopping errand to get a loaf of bread. An Aircraftman home on leave from the RAF visited his relations, evacuated from Beckenham, at West Street. The hooter on the Ironworks sounded the "Immediate Danger Signal" at 1240 hours as eight aircraft identified as six Messerschmidt (Me) 109s and two Focke Wulfe (FW) 190s appeared from the north west at roof top height dropping six 250 Kg bombs all of which exploded on impact. Lewes was now experiencing its most damaging raid of the war. The attackers were part of a large diversionary force that ranged over a wide area of Sussex shooting up villages and isolated homes. Maresfield Camp was hit as was a train near Isfield. Little Horsted, Barcombe, Hamsey, Gote Lane, Ringmer and Seaford were machine-gunned.

North Street salvaging furniture and effects the afternoon 20-1-1943 *RCHME*

Fighter Command Plotting Table designated the raid as No. 411. It consisted of three groups of enemy planes 34 FW 190s at zero feet seen at 1222 hours between North Foreland and Beachy Head which fanned out over a wide area of Kent and East Sussex. This group attacked south-east London, a school in Lewisham receiving a direct hit killing 24 children and teachers and injuring 66 others. The second group of planes identified as Me 109s crossed the coast at Eastbourne at 1234 hours penetrating 15 miles inland at rooftop height before re-crossing the coast at Brighton. The timings suggest that the Lewes raiders were part of this force. A third high level group of 30 aircraft appeared at 1236 hours sweeping down the coast from North Foreland to Dover as a rear cover party. The RAF put up 214 fighter aircraft in response and combats continued across the channel with 14 enemy planes claimed as destroyed for the loss of two RAF planes and one pilot killed. The main target that day was south-east London, attacked by 30 fighter bombers that had crossed the coast at low level between the North Foreland and Beachy Head. The Capital would have been reached in six minutes flying time at 350 mph. Some confusion arose as the planes arrived over the boundary of two Observer Corps areas with headquarters at Maidstone and Horsham, the latter to which the Lewes Observers reported. To make matters worse for London the balloon barrage had been hauled down to calibrate anti-aircraft gun radars. The

German planes which attacked London were FW 190s from Jageschwader (Jg) (120 aircraft) 10/2 led by Oberleutnant Heinz Schumann flying from Arques and St Omer and by JG 10/26 led by Oberleutnant Paul Keller based at Abbeville. Oberleutenant Keller was himself killed by Bofors anti-aircraft Fire on 25th March 1943 during a low level attack on Ashford Railway works in Kent.

The Stag North Street, a gas main blazes 20-1-1943   *R Hallett Sussex Express*

The first of the six 250 Kg bombs fell at the rear of Chandler's Yard in Brook Street damaging the Corporation's greenhouse. In November 1946 a Council war damage claim of £338 for the greenhouse confirms the impact point. The second bomb fell, like most low level released bombs, horizontally furrowing the slates on the roof of a house on the east side of North Street before falling on its side to score the roadway, it then bounced sideways against the wall of the old Naval Prison knocking a hole in the brickwork. Finally it exploded cratering the roadway outside the *Stag Inn* on the corner of East and North Streets. The houses in this part of North Street were of mainly wood framed mathematical tile construction. They suffered badly from the effect of blast, numbers eight and nine had the fronts torn off, opposite, numbers 66 and 67 were reduced to a shambles. The *Stag* next door was badly battered but still standing. Gas from the broken main flared in the crater opposite. Here nine year old Stanley Johnson lost his life. Staddon's the Chemist on the corner of West and Market Streets had lost windows and mathematical tiles. Today the upper frontage is hung with clay tiles the mathematical tiles having been used to patch the gaps lower down. Other shops at this point, Urry's the confectioners, the Co-op Butcher's, and Stevenson's Corn Merchants all suffered damage. Demolition was required of numbers 4 to 10 these stood where the telephone exchange now stands. All seven properties between *The Limes* at the corner of Little East Street and the remains of the *Stag* had to be cleared.

Bomb number three fell at the rear of 8 West Street causing serious damage to the houses there and to those in the adjacent New Street. Here Leading Aircraftman George Henry Pallen of Beckenham was fatally injured. This area is now the site of the West Street Car Park. Across the road the Co-operative store and its baker's shop had lost their windows. The clock on the store had stopped at 12.47 pm. Hyland's general store not only lost its windows but stock and fittings as well. The houses from the corner of New Street, numbers 6, 8 and 12, had to be demolished. No 12 was the home of siren diarist Special Constable Wells. Six houses 13 to 18 New Street also had to be demolished. The demolitions did not always follow immediately after the raid, a photograph taken later in 1943 shows the Home Guard using the ruined houses for street fighting practice.

The remains of 28 New Road 20-1-1943 *R Hallett Sussex Express*

Bomb number four fell behind 39 and 41 New Road, both brick built, causing the fronts to bulge out. Although they withstood the blast effect better than the tile covered wooden framed houses, both had to be demolished. There were no serious injuries here. A planning wrangle developed between the site owners and the Council in 1945. An application to rebuild was refused on the grounds that the area was over occupied at 70 houses and 284 persons per acre, there was no rear entrance to a row of 28 houses and a sixty-foot road widening was envisaged. In 1984 two new houses appeared to fill the gap matching the old perfectly. Alternative road schemes, patience and common sense had prevailed.

Bomb number five landed further up New Road on the opposite side destroying the end house number 28 and starting a fire in the garden of the house behind in Paddock Road. Soil blasted from the gardens covered that part of Paddock Road. Again there were no serious injuries here and what was left of the house was demolished soon afterwards. The property has never been replaced and viewing the site today it is hard to imagine sufficient space for a house. In 1945 negotiations with the Council over compensation for the site ended with the Council's valuation of £10 being paid after firstly a £30 and then a £20 claim had been rejected.

Bomb number six fell behind the houses in Elm Grove seriously injuring some residents, before it landed and exploded. Its near horizontal flight path had caught the chimney stack of the head Post Office depositing a shower of bricks in the road at the top of Watergate Lane. The tail fin becoming detached was later found in a summerhouse behind a High Street property. The explosion wrecked a corrugated iron shed that stood next to the railway tunnel at the bottom of St Martin's Lane. This was used by Harper and Eede to store agricultural machinery for display on Cattle Market days. Again war damage records confirm the impact point with the Council's claim in 1948 for £13 in respect of repairs to the sewer in St Martin's Lane.

Jackson's anti-blast window tape before the bombing *L Davey Sussex Express*

The raiders would have been over the town for no longer than 30 seconds. In that time in addition to the two fatalities there were 11 people seriously injured requiring admission to the Victoria Hospital. There were 34 minor injury cases many having cuts caused by flying glass. A number were treated in their own homes. Property damage amounted to 15 (category A) destroyed or in need of demolition, 56 (category B) seriously damaged, major repairs required, 70 (category D) needing to be evacuated before repair and 230 (category E) needing minor repairs while occupancy continued. The Salvation Army Hall in St John Street and The Forester's Hall in Station Street were used as rest centres for the homeless until alternative accommodation could be found for them. Most of the shops in the High Street from Library Corner to St Michael's Church had lost their shop windows. The roads where bombing had occurred were closed for three days, except to essential traffic, while the clear up operation got under way. North Street remaining closed for several more days.

The Canadian Army units stationed in the town rendered valuable service with the West Nova Scotia Regiment providing lorries to transport furniture and effects into temporary store and willing hands to do the carrying. Empty shops were used as stores for the effects from bomb damaged homes. One of these in Fisher Street is now Seymour's. Shaw's Stores two doors up from the Odeon was also used as also was Curry's empty shop that stood at the corner of Morris Road and the Cliffe. The NFS men also helped move some of the effects into empty houses where the bombed out families were temporarily housed. The Ministry of Works took over the empty Venus Car showrooms at 144/5 High Street at the corner of Westgate Street as a store for items of architectural interest from bomb damaged properties so that demolition could proceed. Some of the fireplaces, doors, windows and the mathematical tiles would have been on the inventory of this store.

Under a mutual aid scheme the Lewes repair squads from the Corporation North Street depot supplemented by local builders commenced first aid repairs to the less seriously damaged houses on the afternoon of the raid. They were supplemented in the days to come by 60 men from repair squads from Eastbourne, East Grinstead and other neighbouring towns repaying the help given to those places by the Lewes repair teams after those towns had been raided. Tarpaulins were placed over damaged roofs, roofing felt was nailed over broken windows and shop fronts were boarded up with many shops receiving a small

Jackson's window bomb damage repair 19-4-43   RCHME

domestic sized window sufficient for customers to know that the shop was still trading. Householders cleared up the mess created when lath and plaster ceilings fell in. The repairmen fitted Essex boarding, the joints being covered with wooden battens. These temporary ceiling repairs may still be seen in some houses today. The Singer Sewing Machine shop opposite the Town Hall had its broken shop front covered with corrugated iron sheeting.

During the afternoon of the raid gas from a broken pipe continued to burn in the crater in the road in North Street until it could be extinguished by the Fire Service and the broken pipe sealed. Later that evening pockets of gas from broken pipes in the *Stag* Inn ignited attracting a crowd of sightseers, and resulted in a further call for the Fire Service. Station Officer Geering hurrying to North Street to man the appliance "Red Major 2" (see under Fire Service) managed to stumble into the water filled crater and arrived on duty soaked through. Two trailer pumps from the Malling Street 31/3Y sub-Fire Station also attended. The fire call can be timed approximately as the air raid alert sounded at 2045 hours dispatching the crowd of onlookers smartly homewards or to the nearest shelters. Nothing more untoward happened and the all clear sounded at 2100 hours except that during the firefighting at the *Stag* a helpful member of the Home Guard tried to assist and was asked by the firemen to fetch a hose branch. Instead of getting the item from the Fire Engine he went to the Auxiliary Fire Station in North Street to ask for one and got an unhelpful response from the crews on stand-by there. This minor confusion was blown up out of all proportion when reported out of context and it took the wisdom and diplomacy of Ald Crisp to restore harmony between the Home Guard and the Fire Service. The final piece of bureaucracy occurred with the arrival of a NFS canteen from Brighton which dispensed hot drinks and sandwiches to the firemen but refused to serve any of the other Civil Defence workers and Police who were still working on the site. Much was made of this later. The WVS canteen was called out and Mrs M Geering and helpers refreshed the other workers.

Bomb damaged Savings Centre, the Singer shop 19-4-43   RCHME

The attack on the Wallands 10th May 1943

At 1813 hours on Monday 10th May 1943 the alert sounded followed four minutes later by the local warning. At 1820 hours two enemy Junkers 88 bombers flew out of low cloud from the north, over the Wallands area amid local AA fire, dropping bombs. The bombs fell in a line 200 yards in length stretching from Hill Road to Ferrers Road. A firepot and two 250 Kg HE bombs and two 50 Kg HE falling 20 yards north of the last house in Ferrers Road. Some also fell on open ground. Altogether that evening there were eight HE bombs, nine firepots, three of which failed to explode, these were dealt with by the Bomb Disposal squad the next day. A small fire started at 17 Gundreda Road and 100 houses suffered minor damage to windows, doors, ceilings and roof tiles. One person was slightly injured in this attack. A firepot consisted of a steel casing similar to a 50-Kg bomb, it contained six tumbler shaped flasks 2 x 3 x 5 inches plus 67 triangular incendiary charges 2 x 1 inches both types of inserts contained Magnesium and to explode and scatter the fire bomblets a charge of 16 lbs of high explosive was used.

"Butterfly" Anti-Personnel Bombs

There were two periods of alarm, the first on the night of 3rd/4th March when 1,400 anti-personnel bombs of the butterfly type were dropped over wide areas of England including Kent, East Sussex and Surrey, and again on the night of 10/11th August 1943. These bombs were dropped in canisters that opened after leaving the aircraft. Each bomb was 3 inches in diameter and weighed about 4 lbs. During descent four vanes opened, two were to stabilise and slow the descent, the other two rotated and armed the device. There were three types of fuses, instantaneous on impact, delayed of 30 minutes' duration and most deadly of all a trembler fuse that remained inactive after impact until the bomb was disturbed when a half second fuse ensured immediate injury or death to whoever touched it. The nearest known fatality to Lewes occurred at Battle in August where a farm worker of eighteen years of age and a keen ATC member, due to enter the RAF two weeks later, was killed by one of these bombs as he crossed a field on his way to work. Schools and the public were cautioned about the danger and in Lewes three blasts on hunting horns would warn the public that this type of bomb had fallen. It was arranged that warning notices for incoming traffic to the town would be posted at appropriate warden's posts and in addition at the junction of Priory Street and Mountfield Road and at the Motor Roads for military traffic leaving the Downs. Clearing operations by No 20 Bomb Disposal Company of the Royal Engineers continued until 1946. It is a sobering thought that after a TV programme in 1979 entitled "UBX" many of these bombs were reported in remote woodlands and some householders owned up to having them as souvenirs.

The V1 "Doodlebugs"

In June 1944 just a week after D-day guarded reports were circulated with advice to school children and adults caught in the streets when "Danger Overhead" threatened, to take cover until it had passed. The reference was of course to the pilotless planes, Hitler's vengeance weapon the V1 which the public soon christened "Doodlebug". The first recorded V1 to land in Sussex was in the early hours of 13th June at Cuckfield not far from the Balcombe railway viaduct. It was the second to be fired by the Germans, with the majority in the early days of their "Rumpelkammer" offensive making landfalls between Dover and Brighton. Of the 775 V1s to land in East Sussex just one came down in Lewes and 16 in the Chailey RDC area. This gave Lewes another peak of air raid alerts in the second and third quarters of the year and a grandstand view of the V1s passing overhead, usually at an altitude of 1,000 feet mostly on their way to London.

The silencing of the V1s pulse jet engine was the sign to take cover before one ton of high explosive descended. The official codeword for the weapon was appropriately "Diver". The one which came down in Lewes fell on 21st July 1944 at 0815 hours. The V1 flying in an east west direction was brought down by AA gunfire at Kingston Ridge the resultant explosion leaving a crater 36 feet in diameter and 8 feet deep. Four houses were damaged.

The Sussex Police incident records show that all the following V1 incidents were the result of aircraft intercepting the V1s. At Beddingham, Littledean Farm on 19th June a V1 exploded leaving a crater 26 feet in diameter and 8 feet deep. On 17th July the Alpha Cement works at

Beddingham suffered damage to a kilnhouse and coal intake when aircraft attacked another V1. The explosion covered the railway with debris for a length of 90 feet putting it out of action for some hours. Golding's Farm Newick had three cottages damaged on the 18th. Wivlesden Farm Chailey suffered damage when the front of the farmhouse was blown in and 300 panes of glass were broken in an adjacent nursery. At Bushey Lodge Farm, The Brooks, West Firle, an impact left a hole 20 feet in diameter by five feet in depth on 28th June.

A 10-foot diameter crater from a V1 warhead was found at Burtenshaw's Farm Barcombe on 1st July the fuselage fell at Scuffleys Farm. A V1 falling on 5th July at Housedean Farm Falmer damaged four houses and cut the telephone wires on the Brighton to Lewes Railway the point of impact was 30 feet from the Brighton Road. On 7th July 18 houses were slightly damaged at Rennies Farm Isfield. At Ripe level crossing four houses and the signal box sustained damage from a V1 on the 11th July, the railway line was also put of action for 12 hours. At Ringmer, on 12th July at Plashett's Farm the farmhouse and cottages were damaged. On 23rd August, also at Ringmer, Paygate Farm and eight houses were wrecked. The NFS dealt with the fire which followed in a haystack.

During the war Lewes did not have static AA protection although it was an important road and rail centre. In 1940 a searchlight and sound locator unit was established on the Downs to the east of the racecourse. In the same year for a time a mobile light AA Bofors gun was located in the field in Ham Lane next to the Convent Field with the Gunners using the Mountfield Road Drill Hall for their meals. Later in 1943, to counter the "Hit and Run Raiders", Bofors guns were located on Cliffe Hill near the Golf Clubhouse, then under military occupation. Another was sited at Mill Road Malling on some level ground which was part of the old chalk pit used pre-war as a bonfire site. A third was next to the Bastion, the Kingsley Road entrance to the Landport Estate, while a fourth was sited on open downland at the end of the unfinished part of Gundreda Road. This fired at the attacking planes during the January 1943 raid. As part of the response to the V1 attack an Oerlikon cannon was installed on top of the railway station.

The fine old Georgian shop front of Lowdell and Coopers, Ironmongers, at 62 High Street was destroyed in the 1941 "Blitz" on Hull. It had been removed in 1939 and placed in a Museum there when the High Street firm closed and the premises were converted for MacFisheries. Today the central pillared entrance is all that survives in Lewes of this once elegant shop front.

****

7. Law and Order

Policing of Lewes was effected from the Police Station in West Street built in 1884 as a Police Barracks on the site of a Mechanic's Institute where a theatre had previously stood. Single and married Police Officers were provided with accommodation there both before and during the war. The building also acted as the Force Headquarters for the East Sussex Area that stretched from Rye to Shoreham and Haywards Heath to Crowborough. The building had been outgrown, hence the Home Office demand for a new headquarters in Mountfield Road. Brighton, Hove, Eastbourne and Hastings County Boroughs had separate forces.

The strength in 1939 amounted to 299 men under the Chief Constable Mr R E Breffit. It consisted of 16 Superintendents and Inspectors and 283 Constables and Sergeants, the latter rank having been increased by five to supervise the air raid warden service countywide. In June 1939 a first police reserve was mainly of retired officers supplemented by seventy-eight War Reserve Constables. Tunic numbers were prefixed with the letters FR and WR as appropriate. Initially both served in civilian clothes until uniforms became available. All policemen were issued with service type box respirators and steel helmets painted navy blue and lettered "Police" in white. The force was further supplemented by the Special Constabulary, a time proven group of unpaid volunteers, although in December 1939 only four would be retained full-time. The rest would receive a boot allowance of twopence per ten hours of duty and a clothing allowance of one and a half-pence per hour. By 1942 the number of "Specials" stood at 54. In late March 1940 the War Reserve constables were still waiting for uniforms but were being paid £3 per week plus 1/- boot allowance. Women were first recruited in 1941 to help with administrative duties, the Women's Auxiliary Police Corps (WAPs) and the Police Auxiliary Messenger Service (PAMs), the latter being young women of 17 and 18 years of age.

Sussex Daily News
Constable in air raid alert order Fisher Street 1939

These arrangements may have sufficed for peacetime but the stress of war called for change. In 1942 proposals were put forward for an amalgamation of all the Police Forces in the County to secure greater effectiveness during the forthcoming invasion of Europe. On 1st April 1943 the amalgamation took place with the former Chief Constable Mr Breffit becoming an Assistant Chief Constable in charge of No 1 East Sussex Police District comprising Lewes and most of the area covered by the present day Lewes District Council. The Force commander was Major John

Fergusson of the Metropolitan Police with headquarters at *Fairmile*, Oathall Road, Haywards Heath. Additional accommodation at Lewes was found at *Roslyn*, 22 King Henry's Road, that subsequently became the administration offices of the East Sussex Fire Brigade. Of all the component forces the No 1 Lewes District had the best preserved set of wartime records handed to the East Sussex Record Office by the Sussex Police Authority.

LEWES DIVISION SPECIAL CONSTABLES

Members attending a recent parade.

The "Specials" made a significant contribution to wartime policing 17-11-44   *Sussex Express*

Several members of the force were called up during the war. To cope with the increased police work concerning the "Second Front," as the D-day Normandy landings were known, until 6th June 1944, a reinforcement from other forces took place. Much of this work was in traffic control duties concerning convoys of military vehicles passing to and from holding camps and the embarkation ports. Communication between Police Headquarters, Stations and Officers on duty was rudimentary. Telephoned, handwritten or verbal messages passing between officers sufficed, radio did not appear until 1946. Between 5th May and 31st August 1944 sixty officers from the Yorkshire forces were seconded to help the Sussex Police. They came from the West Riding, York City, Leeds City, Huddersfield City and Halifax Borough forces.

The Observer Corps

The Observer Corps had come into being in 1926, the members being enrolled as Special Constables. They wore civilian clothes and police duty bands, an armband of white stripes on blue. These were also worn by all uniformed constables when on duty, lawbreakers found that the absence of armbands did not bring immunity from apprehension. The observers had three states of readiness. Firstly, Post Manned and plotting instruments ready. Secondly, Alert, half manned with two observers at each post within telephone bell hearing, the rest within recall reach. Thirdly, Released but within two hours readiness. A secret mobilisation of the Corps took place on 26th August 1939 eight days before the outbreak of war. The members were paid from that date £3 per week when the Air Ministry took over the responsibility from the police. Their duties were to plot the bearing, number, altitude, and type of enemy planes, using a gridded map table with a sighting arm and height bar and to relay this information to the control room at Horsham.

Fighter Command at Stanmore issued orders to Fighter Groups to make the necessary response to enemy air attacks. Aircraft plots from Observer Corps control rooms throughout the country provided the vital information. The air raid warning system was operated from Stanmore but the twenty minutes' warning could not always be given. By 1942 thirty-one posts were authorised to issue warnings to siren control points direct to prevent warnings being given after attacks had occurred. This enabled Lewes Castle to notify the Lewes Town Hall and Pelham House, East Sussex control rooms direct.

The Lewes Corps had 65 members who worked in shifts of three, round the clock, seven days a week, a constant watch being maintained. During the war there were two Chief Observers Mr A C Broadbent and Mr A C Channon. One of the senior observers was Mr C G Kraushaar, custodian of the Castle, who in 1944, volunteered to act as a seagoing observer with the Normandy invasion fleet. Mr J A Davies, Pleasure Ground's Superintendent, was another member of the corps who was released in October 1944 to help with the reinstatement of the Corporation's recreational facilities.

Besides reporting enemy aircraft the observers had other duties, lights flashed from aircraft, seaborne or airborne landings, aircraft in distress, aircraft crashes and suspicious persons or events all had to be logged and reported. An instruction to fire rockets, red for air and green for sea landings, during a German invasion remained in force until December 1944.

Observers J A Davies and C G Kraushaar at the Castle 1943 *J Carvill*

The Corps was issued with blue battledress uniforms in 1942 and on 9th April 1942 received the title "Royal". The Lewes post stood down on 12th May 1945. In November 1953 the observers left the Castle for a new underground bunker on the Race Hill with a capability for nuclear observation.

Records and Regulations

Wartime police duties included keeping records for the Home Office of every bomb, or other item dropped from the air, and a record of all air raid deaths and severe or slightly injured casualties. A categorised list of properties damaged by enemy action, from destroyed to those slightly damaged was also needed. In coastal areas records were required of explosions, air crashes, bodies and other items washed ashore. The Defence Regulations promulgated during the war numbered well over 100. On 9th May 1944, the day after "VE" day, 84 were revoked entirely and 25 others relaxed. These "Orders" as they were known covered almost every aspect of life, the supply and use of rationed food, fuel, clothing and other commodities. Freedom of movement of both aliens and natives, control of occupations, restriction on lighting (The Blackout), control of noise (Church Bells) and the opening of cinemas on Sundays. Some were well known, 18b used to intern aliens on The Isle of Man, others less well known. No 33 was familiar to health workers. Any two persons having acquired a Venereal Infection from the same third person could lay information against that third person that required him or her to undergo compulsory treatment or face prosecution.

Quite early in the war on 20th October 1939 a Hindu jute trader was intercepted as he was about to board the Dieppe Ferry at Newhaven. A personal search produced a letter that was being taken abroad for onward posting to avoid censorship, a punishable breach of the Defence Regulations.

The Police would have a heavy workload in dealing with the usual calendar of offences plus the added burden imposed by the wartime regulations. Probably the commonest offence was that of contravening the blackout regulations. Inadvertence, failing to draw curtains, lights switched on before the blacking out time in rooms with curtains undrawn and sheer carelessness resulted in a procession of cases through the court. The culprits ranged from housewives to professional men, three men of the cloth and two court officials. Corporate guilt emerged when one of the summonses related to a light left on by a prisoner in Lewes Gaol. The fines were usually in the order of 10/- (50 pence), a day's pay, but repeated appearances of the same offender would rate fines of £2 or £3 that equalled a week's pay.

Most consumer goods were scarce during the war, photographic supplies included, but this did not prevent some people being caught, photographing the forbidden. In 1940 a honeymoon couple from Reigate were seen by a police inspector at Newhaven snapping ships in the harbour. These were on a prohibited list. The couple were traced through the car number, a penalty of £1.50 fines and costs was imposed. On 22nd July 1940 a clergyman, a native of Nigeria, was visiting Lewes on a preaching engagement and chose to take a stroll on Cliffe Hill. While enjoying the view he decided to take a picture that included the Lewes Gas works, he was fined ten shillings. Another resident of Lewes who took a picture of his workplace was also fined £1 at the same hearing. The chemist on developing the film had informed the police of its content. In June 1942 a column of medium tanks was passing through Newick when an NCO saw something glinting through a hedge, investigation revealed a photographer who was placed under arrest. Later in court the man explained that he was taking the pictures for a nephew who was "Mad on Tanks". On conviction he was fined £2. In 1944, prior to D-day, an air raid warden at Firle was seen, by a member of the armed forces, using a pair of binoculars at an upstairs window. A plea of ignorance of the regulations governing the use of such items in a restricted area failed to save him from conviction.

Motoring Offences

Two motorists were fined 5/- each for leaving cars parked without lights, one in the High Street the other in Mount Place. As an anti-invasion measure, from June 1940, all motor vehicles, when left unattended, had to be immobilised by removal of the rotor arm from the distributor. In August 1940 a motorist who left his car unlocked and not immobilised was fined 5/-. Petrol was rationed from the outset of the war. Until 1942 a small ration was allowed for private motoring but this ceased and essential petrol allowances could only be used for the purpose specified on the ration book. A local filling station had been taken over for use by the army in 1940. The premises had been under observation by the police and they saw customers obtaining fuel in cans. In court it was said that it was thought the substance was paraffin and if it was petrol then it was residual petrol in the garage tanks from civilian ownership. Charges of stealing and receiving War Department petrol were dropped but a conviction was obtained on the supply and receipt of petrol without coupons. Fines of £2 and £5 were levied.

In February 1943 a Lewes motorist was stopped in Brighton. It transpired that a new engine had been fitted to the car and a running in trip had been deemed necessary. The fact that there were two couples in the car who both admitted to having had a convivial evening after visiting the *Theatre Royal*, failed to impress the bench and a conviction followed for the misuse of petrol. Fines for the owner and driver totalled £10. A Fuel Inspector was caught at a dance in June 1944 and fined £10 for parking on the wrong side of the road after dark, failing to immobilise her car and using petrol for improper purposes. Another dancer visiting a class at Hamsey having journeyed from Cooksbridge received a fine of £1, an expensive short distance trip. Lewes tradesmen suffered the restrictions on deliveries which petrol rationing had imposed but were put out when a van from Brighton was seen in the town selling ice cream. Their good record was slightly dented when a police routine check stopped a tradesman's delivery van in Nevill Road. It was found empty and the owner admitted using it to travel home for his midday meal. He was fined £1. By 1944 fines had increased, a Plumpton couple caught in a police spot check were fined £50 for the misuse of petrol. Two Streat farmers were prosecuted for misusing petrol issued for farming. Their plea that they had travelled to ARP and Home Guard duty was not accepted.

Food rationing regulations and price controls were full of hazards. Three months after meat rationing had started in January 1940 a local butcher was fined £1 for overcharging on breast of veal by 2d a pound and best end of neck of mutton by 1d per pound. This butcher appeared in court again in September 1944 for supplying meat to certain customers in excess of ration books held. A total of 61 summonses were heard under the Food Control Order. After fines of £60 and costs of £53 had been imposed, the court heard that the firm had been fined on three previous occasions, 1940, 1942 and 1943.

Food Controls and Rationing

A greengrocer in Malling Street in October 1941 was prosecuted over charging incorrectly for blackberries. The controlled price for cultivated berries was 10d a pound while that for wild fruit was 5d a pound. Cultivated berries could only be sold to a commercial preserver, while the defendant had both kinds for sale at the higher price. A food inspector from Tunbridge Wells gave evidence of a trial purchase, and a conviction on technical grounds resulted in a ten shilling fine.

Technicalities continued to entrap the unwary. A Newick market gardener was fined £4 for planting strawberry plants contrary to instructions given to him by the War Agricultural Committee under the Defence Regulations. A dairy in Fisher Street was fined for supplying milk to an unregistered customer, apparently a casual helper in the shop had made the mistake. A local woman was convicted in September 1941 for receiving food stolen by a soldier from an army cookhouse.

In March 1944 a man was apprehended in a shop in Fisher Street. In his possession was a bag containing two bacon backs and 36 eggs to the value of £5, the property of I G Beer & Co of the Maltings Castle Ditch Lane. Both the man and the shopkeeper were fined £50 with costs for supplying and purchasing items contrary to the food regulations. A shoemaker was brought to court for failing to comply with footwear repair regulations in that he repaired a pair of shoes with a through sole, a piece of leather from toe to heel instead of using separate pieces. A market gardener was fined for sending cartons of tomatoes to Leeds that was outside the permitted transport zone limits for Lewes.

Restricted Areas

Following the fall of France in June 1940 and again in the run up to D-day in 1944 a strip 10 miles in depth of the Sussex Coast was declared a prohibited area. It was out of bounds to all except residents and those with a bona fide purpose for entry. Identity cards were checked at the Railway station and on the roads leading into the town at the Home Guard checkpoints. Those who objected to the challenge or who evaded it and were later caught inside faced prosecution. On 11th July 1941 a motorist from London was stopped at Uckfield and was cautioned by a police officer for attempting to enter a prohibited area. The motorist was told to turn round, instead he sped off pursued by an officer on a motorcycle and eventually caught. The escapade cost him a £5 fine. Two Uckfield men were caught in a prohibited area and each fined ten shillings. They were found during a random check carried out by the police in the foyer of the Odeon Cinema. Their plea that there was no Sunday Cinema in Uckfield found no favour with the court. In June 1944 a Red Cross worker from London was intercepted at Newick and was unable to provide satisfactory evidence for being in a prohibited area she was duly convicted.

Roistering Servicemen

Service personnel visiting Lewes when off duty in search of entertainment posed problems on occasions for the police. Canadian soldiers seemed to figure largely in the disturbances. This was due to the high concentration of the Canadian Army in Sussex. There was also the novelty for them of the English Public House. Back home in Canada a form of prohibition on alcohol sales had existed long after it was abandoned in the United States. Many of the Provinces had "Beverage Rooms" soulless places where only beer was sold. Music, dancing, singing and all other forms of amusement were banned.

For security reasons a soldier's nationality was often hidden by the term "An overseas soldier". This was the description applied to a Canadian Earle W------ age 27 who, in June 1942 was arrested in the High Street after P C Gard, when on duty heard the sound of breaking glass at No 15A, the premises having been left secure. A witness inside saw a hand trying to unbolt the door through the broken panel. When charged the defendant replied "What window. I have no recollection of it at all". Penalty, fined £1 plus costs.

In the same court Corporal Walter Alexander W------ was charged with being on enclosed premises without just cause. He had apparently entered the *Red White and Blue* public house in Friars Walk by climbing a six foot wall, and jumping a four foot gap over a twelve foot drop, in all quite a feat from someone whose defence was drunkenness. A plea from his unit officer secured his release after payment of the fine £1.

On 21st July 1942 premises at Library Corner were seen to be secure by War Reserve Constable John Miller at 10.40 pm. Shortly afterwards paid Firewatcher Ernest Whitham drew the constable's attention to a damaged plate glass door at the offices of the Lewes Building Society and to the flight of three soldiers towards Cliffe Bridge. Richard Carlton W------- a Canadian soldier was seen at Cliffe Corner with a bleeding wrist. He was arrested and treated at the Victoria Hospital. In court he admitted being drunk and was fined £1 with fifteen shillings costs. In the same month another two from Canada, Paul Auguste P------ and Jean Le------- who had been drinking in the *Pelham Arms* started arguing at closing time and refused to leave the premises. Special Constable Mann was called and ejected them when they smashed the door panel. They were then arrested by Inspector W Lamberth. In court an officer from the men's unit gave good character references for them and they admitted being drunk. Each was fined fifteen shillings with thirty-five shillings costs.

On Christmas night 1942 three Canadian soldiers had been on a round of the town's pubs and had ended up near closing time at the *Dorset Arms* in Malling Street. They asked the landlady if they could have a room for the night. This was provided and the visitors' book signed. The trio and their hosts retired to their bedrooms. During the night breaking noises were heard downstairs in the bar where the three soldiers had resumed their drinking, but without the landlady's permission. Difficulties followed and the police were called. However before their arrival all three departed along South Street. By now it was 4.00 am, PC John Carter pedalled off on his bicycle, in pursuit, towards Southerham in the bright moonlight. The pursuit ended in Ranscombe Lane when the constable caught up with Private Sherman John D----- age 25, who was arrested and handcuffed by the resourceful officer to a telephone pole while he went after the other two. Private John Alcon R------- age 24 and Private Leslie Joseph D------ age 26 threw away most of the bottles as they fled. One fugitive was arrested in Brigdens Hill shortly afterwards. By the next day the third was in custody at Lewes Police Station. In court the arresting officer PC Carter described recovering bottles of spirits discarded during the chase and that the value of the stolen goods amounted to £13. Each defendant was fined thirty shillings.

Penalties generally for drunkenness and damage did not seem unduly severe. Where violence was offered, sterner punishments were handed out. During the night of 23rd August 1943 PC Rodgers was patrolling in Malling Street. At 12.30 am he heard the sound of bottles breaking near the Cliffe air raid shelter. Later at 1.30 am he heard shouts of "I'll kill you" coming from the river bank near Harvey's premises in the Cliffe. Three soldiers were seen trying to throw a fourth in the river. PS Hullock attended the disturbance to render assistance, he knocked out one of the attackers with his truncheon and went for additional help. Before he returned PC Rodgers was thrown to the ground and jumped on. Help arrived and PS Hullock adopted a ruse, by shining a torch in the faces of the combatants he blinded them telling them that they were covered with a loaded rifle. The arrests were completed and the next day Bernard Howard T------, Thomas E-------, and Joseph Gerard P-------- appeared in court pleading guilty to being drunk and disorderly and assaulting a Police Officer. P------- made his appearance with his head heavily bandaged. Along with his compatriots he was sentenced to one month's hard labour despite an eloquent plea from their Officer. The fourth man, the victim of the attack, was never found.

War Reserve Constable Munday made an arrest on 7th May 1943 when he found George Cyril Mc C----- a Canadian Soldier age 22 with his hand through a broken window at 126 Malling Street. A modest fine of thirty shillings was imposed by the court. In July 1943 two Canadian soldiers, Henry Le------- and George Oliver D-------, who both were the worse for drink, caused a problem on School Hill, when they marched round with a bicycle above their heads looking for some Home Guards to fight. Police Constables Norris and Ridley were called to a shop at 69 High Street at 9.30 pm where a door had been damaged and the handle broken. Witness Mrs Alice Briggs said that earlier the premises had been secured for the night. Bad language was used and PC Ridley was hit on the chest and neck. Police Sergeant Mills arrived to assist with the arrest and was told by Le------- that he was the champion boxer of Canada and that the Sergeant should take his hat off and get ready to look after himself. This defendant then threw his paybook in the police officer's face. They were ordered to pay for the damage to the door, £6:12 shillings and each sentenced to three months hard labour. It was observed in court that there were normally only two Military Policemen on duty in Lewes at night, insufficient to supervise the behaviour of the troops in the town.

British Miscreants

A case with some unexplained issues occurred at Christmas 1941 when two soldiers from the Suffolk Regiment went to an Outfitters shop in Lansdown Place where one asked to be measured for a suit, which was to cost £8, just before the shop closed on Saturday 20th December. This was done and the shopkeeper closed and secured his shop in the customary manner. After the weekend it was found that the shop had been broken into and the safe with valuable contents had gone.

The safe had contained £105 in cash, Savings Certificates, Savings Stamp books, four cheque books and title deeds the property of Mr Ingram, the owner, of South Way. The two soldiers were arrested at Crewe Railway Station and returned to Lewes for a court appearance. It was revealed that the safe had been opened by them and the contents burnt except the cash and the Savings Certificates. The safe minus its door had been left by a stable at the *Elephant and Castle* while the door of the safe had been dumped by the river near the Pells. The two each received sentences of three months hard labour.

There were three unanswered questions in the case. Where had the soldiers obtained the clothing coupons for the suit? A retailer when taking an order for a suit would require both, a cash deposit and the coupons. Clothes rationing had started in July of that year and service personnel did not have coupons issued to them. What were the pair doing in Lewes? No local family connection was established and no record has been found of the Regiment being stationed locally. Why did the men travel to Crewe? An important railway junction would have had far too many "Redcaps" (Military Police) and Railway Transport Officers checking army travellers to make it a place to be without good cause.

In March 1944 two Sailors had been drinking in the *Elephant and Castle*. After they had gone, a Red Cross Collecting Box was missed from the bar. Later they were seen by War Reserve Constable Munday who was on duty in Market Street where he heard them rattling a box. The sailors made their way off down Station Street when challenged. Eventually they were caught up with at the Railway Station. Police Sergeant Oldfield arrived to assist with the arrest when the pair assaulted him. Subsequently in court they were sentenced to two months hard labour.

A resident of East Street was found to have without authority an army lamp in March 1943 and as a result was fined five shillings. In May two Lewes men, one a shoe mender, the other of unstated occupation, living at the New Levels were each fined ten shillings for improperly having in their possession Canadian army boots. Souvenir hunting was both hazardous and against the law. Any item found dropped by aircraft, or belonging to a crashed aircraft, German or British, had to be handed into the police. Similarly any item of equipment, ammunition or War Department property had to be handed in. A Lewes teenager was prosecuted for failing to hand in ammunition and an Uckfield resident was fined for failing to give up a compass from a crashed German plane. In 1943 the bomb damaged *Stag Hotel* Tontine Club had difficulty in meeting its Christmas pay out. The funds being unavailable, as is usual in such cases, the Brewers made good the shortfall. In the same year the body of a newly born infant was found in a shallow grave in Juggs Lane but no record exists of court proceedings in this matter. Another case found its way to the local court. A family was sheltering one of their sons, a deserter from the army. The father received a fine and the deserting son was kept in custody to await a military escort. This was the only case of its kind in Lewes but similar cases often made news in larger towns elsewhere.

The Prison Mutiny

Residents of the Western Road area were alarmed to hear the bell on the Prison ringing intermittently on Wednesday 21st October 1942. The bell's original purpose was as an alarm to be raised in case of an escape. Since 1940 it, like church bells, had been kept silent, to be used only in case of a German invasion. A crowd of over one hundred gathered at the Prison on a wet afternoon to watch four prisoners on the roof. A protest by servicemen who were inmates was under way. Ladders being used by contractors provided easy access to the roof and after reaching the top these were then thrown down to foil pursuit. Shouts of protest made it clear that those aloft were Canadians who called "That they had come to fight the Germans and not to be shut away in prison". Slates and lead were thrown down and soon both the Police and Fire Brigade had arrived. Persuasion and the weather eventually induced the protesters to descend.

A bonus of the incident for historians is to be found in the newspaper photographs of the incident. The Sussex Express and the Sussex Daily News both carried pictures of the crowds, the men on the roof and in the foreground a forbidden subject, which because of its camouflage was missed by the censors. The type 22 Pillbox which was painted to resemble the Gothic flint prison buildings. Its field of fire covered the crossroads at the prison and at first glance resembled a gatehouse. It was considered to be a unique siting and style of camouflage painting.

8. The Fire Services

Pre-War Arrangements

Fire Brigades have always been a source of municipal pride and have fostered a strong loyalty between the members. The Lewes Fire Brigade was no exception. Pre-war the town was served from the fire station at the lower end of North Street by the Corporation Yard. The engine house had two bays each with a pump escape. Appliance Number 1 was a Dennis motor pump escape with solid tyres and a Braidwood open body newly purchased in 1922, the town's first motor fire engine. The crew members sat on benches on either side of the engine, while there was space for another fireman, who would ring the large brass warning bell, alongside the driver. Engine Number 2 also by Dennis with a Braidwood body was bought in 1934 at a cost of £1,312, it developed 80 horse power. The pump could deliver 300/400 gallons per minute, a first aid 120 foot hose reel coupled to an onboard tank of 40 gallons of water and a 50 foot telescopic detachable escape ladder were up to date features. These appliances were to be identified as Red Major One and Red Major Two by the NFS (National Fire Service).

The Brigade was under the command of Chief Officer George Carter with Lieutenant J Morris as deputy, Engineer E Ovenden was the only full-time staff member. In addition there were 14 retained members whose employment enabled them to respond to the call out maroon when their services were required. A further 11 standby men could be called upon as necessary. The skill and pride of Lewes Brigade were amply demonstrated during the inter-war years by successes in winning drill competitions, smart turnouts for civic occasions and prompt and effective fire fighting when needed. The brigade served the Borough and by arrangement with the Chailey Rural District Council provided cover for Kingston, Ringmer, Chailey, Firle, Glynde, Rodmell and Southease. Through the Chief Fire Officers' meetings, usually held at Brighton, mutual support arrangements were available between adjoining brigades.

Call outs were usually as a result of a telephone call to the station or the operation of one of the glass fronted Alarm Call boxes located at various points in the town. One was outside the main entrance of the Town Hall. Others were at Cliffe Square, the *Kings Head Hotel* Southover, St Anne's near the *Black Horse Hotel* and in Offham Road opposite the corner of Prince Edward's Road. These boxes survived the war and were removed in July 1945. Retained men would have call bells fitted in their homes. This was a satisfactory system for peacetime at modest cost but inadequate for the demands of war.

The Chailey RDC Fire Brigade

Early in 1940 Chailey Rural District Council (RDC) had asked the Lewes Brigade what level of help it could provide in the event of serious enemy action in the Chailey area. The reply from Lewes was that if the Brigade was occupied in Lewes the town would receive priority. The Chailey response was that it would then form its own Fire Brigade to take care of its needs. A new appliance had been ordered by Chailey to replace the obsolescent Barcombe Volunteer Brigade's engine. This was allocated to a new Lewes Fire Station of the Chailey Brigade. The proposal had provoked outrage among the Barcombe volunteers who had bought the original engine and now saw themselves as supplanted. A reconditioned appliance was obtained and the Barcombe Volunteers regained their role, although under the RDC's control.

The Chailey Brigade's Lewes Fire Station was located at 11a St Nicholas Lane in a garage belonging to Mr C Geering, the signwriter and coachpainter, who had been a retained member of the Lewes Brigade since 1911. A Gilbertian situation now arose. The service conditions for the Chailey Brigade being better than those that applied to Lewes. Eight members of the Lewes Brigade applied to transfer, which would have left Lewes short of experienced men. A meeting took place between the Mayor Ald Crisp and Colonel Churchill Hale, Chairman of the RDC, and it was agreed that the two Chief Fire Officers, Mr C Geering and Mr George Carter, would meet Mr H Woolard a senior ex-fireman and Mr R P Cheale Chief of Chailey Fire Brigade to resolve the problem. After due deliberation it was decided that four men would transfer and the method would be for each Chief Officer in turn to pick a man. There is no record of how first choice was decided!

The new arrangements commenced on 10th May 1940. Pictures taken on 11th September of the crashed Messerschmitt 109 at Houndean Bottom show the attending fire appliances to be from the Chailey and Ditchling Brigades. The first real test of the new brigade came on 2nd February 1941 when at 0132 hours a report was received that a fire had broken out at the Racecourse, just outside the Borough Brigade's area. Chief Officer Geering and Section Officer Pound attended, an additional pump was sent from the Ditchling Fire Station to help and water to fight the fire was drawn from a reservoir under the grandstand. Two mobile dams were sent from Brighton but these had to be filled, when erected, from hydrants on the Downs Estate. The fire was under control by 0430 hours but not before damage estimated at £2,000 had occurred to the Steward's Stand. Not long afterwards a small scale disaster occurred, which emphasised the risks of two Fire Brigades in the same town serving two different areas. On 8th August 1941 the Lewes Manual Telephone exchange received a call saying that a property was on fire but failing to give the location, the telephone operator alerted the Lewes Brigade which stood by for action. A few minutes later another call was received at the exchange giving an address in Kingston, the operator this time correctly called the Chailey Brigade from St Nicholas Lane. A slight delay occurred in turning out. No budget had been allowed for paying standby messengers so twelve minutes elapsed before sufficient men could be found to man the fire engine. On arrival the bungalow was well alight and a poor water supply meant that little could be saved. An Auxiliary Fire Station to the Chailey Brigade was set up in the Ringmer Motor Works but like its parent station in St Nicholas Lane it disappeared during the reorganisation of 1941.

The Lewes Brigade

The first wartime fire call for the Lewes Brigade came on Monday 4th September 1939 to the Tip at the Outfall works where the customary burning of household refuse produced a glow thereby breaking the blackout regulations. Five hours pumping with a trailer pump was required to put out the blaze. On Saturday 18th January 1941 the Lewes Fire Brigade were alerted at 0130 hours by a telephone call from the Horsham Observer Corps Control Room that their observers on Lewes Castle Keep could see a large fire blazing in the direction of Malling. The only telephone line from the observers' post was a direct line to Horsham. The Brigade turned out with one of the AFS trailer pump crews to find The East Sussex Steam Laundry at the corner of Malling Hill and Mill Road was well alight, the roof having fallen in. Little could be saved, three-quarters of the customers' work had been destroyed together with the building. Some soap and motor tyres were saved. The Wick Laundry from Hove provided an emergency service for customers and eventually bought out the business. Today Council flats occupy the site.

A postscript to the episode provides an interesting legal precedent as the Laundry Company was required under the Fire Watching (Business Premises) Order to maintain a rota of firewatchers for the hours when the premises were closed. When the fire occurred there were no firewatchers on duty so the Council took the Laundry owners to Court. The prosecution failed on a technicality, the Company had complied precisely with the order that simply said that the owners must arrange a rota of firewatchers, nowhere did the order place a responsibility on the owners to see that the rota was filled. The Home Office was obliged to amend the Order to close the loophole. An electrical fault was found to be the cause of the fire.

The Auxiliary Fire Service

The Home Office in its preparations for war, recognised the need for increased fire protection by forming the Auxiliary Fire Service (AFS). Under The ARP Act of January 1938, a body of volunteers was trained and ready to support the regular brigades in time of war. The principal equipment would be a light trailer pump that could be towed by a medium sized car or lorry. The pump was de-mountable and equipped with lengths of suction hose with a basket filter to draw from rivers. It would throw two jets of water about 150 feet. By the outbreak of war the town would have three on hand, made by the Coventry Climax Company and an additional seven more were to follow plus two of a larger type making eleven in all. By 3rd September 1939 over 50 men had been enrolled and trained. These men were mobilised for full-time duty by a broadcast announcement after the 9.00 pm news that night. They were stood down on 17th May 1940 just as the tempo of war began to increase. The situation was reversed in October 1940 when further strengthening of the service became necessary. It was decided to appoint ten members of the AFS to full-time paid duty.

Sussex Express

AFS light trailer pump at *Shelleys Hotel* action station with Mr R Heriot 4th left 25-7-1941

As the AFS expanded in both men and equipment more accommodation became necessary. The Home Office instructed the Council to look for premises suitable for an auxiliary Fire Station and a Civil Defence Mortuary. An arrangement was reached by the council to rent part of Richardson's Marine Store at 15 North Street, now the home of Gorringe's Auction Rooms. The Home Office then tried to cancel the arrangement saying that it intended premises to be earmarked and not contracted for, however an agreement to continue with the lease was secured. The AFS had further difficulties to surmount. From 12th June 1940 it was decided to decentralise the accommodation of the trailer pumps, some of which had stood in the open at the corporation yard, by creating "Action Stations" in different parts of the town. The Market Tower, *Shelleys Hotel* Garages, the Cliffe Square home of the old Cliffe Fire Brigade, *Saxonbury* Kingston Road, Elm Tree Stables Southover, Hayward's builder's workshop at 13 Chapel Hill and the garage of 3 De Warrenne Road were all taken over.

A test call out of the AFS took place on 21st June 1940 that required the trailer pumps and crews to go to "Incidents" in various parts of the town from the action stations. The arrangements for the towing vehicles hardly met the requirements of wartime, each time an alert sounded or a trailer pump call out was needed the towing vehicles that traders in the town had offered on loan had to be recalled from their normal commercial use.

Towing vehicles had to be unloaded and were then driven to collect the trailer pump. Six months earlier in January approval had been given for six ARP vehicles to be fitted with tow-bars and shackles, but this still had not been completed. Jesse Hunt's coal lorry was one of the vehicles borrowed, another belonged to Harvey's Brewery that recorded thirteen off-loadings and re-loadings of beer barrels in the six month period. The test showed the impracticality of this arrangement. The best timed attendance at the "Incident" was thirty minutes and the worst nearly two hours. Voluntary effort solved the problem. Mr M R Heriot of *Shelleys Hotel* gave the money to buy a secondhand lorry and started a fund that raised sufficient money to buy three more. The practice recalled that of the early years of this century when the horse drawn Lewes Steam fire engine used the horses from the corporation refuse cart for motive power. A wait ensued for the horses to return to North Street Fire Station before answering a fire call. A council minute records that a motor boat had been offered to the Fire Service for use as a fire float. Mr George Carter, the Chief Officer reported that the boat was satisfactory but nothing further is mentioned about the town's first and only fire float.

Through the mutual support arrangements the Lewes AFS was sent out of the town four times during the fire raids on other towns during the winter of 1940-1. On 30th November a trailer pump and crew were sent to standby at Fratton and then

AFS wet trailer pump drill, the Pells 1941　　　　　　　　*R Thomas*

went into Portsmouth to fight fires in the City. The same unit then stood by with a replacement crew at Cosham and on 3rd December fought fires in Southampton. On 29th December a call was received for a pump and crew to stand by at Leatherhead and they subsequently went into action at Epsom. On 11th January 1941 help was rendered again when a pump and crew standing by at Cosham, were called forward to Fareham and then went into action at Gosport.

There were serious gaps in the nation's fire fighting arrangements and these extended to Lewes. The experience of the Fire Blitz on London in 1940 underlined the need for adequate emergency water supplies to counter bomb damage to mains' supplies. Empty properties, especially in business areas at night were vulnerable to fire. A person on the spot was needed to prevent small fires becoming big ones. Mutual assistance between brigades often faltered through the lack of standardised equipment such as hose couplings and hydrant fittings. Effective fire fighting would need planning and organisation along military lines. This had become a necessity to deal with the Fire Blitzes of 1940-2.

The National Fire Service

1st August 1941 was Nationalisation day for all the country's 1,600 Fire Fighting Forces, full and part-time municipal brigades and all their respective auxiliary units. Designations and ranks that had varied widely became standardised. The Fire Service was, nationwide, organized into thirty-two areas. Lewes was subdivision 3 of Area 31, with Area Headquarters at *Southlands* Burgess Hill. The Fire Force Commander for this area was Mr C Birch former Chief Officer of the Brighton Fire Brigade. Mr G Carter the Lewes Chief Officer became full time Section Leader at Lewes. The Fire Stations in the town were later identified as 3Z North Street, 3Y Malling Street and 3X Elm Tree Stables, Southover. Malling and North Street Stations were manned full-time Southover was manned at night. A clue to the size of the establishment at Malling Street is given in a report of a St George's Day Church Parade at South Malling Church in 1944 attended by 60 firemen and firewomen. Much change was to follow, the most significant was the upgrading of the EWS arrangements that continued until 1944.

Although officially now the National Fire Service (NFS), the Council did not record the receipt of documentation until December. The Lewes AFS carried out on 31st August 1941 a wet relay exercise in a most professional way. They demonstrated their abilities and equipment by using all seven trailer pumps, 3,000 feet of hose and a 1,000 gallon portable dam. Water was pumped from the Pells where one pump was located to another at the bottom of The Avenue. A third was at Park Road and a fourth at Bradford Road. This line fed the mobile dam in Gundreda Road where three more pumps provided a spectacular jetting display outside the Mayor's House *Franche* 2 De Warrenne Road. This exercise pointed the way to further significant improvements essential to afford adequate protection to a town with so many old wood-framed buildings.

The recorded establishment for the early days of the NFS in Lewes was eight part time firemen and three messengers for each of the five action stations. This would be in addition to the thirteeen full-time members and those who were on a retained basis. Station 3Y Malling Street was located on the north side of the South Malling Church Hall and opened in February 1942. The Chapel Hill Action Station that had been transferred to the Old Southdown Brewery in Malling Street in April 1941, now closed.

NFS crew at the North Street fire station, 3Z with a heavy trailer pump 1943   *J & S Geering*

Emergency Water Supplies

In November 1940 the Lewes Corporation Water undertaking was linked to the Chailey RDC's system by a new main from Nevill Road to the Hamsey pumping station. Chailey was linked in turn to the Burgess Hill undertaking. This brought about a mutual strengthening of supplies. Improvements in fire fighting arrangements continued steadily. In June 1940 attempts to place a sump in the river bed at the Town Wharf by Martin's Garage had failed owing to the presence of pipework in the river bed. Success was achieved by sinking the sump at the Electricity works' wharf. The sumps were large-diameter spun concrete drain pipes set upright with a lip just above the river bed that would provide at all states of the tide sufficient water depth for a fire pump.

In March 1941 four sectional steel 5,000 gallon emergency water supply (EWS) tanks were ordered. Within a month they had arrived and had been erected on concrete bases. They were eight feet wide four feet high and thirty feet long. In time the water became stagnant, rubbish was often thrown in them, although later they were covered with wire netting to reduce this nuisance. Eventually they acquired two strands of barbed wire to deter children from getting into the water. They were sited on vacant ground in Westgate Street, in Abinger Place opposite the *Elephant and Castle*, outside the Museum, now the Library, in Albion Street and most remembered of all, in the High Street opposite the County Hall outside Boots the Chemists. This tank was numbered "3", Albion Street was number "2", the numbering of the other two is unclear. In 1943 three more tanks of this type were installed, at Cliffe Corner on the site of Shaw's Stores, in the car park of *Shelleys Hotel,* and on the raised area outside Southover Church. Other water sources were secured by damming the Winterbourne stream at the Pinwell Road Railway Arch and by filling one of the disused drainage culverts in the Cliffe.

Static emergency water tank No 3 High Street 19-4-43   RCHME

In September 1941 a 100,000 gallon EWS was planned for Castle Green. The proposal caused considerable concern to members of the Bowling Club who had agreed earlier to two concrete sectional air raid shelters being dug into the north-east corner of the green. The first site proposed was next to Castlegate House. After objections it was finally sited in the south-east corner next to the Maltings. Just as hurried construction allowed water to penetrate into air raid shelters, water loss through seepage was a problem with the Castle Green tank, the largest in the town. Keen observation today at the Green will show the undulations of the excavations for the air raid shelters by the small gate near the Maltings entrance and the thirty yard square EWS in the far corner near the store shed. In June 1942 a six-inch steel pipeline (pipeline "B") was installed from a sump in the Pells by the Baths to top up the Castle Green tank for emergency use. After passing under Pelham Terrace, the line ran in the gutter up St John's Hill under the Toronto Terrace junction along St John's Terrace again in the gutter, under the road in White Hill where an outlet header was located, up Castle Banks and under Castle Ditch Lane to the tank on the Bowling Green. The Pells being spring fed was deemed to be an unreliable source so the pipeline was extended to the river in November 1943 where a fixed 750 gallons per minute pump (gpm) was sited.

A 700-900 gpm fixed pump at the military (Bailey bridge) which spanned the river between Hoopers Lane and Bridgman's Wharf supplied two lines. Pipeline "J" ran to a point by No 44 Malling Street terminating in outlet valves. In the opposite direction the pipeline "R" ran under Eastgate Street up the north gutter of East Street under North Street to feed a 10,000-gallon tank No 73 on the bombed site where the telephone exchange now stands. There were outlet headers in East Street and Eastgate Street and the length was 1,200 feet, the working pressure being 100 lbs per sq in Besides the fixed pump two trailer pumps were needed inline for a maximum flow of 1,500 gpm.

Pipeline "S" ran from the Cockshut by the Southdown Tennis Club's Pavilion under the railway bridge up Cockshut Road under Southover High Street through the playing fields of the County Secondary School for Girls', now Southover and Western Road Schools, emerging to cross under Grange Road. It continued up Keere Street on the surface, under the High Street and across the cleared site, now the Westgate Street car park, past warden's post No 5, and the Gas Decontamination Centre to EWS tank No 74. This had a capacity of 20,000 gallons and was installed at the northern end of Westgate Street in 1943. A branch fed tank No 8 of 5,000 gallons in Southover High Street near St John the Baptist Church.

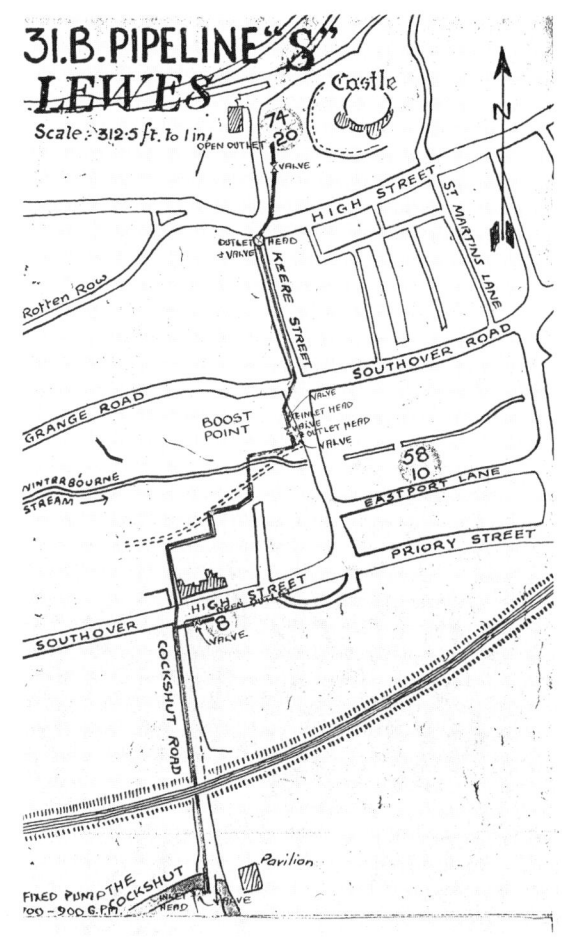

Fireman's pumping diagram   *J & S Geering*

The total length was 2,500 feet, there were two outlet headers, one at Southover Grange and the other at the High Street. A fixed pump at The Cockshut would deliver 700 gpm at Westgate Street but with three large trailer pumps at the booster points the maximum of 1,100 gpm could be delivered. These pipelines were of welded steel construction six inches in diameter, laid in the gutters or elsewhere on the surface being buried only where roads had to be crossed. The depth below the road surface was no more than six inches. Great consternation was caused in 1967 during the road construction for the Phoenix Causeway when a large unmapped service pipe was uncovered, careful excavation revealed two unsealed ends being an abandoned under road length of the wartime EWS pipeline "R" installed in 1943. A subsidiary line ("F") from the lifting bridge over the Cockshut near the Outfall works fed a circular concrete tank in a field near the end of Mountfield Road for firefighting in the railway marshalling yards.

EWS tanks appeared to spring up everywhere, in September 1941, 24 circular concrete tanks were installed at strategic places, including Nevill Green which contained 10,000 gallons, the Grange Gardens by Eastport Lane, Cross Way, Eridge Green, North Way and Mount Harry Road, where concern arose over the possible flooding of an adjacent air raid shelter. The Sussex Express regarded it as noteworthy that small boys had hooked a three-inch fish from the tank at the Windover Crescent North Way corner in July 1943. The gardens of Pelham House sported three circular tanks. A dam was constructed at the bridge at Winterbourne Hollow in 1942. Thirteen numbered sites, were identified along the river as suitable for pumping in an emergency, examples being No 29 at the Corporation yard and No 34 at Eastwood's cement works. To provide an additional water supply for the Downs Estate a hydrant was fixed at Number 4 reservoir at the Race Hill. Area 31 reinforcements were available from two hutted camps each of which had personnel and transport for fifty trailer pumps, the nearest to Lewes being Crowborough. This completed the professional fire fighting arrangements for wartime Lewes. An agreeable feature of fire service life was the summer training camps held at Glyndebourne.

Fire Watching

Self help was the order of the day and first aid fire fighting, particularly of incendiary bombs, was always encouraged. Each street had its stirrup pump team. A card was displayed in the window of the house where the pump was kept, bearing the letters "SP". The file of William Geering the signwriter contains accounts for three orders totalling four gross for "SP" signs. Training began in earnest in June 1940. A variety of equipment ordered in March now arrived including rakes, scoops, sandbags, sand-mats and axes. In September 1941, The Clearance of Lofts Order was announced which required all inflammable material to be removed from lofts and unoccupied upper rooms. Coupled with this was an instruction in July 1942 that unoccupied buildings must have the upper windows left unobscured so that any fire developing might be seen early and dealt with.

FIREGUARDS' MECHANICAL PUMPS

Sussex Express
New equipment rear of Town Hall 3-10-43

Possibly the most disliked wartime duty was fire watching. This involved one night's duty a week at a fire watch post. A proportion of that night would be a wakeful watch patrolling an assigned area. The remainder could be spent asleep at the post but available for stirrup pump firefighting of incendiary bombs if required. A small subsistence allowance was paid. Fire watchers would be expected to go to work as usual the next day. Business premises where there were more than thirty employees had been required from January 1941 to have a rota of firewatchers. In Lewes 52 firms operated schemes, Every's Phoenix Ironworks had its own trailer pump to form in effect the work's fire brigade. In April firewatching was made compulsory for all men between the ages of 18 and 65. Exceptions were made for certain categories of those in Civil Defence, Home Guard, doctors and nurses.

The Fireguard Service

From September 1941 a Fireguard Service was started, as part of the warden service, under the control of The NFS but with Mr C G Sains Chief ARP Officer as Head Fireguard with Clr H C Woolmore as deputy. A hierarchy of officers was set up, one senior officer, one deputy senior officer and fifteen senior fireguards. It was estimated that 1,817 fire watching members would be needed. The service operated from the ARP store in Lancaster Street, the County Secondary Schools for Boys' and Girls', the Labour Exchange in the old Central School, Mountfield Road Schools and The Pells School. In September 1942 the Fireguard began forming street fire watching teams. The strength of the full-time fireguards is confirmed by the order for eleven uniforms in December 1942. Also two Siemens wheelbarrow pumps were ordered.

Sun Street 29-1-43 each house has a doorstep water can for stirrup pumps. "S" is for cellar shelter *RCHME*

In July 1942, 5,000 surplus rectangular army petrol cans, the army now was using Jerricans, were obtained. They were repainted with bitumastic paint for which Geerings charged 2d per can. A large hole was cut in the top and each household was provided with one with instructions not to overfill with water to allow space for freezing. The front door water can became as familiar as the doorstep milk bottle. Lewes had scored another first, credit going to Ald Crisp for the idea. Residents were asked to keep baths and buckets filled with water at all times. In 1944 to supplement these supplies eight 500 gallon tanks were installed; one being placed on the School Hill side of the war memorial. In addition twenty-six surplus 40 gallon oil drums were filled with water and placed at strategic points specifically for the fireguard service to use. These water drums were, with military precision, mapped and numbered, by the NFS, 601 to 626 inclusive. Like all static water supply tanks, large and small, they proved to be breeding grounds for mosquitos. A regular inspection and addition of insecticide was a routine task for firemen. The main purpose of the fireguard service was to provide information to the NFS about the location of fires and to tackle any small fire to prevent it becoming a large one.

With the coming of the NFS it was a natural consequence that the firewatching arrangements would become more organised, the Lewes ARP service losing control of the arrangements. A new type of civilian duty steel helmet appeared, somewhat cheaper at six shillings as opposed to ten shillings for the standard army pattern, 161 of these lighter higher crowned type were ordered. They were regarded as a lower status symbol than the army type that all the other Civil Defence services were issued with. Firewatch observation posts had been established on the Old Brewery Malling Street, Southover Church Tower, Lewes Motors, now Caffyn's, and Mr G F Burtt's garage at 31 South Way. This latter was fitted with a bomb proof shutter. The Town Hall roof observation post supplied by Every's Ironworks at a cost of £80, was fitted with Perspex windows. It remains in position to this day. The Fire Station training tower was also used as an observation post as was the warden's post at the Bastion. Expenditure on the posts amounted to £260. Fifteen fireguard sector posts were located in town. Few details of them survive but in true NFS fashion they were all numbered. No 512 was at Mr R Vinall's Nevill Stores, No 503 at *The Limes* a guest house, that survived the bombing of 20th January 1943, to stand in isolation at the corner of Little East Street and North Street, No 504 25a Priory Street and another its number unknown in a room over Culverwell's garage in Thomas Street. A senior fireguard was in charge of each sector with a deputy and up to 60 Firewatchers to maintain the watches. On 6th August 1943 the NFS gave up the control of the fireguard service and it reverted to ARP service.

8 Thomas Street 1943 with Robert Towner, *Claude* and stirrup pump sign in window *R Towner*

As the war progressed the demands for labour produced situations where essential services were hard put to keep up to strength. From the beginning the ARP service had been staffed by women in the traditional areas of nursing, first aid, clerical and welfare. The previous all male preserve of firefighting was broken when the NFS recruited women for drivers and telephonists and as fire-crews. By September 1942 it had become clear that it would be impossible to recruit sufficient male fire watchers. It had been observed that compulsory enrolment in the Home Guard had a detrimental effect on the fire watching service. All women between the ages of 20 and 45 years were required to register for National service.

The results of the registration in Lewes were somewhat unexpected. Out of 2,201 registering only 254 were available for duty.

Registration of Women for Fire Watching in Lewes September 1942

Persons with a child under 14 years of age	1,002
Members of a residential fire watching scheme	353
Members of a business premises scheme	245
Enrolled in NFS or Civil Defence	124
Unfit and or in hospital	154
Nurses, shift workers and expectant mothers	69
Not claiming exemption and liable for fire watching	254
Total women in age group	2,201

It was stipulated that women fire watchers would only be employed in the roads where they lived and compulsion would not be used while men were available. Eventually there were 24 full-time fireguards 12 with the specific responsibility for the welfare of the fire watchers, particularly that the rest rooms and posts had clean blankets and that there were beverage making facilities available. A less agreeable task was that of ensuring that rotas were filled and that absentees were followed up. Absence from assigned duty without adequate reason would lead to prosecution. A 25 year old man who was found asleep at The Pells School when he should have been on wakeful watch, was fined £5. Several other residents failed to turn up for duty without reasonable excuse. A lady was fined and a Reverend Gentleman when reported for absence from duty escaped a fine by complying with the order before the case came to court. Another resident on strong conscientious grounds refused to firewatch. A succession of court appearances followed, on one occasion King's Counsel appeared for both sides. Nine attendances in all with three committals to prison for non-payment of fines resulted. Ten Members of Parliament tabled a question in the House of Commons on the matter. In desperation the Lewes Magistrates imposed a nominal fine on the last occasion and both parties were saved further dispute when on 29th April 1944 all firewatching duties were suspended. The German fire threat from the air was deemed to be over. Despite this a further distribution of sand-mats and sandbags took place on 10th May 1944.

Firemen laying emergency water lines 1943 — *Brighton &Hove Herald*

The war brought additional fire risks. Army petrol, ammunition and toxic chemical dumps being examples. The RAF used liquid Oxygen, a potent fire hazard. These stores were often in barns and empty properties which in peacetime would not have been acceptable. Small garages carrying out turning of Magnesium pressings produced much inflammable swarf. For D-day the NFS installed fire points of extinguishers and sand buckets at quarter mile intervals on the roads from the holding camps to Newhaven.

The wartime fire services for the town had been built up over a period of five years to a peak of efficiency by D-day. An equipment review listed two major heavy pump escape units, four heavy trailer pumps and seven light trailer pumps. A hose carrying unit with fan folded hose for high speed laying, with 6,000 feet of three inch hose and a further 4,000 of other size hose. It was calculated that in a major fire situation these units would require 2,550 gallons of petrol to sustain fifty hours pumping, fortunately this was never to be put to the test. On 31st May 1943 the action stations were closed down and the men and equipment were concentrated at Station 3X Elm Tree Stables Southover under Section Leader C Geering. Two heavy and four light trailer pumps with 70 men all part-timers and 30 Firewomen under Leading Firewoman Hullock were based there providing fire cover from 2000 to 0600 hours each night. A rapid rundown followed, the Malling Street Fire Station closed on 27th December 1944. Elm Tree Stables Southover was manned at nights only, the town was covered by three full-time and two part-time pump crews. On 25th February 1945 the Lewes Sub Division "B" of the NFS ceased to exist. On 10th May 1945 Station 3X Elmtree Stables, Southover was closed and the personnel offered discharge. In all this change the Chailey RDC's Fire Brigade had disappeared from view absorbed into the NFS This notion is supported by a member of the Lewes NFS recalling his attendance at an aircraft crash fire at Firle in 1942.

The last wartime fire broke out in the Civil Defence Store in Lancaster Street at 2220 hours on 5th February 1945. Fifty bags of creosoted sandbags each weighing over three hundredweights had caught fire. The fire was prevented from spreading to the main building where blankets and bedding belonging to County Control were kept. Two hose lines from the Red Major 2 appliance quelled the blaze. Besides the sandbags several stirrup pumps were lost in the fire. The National Fire Service besides providing an efficient fire service had also been of use in providing a pre-service training for many young boys who had been messengers, up to twenty at a time being on the strength. Socially the members made a contribution to the life of the town. The dances held by them in the Old Naval Prison helped brighten the dark days of war. The recreation room at North Street, where a full size billiards table was provided, in 1942, was a popular venue. The Fire Brigade Act of 1947 redeemed a wartime promise to return Fire Brigades to municipal control but not to the smaller towns and villages. Lewes did not see its Brigade re-established, fire protection for the town being provided from that date by the East Sussex Fire Brigade, one of 147 brigades to emerge from the national service, in April 1948.

87

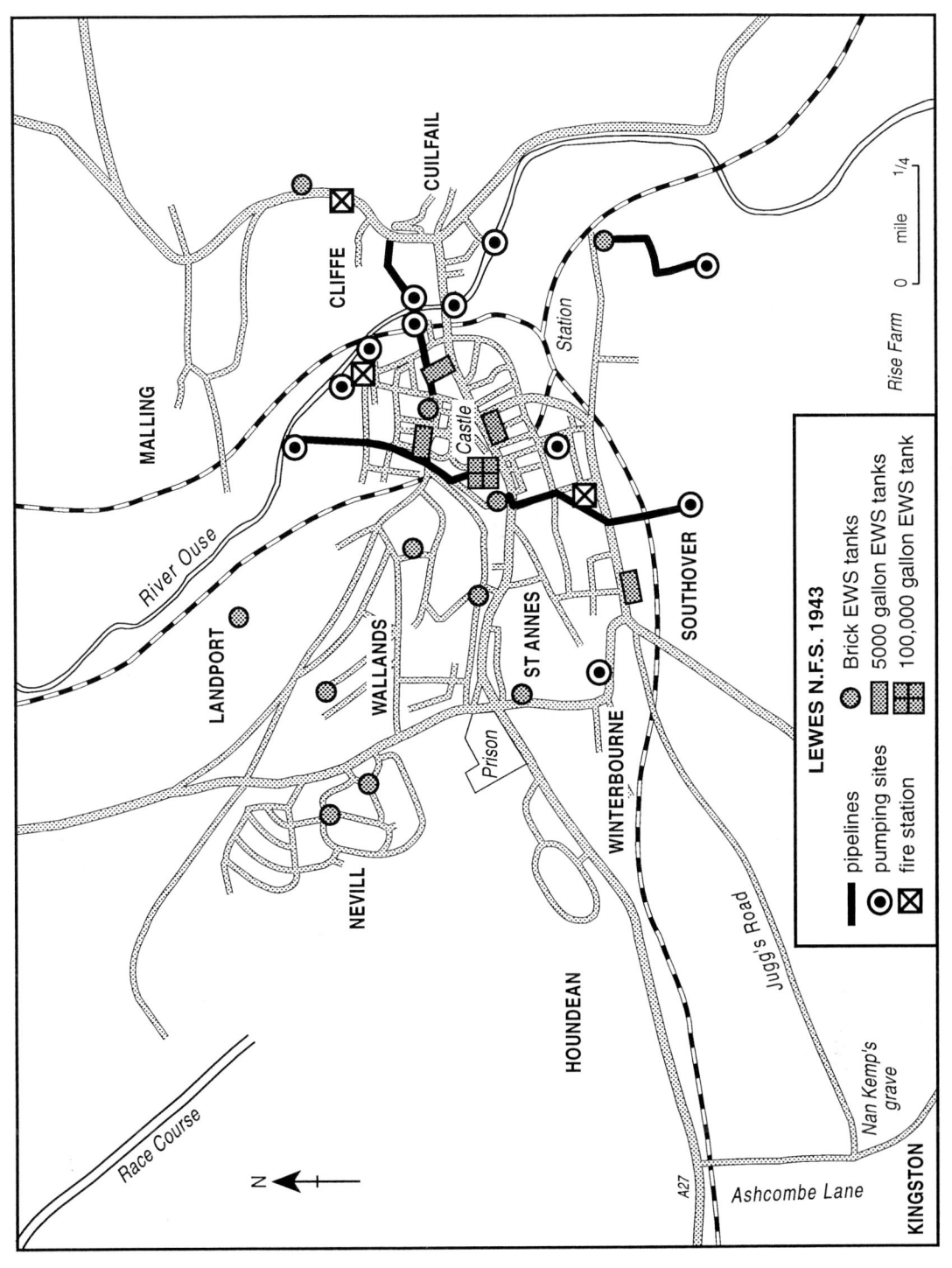

LEWES N.F.S. 1943

Map by Susan Rowland

9. Civil Defence

When Ald Charles Doland Crisp OBE accepted the Office of Mayor for the year commencing May 1938 he realized that war would come. He could not have foreseen that his term of office would extend until 1945 giving him seven consecutive years in office besides three years between 1924-26 before a final year in 1949-50. Lewes was designated a sub-area of East Sussex for Civil Defence the Mayor became the sub-controller. County Control was located in the basement of Pelham House. Lewes Control was in the basement of the Town Hall. The control room was fitted up with sleeping accommodation and with limited welfare and recreational facilities including a dartboard. The rooms were heavily strutted with timber and equipped with maps of the town, situation boards showing the strengths and locations of the services directed and telephones, two of which were reserved for outgoing calls only.

Normally the complement of the Control Room would consist of the controller or his deputy, who was Clr W J Hoyle of W H Smith's Station Bookstall, Mr C T Butler the Borough Surveyor, The ARP Officer Mr C G Sains, a member of the Police Force, a member of the Fire Service, a secretary, telephonist and messengers. Other officers of the Council would also supplement the staffing of the control.

The control was manned continuously throughout the war, with a standby watch who would sound the air raid alert, upon which the control room would be fully manned. A staff car, either a Humber or a Buick, would be sent to collect the controller, most of the rest would proceed on foot, but the ARP Officer would use his official car. Mr Sains an ex-Navy man arranged to sleep in a hammock otherwise it would be camp beds for those not on active duty. This seemed satisfactory but the Home Office thought differently and insisted that an above ground control centre should be set up. An agreement was made with Barclays Bank to have the use of a small piece of the garden behind the High Street branch on payment of a peppercorn rent of £1 per annum with the understanding that it would be for the duration

St Anne's First Aid Post 1939   *Sussex Daily News*

of the war only. A reinforced concrete bunker was built at a cost of £720 and was first occupied on 2nd September 1942, it became operational at 1500 hours that day. As a backup a shadow control room was set up at the Isolation Hospital in Nevill Road. The Council kept its promise and immediately the war was over arranged for the bunker to be demolished. In May 1953 when the Cold War led to the rebirth of Civil Defence the Home Office agreed to a control room being sited in the Town Hall basement that now appeared to be suitable!

Much organisational change took place before a well honed set of services emerged. The town had a succession of ARP Officers, Mr W Barsby from 1938 then Mr W W Masters, who left in September 1939. He was followed by a duality of Mr W R Johnston as Head Warden and ARP Officer with Captain H Mellard Smith as Honorary Organiser, an arrangement that ended in disagreement, and finally Mr C G Sains from Essex, one of 61 applicants for the post, in April 1940, who remained in service through the rest of the war. The police who had taken over the supervision of the warden's service in April 1939 returned it to Council control in February 1941, the Head Warden being Mr E C Russell. The formal adoption of the title Civil Defence took place in September 1941 on government instruction.

Despite the excellent organisational arrangements for Civil Defence the residents of Landport expressed concern that their characteristic lozenge pattern road layout would make a good target for German bombers. The request of 5th August 1940 to have roads painted black came to naught. The Council's generosity in providing 500 sandbags to the Victoria Hospital rebounded when a bill arrived from the Ministry of Home Security early the following year.

The Warden Service

Originally the town was divided into twenty sectors for Air Raid Warden supervision, each had a warden's post, but eventually these were reduced to twelve.

1	Malling Down	2	Cliffe Corner
3	Market Tower	4	New Station Inn
5	Westgate Street	6	Swan Inn Southover
7	*St Brelades* Houndean Rise	8	Prison Cross Roads
9	Corner Offham/Paddock Roads	10	*White Cottage* The Avenue
11	The Bastion Kingsley Road	12	Nevill Road Stores

Each would have a rest room if not at the post then in a property nearby. The No 2 rest room was in Fuschia Cottage in South Street, No 4 was in the GPO garage in Pinwell Lane, No 5 was in Dusart's Hairdressers 85 High Street, No 8 in St Anne's Parish Rooms First Aid Post, No 9 Warden's used Miss Boyles house at 7 The Avenue and No 11 rested at 34 King Henry's Road. If there was no proper building where the post was located sandbagged night watchman's huts were used. At Malling Down an allotment shed was pressed into service. The sandbags soon rotted and purpose built brick and concrete replacements were provided. No 1, in the bank by the south side of the burnt out Laundry, No 2 at the rear of the Cliffe Corner toilets, No 4 was in a strutted basement below the now demolished inn at the corner of Pinwell Lane and Lansdown Place, No 5 in the corner of the present car park behind the High Street shops. The outline of the doorway and the concrete slab roof still exists in the flint wall opposite the garage in Western Road of No 8 and No 9 survives today in the Gentlemen's toilet at the corner of Paddock Road. The posts were manned when the sirens sounded. They were equipped with first aid kits, rattles, handbells, whistles, and log books. Electric light and sometimes gas heating were provided. A canteen was started at the Town Hall but encountered some problems due to finance and for a time was abandoned but was restarted due to popular demand in December 1942. The Air Training Corps provided 32 Messengers for the Civil Defence Service. An important function for them was a bicycle delivery of sandwiches and Thermos flasks to each of the wardens posts at 2100 hours.

Initially the wardens wore civilian clothes with an armband, later blue dungarees were supplied. For those carrying out more than 48 hours of duty per month navy blue battledress, boots and anklets were issued. Those with outdoor duties were provided with an overcoat. Service type steel helmets were worn and some wardens had service box type gas masks, others made do with civilian duty respirators, a more rugged version of the civilian type. Again the type of respirator was regarded as a status symbol, everyone was keen to get a box type. In October 1940 an order for 50 more steel helmets and 280 oilskins was held up, the army having priority for supplies. Steel helmets were usually painted grey and often had the owner's name signwritten on them together with their designation. Signwriter Geering was kept busy repainting and writing over 50 helmets in 1941. Depot Superintendent in black, FAP, (First Aid Post) white with black stripe, Ald Crisp's helmet was painted red with two black stripes and titled Sub Controller, Mr Sains also sported a red helmet with one black stripe, Auxiliary Fire Service helmets were grey with white letters, a Civil Defence heraldry was emerging.

Wardens at *New Station Inn* 18-3-41 *Sussex Express*

The wardens had regulatory and reporting functions. Enforcement with the Police of the blackout regulations gained them some unpopularity. They would observe the fall of bombs, if a gas attack developed they would use rattles to give warnings and ring handbells to signify when the danger of gas was past. Wardens would unlock the air raid shelters when an alert sounded and people in the streets would be shepherded into them if an air attack developed. Bomb explosions were called "Incidents". Wardens would help with the rescue and first aid services at the scene and provide information about who might be in a damaged building. The full test of their function occurred on the occasions of the three air attacks on the town. For most of the war it was a routine of standing to when the sirens sounded, training practices and much boredom of long night watches. On 28th February 1941 an exercise took place that almost anticipated events that were to follow two years later. Bombs were said to have fallen on Nos 1-17 East Street, and the Museum in Albion Street. *The Stag* at the corner of East and North Streets being destroyed and water mains broken. A realistic response was made by the ARP services and the AFS.

Civil Defence staffing had its problems, in May 1940 a volunteer typist was replaced with paid help. This caused a storm of protest in Council. The following year wardens complained that they performed their duties voluntarily whereas the compulsorily recruited fire watchers received three shillings per night subsistence. Eventually all the Civil Defence members, Auxiliary Firemen and Home Guard were treated alike. In 1944 long service chevrons caused difficulties. They were issued one for each year of service and wardens complained that they were not being issued to them as some head wardens, because of recent entry, would not be

St John and Red Cross on Home Guard Sunday 12-4-42 Southover Road *L Davey Sussex Express*

entitled to them and had therefore held up the issue. Mr Sains was able to smooth this problem over within a short time. As competition for manpower by Home Guard recruiting had by 1942 caused manning problems for the Civil Defence services, it was decided to form a Home Guard Civil Defence Platoon. The men of this hybrid unit were fully trained and equipped as Home Guards, where their first call for duty would be. They would, however, be available to support the Civil Defence at other times.

First Aid Services

Provision for the injured was made initially through mobile first aid parties, composed mainly of members of the St John Ambulance and the British Red Cross Society, or others trained by them. These parties would go to the scene of an incident and render first aid. They would help remove the casualties in Civil Defence ambulances. These were large cars converted to resemble a van. Twenty pounds had been allowed for each conversion, the vehicles would take four tubular mesh steel stretchers on a framework. Lewes had two civilian ambulances kept in Martin's Garage at Cliffe Bridge. One was reserved for infectious diseases. The St John Ambulance had one vehicle that was better equipped than those of the town and in April 1942 took delivery of a second new vehicle. The Civil Defence supplement amounted to four converted cars and five sitting case cars with seventeen drivers and attendants. With the reorganisation of the fire services part of the auxiliary station at Richardson's in North Street became available and was used as a transport depot for the Civil Defence ambulances and cars. A second was located behind the Cliffe Corner toilets in Rushbridge's Yard. In August 1940 the Mayor received two new fully equipped trailer ambulances, a gift from the USA. No record of their fate survives but the many narrow streets of Lewes would have made their use difficult.

The first aid posts were at St Anne's Hall and Cliffe Parish Rooms, both of which could take 20 patients each. They were staffed with members of the St John Ambulance and the British Red Cross augmented by volunteers and members of the nursing profession, St Anne's had two Registered Nurses with 42 female and two male first aiders. Cliffe had a staff of three Registered Nurses supported by 41 female and five male first aiders. Casualties would have been seen first by the mobile First Aid parties and then sent as appropriate to the posts or to the Victoria Hospital that could take 38 less seriously injured. The most serious cases would go to the Royal Sussex County Hospital Brighton. In the event of many casualties two basements had been fitted out as emergency hospitals or casualty stations, Market Tower with 14 bunks and Fuller's at 19A the High Street had been equipped to take 24. There a hand operated lift made by Every's Ironworks would lower patients down for treatment. Staff available for these posts were four Registered Nurses and three assistants between Fuller's and the Market Tower. The latter post cost £817 to equip and Fuller's was cheaper at £189. For the fatal casualties a supplementary mortuary to the Borough Mortuary at North Street was provided at the rear of the Auxiliary Fire Station formerly Richardson's. This would be in the charge of Mr A W Moorey the Cemetery superintendent. Specially printed identity labels were provided by the Home Office and arrangements for photographic identification by relatives was planned. It was fortunate that these facilities were needed for only the two victims of the January 1943 air raid whose death certificates carried the standard record from the Coroner "Death due to War Operations".

Gas Decontamination

The threat of gas attacks required the provision of special facilities for the treatment of those affected by skin blistering agents such as mustard gas. Decontamination stations were set up consisting of shower baths, changing rooms and store rooms for spare clean clothing. Two were provided for the town one by a conversion, planned in 1938 of part of the old Southdown Brewery Maltings in Davey's Lane. Full plans of the work carried out survive in the East Sussex Record Office at the Maltings. The other, erected in 1941 was located on a slum clearance site in Westgate Street opposite the YMCA Gymnasium. Today a vestige of the chimney stack in bright red brickwork is incorporated in the retaining wall. Mann's the cleaners and dyers in Lansdown Place were under contract to provide a cleaning service to deal with contaminated clothing collected at the cleansing stations. These cleansing stations were never called upon to fill their planned purpose but in the run up to D-day with many troops in tented holding camps outside the town the shower baths were put to good use. Council minutes record with satisfaction that by military use the equipment was maintained in good order. By 21st June 1944, 6,222 soldiers had used Westgate Street. One month later the minutes recorded that the numbers were significantly down.

Rescue and Repair

The rescue and repair service was staffed by the Borough Surveyor's department both professional and artisan. In case of property being damaged, the rescue of those trapped inside would be the priority. After that shoring up and making safe dangerous structures would come second. Emergency repairs would follow on houses that could be made habitable and finally the demolition of buildings badly damaged beyond repair. The building firms of the town would also be called on to supply much of the labour for the work carried out after the three air attacks and on other occasions when explosions outside the town caused damage to property. Their service was also required when damage occurred as the result of military activity, usually vehicle contact with buildings or road damage due to tracked vehicles. Stockpiles of building materials were maintained at the North Street Depot including 20,000 roofing tiles and 250 sheets of Essex board for repairing ceilings

The Women's Voluntary Service

Lewes had a close connection with the foundation of the WVS. In the Spring of 1938 the Home Secretary invited Lady Reading of Swanborough Manor, Kingston to undertake the creation of a voluntary service of women, mainly housewives, to undertake duties of a welfare nature as part of the Civil Defence programme. Region No 12 covering East Sussex was set up in September 1938. Between March and May 1939 all the local authorities were written to by the No 12 regional organiser, Lady Rachel Edgerton of Uckfield, asking if they would be interested and supportive of the new organisation. All the councils responded warmly and with limited government funding for rented accommodation, stationery, armbands and badges, the women of Sussex began finding tasks to take on. On many occasions during the war the Lewes WVS played an important part in visiting homes to find additional accommodation for evacuees. The initial idea was for them to provide a leading role in the welfare provision for the victims of the mass air raids expected. In the areas adjacent to London and the big cities they were in the forefront of this work particularly in the winter of 1940-1.

The housewives' service was organised by the WVS. Their role was to help the warden's service by notifying absentees from home. In the case of a damaged house this would have saved time being wasted digging for non-existent casualties. This required the keeping of records of the usual number of occupants of houses including guests. Other responsibilities included the locations of shelters, fire fighting equipment such as sand mats, stirrup pumps and water buckets, keeping spare blankets and hot water bottles and being prepared to take the homeless in for rest and shelter. This service was expected to play a part in welfare work should an invasion occur.

Stirrup pump practice 1939 Southover *Sussex Daily News*

The WVS was not allowed to raise funds and continued to receive state funding until 1994 when it became a registered charity. This did not deter the women of Sussex and when ambitions could not be realised and needs met from allocations, subscriptions and interest free loans were soon arranged. Some of the first mobile canteens that toured the outlying areas to serve refreshments to the troops were funded by loans from the husbands of the better off members. Static canteens such as the ones in the High Street and Albion House called for much effort by the organisers in obtaining the furniture, equipment, food supplies and the helpers to fill the rotas. When in April 1943 the Council needed to revise the register of housewives willing to take evacuees it turned to the WVS to carry out the task. They sent out 3,750 enquiry forms and received back 2,893. The rest were patiently followed up. The survey found 3,600 possible spare beds.

Shelter welfare and emergency feeding and clothing for the bombed out required the maintenance of appropriate stocks. Incident enquiry points were provided and staffed at the sites of bombing. Although Lewes in comparison suffered little in this respect, when the call came the WVS was there. In 1943 a clothing exchange was opened in a shop at No 36 Cliffe High Street two doors from the Odeon Cinema. This was mainly to help mothers clothe growing children. The following year the WVS was prepared to receive and care for French refugees who might have to be evacuated from the Normandy fighting area, but this proved to be unnecessary. The welfare role came to the fore again in 1945 when the WVS were asked to help at reception camps for returning prisoners of war. In 1945 the government asked the service to continue for another two years but in the event their "Stand Down" came at the end of the "Cold War" and only in 1994 was the state funding reduced.

The Air Raid Shelters

Air raid shelter accommodation was provided for most of the population by the end of 1941. Initially the Munich trench shelters had been reopened and the sides strutted with timber. As the war progressed the timbers rotted and they were eventually declared to be unsafe. The curved corrugated iron Anderson shelters for digging into a garden were supplied to many homes. Later where this was not practical the Morrison steel table shelter for indoor use was issued. It was made with angle iron legs a thick steel plate top and steel mesh sides. Lewes was fortunate in that many of the older Victorian houses and cottages were endowed with cellars. The Council pursued a vigorous policy of timber strutting these cellars, a condition for this was that the householder would allow them to be used by the public during raids. Wartime photographs show houses with a black plate with the white letter "S" denoting a shelter. By June 1941 basements in 440 houses had been strutted to hold over 4,000 persons, a further 850 had places in Anderson shelters and 788 in 44 brick and concrete surface shelters.

Brick surface shelter Pelham Terrace *F Burgess*

There were public trench shelters of varying construction, lined with concrete, timber, or steel. Rugg's Garage basement was entered from a sandbagged protected entrance in St Nicholas Lane until it was requisitioned by the army in 1941. Together these would hold nearly 700 persons. The 15 locations included Bell Lane Recreation Ground, Church Lane Malling, Bradford Road, Grange Road, Lancaster Street and Pinwell Road. Every school had its own shelter accommodation either in the grounds or near by. These were mainly trench shelters lined with concrete or of brick surface construction. In total school shelters would accommodate 2,276 persons.

Lewes became the home of 69 BCF Shelters each holding fifty persons. These were located at 44 sites, examples being on the verge at the Prince Edward's Road-Ferrers Road junction, on the vacant site at the corner of Garden Street and Priory Street. Another stood in Grange Road on the island at the junction of St Pancras Road, with two more at the rear of the *Thatched House Inn*, in Union Place at 39 South Street. The gardens of *Locarno* Southdown Avenue and *Fosdyke* Houndean Rise were also equipped. More were placed at the rear of the sports pavilion in Paddock Road and the YMCA garages in Westgate Street. The Avenue Children's Home and *Treetops* in Bradford Road had one each. Highdown Road had five, one behind the Church Hall, one at the side of No 29 and three on the downs at the rear. Thirteen more offered protection in other parts of the Nevill Estate, seven in roads with houses backing onto the Downs, two on Nevill green and one in the garden of 49 Middle Way. In total BCF shelters offered protection to 3,265 residents.

Interior BCF Shelter *Treetops* 1985   R Woakes

The BCF shelter was a product of wartime co-operation between the makers of precast sectional concrete buildings who came together in 1939 as The British Concrete Federation to advise the government on the best way to meet its war needs in concrete structures. BCF shelters were made of reinforced interlocking side beams 8 feet tall by 11 inches wide and 4 inches thick, roof beams of the same section completed the structure that was internally braced by sectional steel members bolted together. The whole was half buried below ground with the excavated soil forming a protective bank on the roof and sides. Five concrete steps led past brick flank walls to the entrance door which was provided with a gas curtain, to the right of which was the switchboard for the battery lighting. The floor was made of standard paving slabs while the roof was waterproofed by hot laid asphalt. At the opposite end to the door were two cubicles made from asbestos sheets each with an Elsan chemical toilet, between these cubicles there was space for the escape ladder to a ventilation shaft with a drain cover as a closure. Wooden slatted seats on each side seated fifty people. The internal dimensions were seven foot six inches high by eleven feet wide and thirty feet long. One of these shelters survives today and is behind *Southdown House* in St. Anne's Crescent, the one at *Treetops* Bradford Road lasted until 1985.

Yet another type of communal surface shelter, built of brick, catered in total for 1,868 persons, three were in the Odeon Car Park (120 persons), others were at Harvey's Brewery (48) in the Cliffe, at the rear of the Jireh Chapel in Malling Street (24), at the end of Morris Road (48), Jubilee Recreation Ground at the Pells (48), Westgate Street (24) between the YMCA and the Women's Institute building, this one is still there, having been converted into a pair of garages. At Landport 29 brick surface shelters were situated between the houses, Evelyn Road having seven and Eridge Green having three. The number of shelter places included 468 in protected passageways, where Council houses had been built in groups of four, a central passageway had been provided for rear access, these had a full height blast wall built at both ends that provided good protection against splinters and blast.

The last group of shelters were the brick individual type with accommodation from nine to twelve persons, most of them being built at Landport. With this amount of construction in hand over a two year period between 1940 and 1941 the Council were forced to employ a temporary Building Officer to oversee the works. Most of the local builders used to construct the shelters were household names such as Burfoot and Son, Erry and Son, J G Hayward, B W Kent, C L Muddell, Philcox Bothers, the Ringmer Building Works, P R Wicks and A Wycherley. Messrs Burchett's hauliers of Lancaster Street, had the task of delivering the sectional Anderson shelters. Ultimately the whole of the population of Lewes, then numbering 12,000, had been provided with shelter accommodation.

The shelters brought with them problems, in June 1940 it was reported to the Council that some shelters had been put to unspecified "Improper Uses". In future they would be kept locked with the key in a glass panelled box that could be broken for emergency access. Later Mr C Bell, Bath Keeper was assigned the task of visiting the shelters regularly when the Swimming Bath was closed for the winter. He would ensure that essential maintenance was listed and that they were in a clean condition, for which he would receive additional remuneration. In August 1942 "Comforts" were supplied for the public shelters. These took the form of battery powered electric lights and chemical toilets. Two young lads on their way home from school vandalised the light fittings in shelters at Priory Street and St Peter's Place. A Court appearance resulted in probation and an award of costs against the parents of three shillings. The Sussex Express under the headline, in June 1944, "A Copper Too Many" gave an account of a Court appearance of six young men from the Brook Street area caught by a Policeman in a shelter at the Pells playing cards for money. They were fined five shillings each and the stake money was confiscated and placed in the Court Poor Fund Box. Baxter's raised the question of damage that had occurred at their sports ground in 1944 in connection with the public's use of two air raid shelters. Vandalism is an age-old problem. These shelters survive to this day and are used to store sports equipment.

The five years of war had run up a bill for Civil Defence of £52,614 for the town of which £29,096 had been spent on shelters. Almost 95% of these costs had been borne by central government. But for the considerable amount of voluntary work in all the Civil Defence services in the town the cost would have been much greater. If the build up had been gradual and steady, the run down, as the war took a successful turn in the months after D-day, was precipitate. As early as July 1943 a reorganisation of the heavy and light rescue squads had taken place, reducing them in numbers and combining them with the first aid parties. In October 1944 all training was suspended and there was a 50% reduction in full-time paid personnel with one night in twelve on duty for those remaining instead of one in six. From this date all fire guard posts were closed. The timber lined trenches at Malling Street, St Anne's and Highdown Road were closed as unsafe. In the interest of economy all unnecessary telephone lines to wardens' posts and the Shadow Control Centre at the old Isolation Hospital, now St Mary's Social Centre were disconnected. One of the first aid posts and six of the wardens' posts were to be closed. Applications had been received from St Anne's Church for the return of the Billiard Room at the Church Hall. The Cliffe First Aid Post was closed in January 1945. On the same day permission was given for each Civil Defence vehicle to have one of its headlamp masks removed. It was reported that, during the war, the control room had been manned for a total of 47,370 hours. Civil Defence was stood down on 4th May 1945. A request made at this time to Region for permission to remove strutting from basements was turned down without explanation. The final act was the return of all Civil Defence equipment to the Town Hall in June 1945. This was followed in September by a two-day sale of the surplus items. Part of the sale included some large tins of Fish Roll intended for emergency feeding each weighing thirty-two pounds. Lewes residents were saved from temptation as the sale was restricted to licensed catering establishments only. An instruction was issued to County Control staff that all special endorsements on Identity Cards relating to Civil Defence Offices held must be cancelled on "Stand Down".

In recognition of his services to the town throughout the war both as Chief ARP officer and in other civic duties Mr Charles Gibson Sains was awarded the British Empire Medal.

The often used cliché to go out in a blaze of glory came to fruition on 15th February 1945 when at 2220 hours a report was received at the Fire Station that the Old British School in Lancaster Street used as an ARP store was on fire.

On 24th November 1944 it was reported that Mr Walter H Godfrey the Lewes architect, historian and writer of the town's guide had been commended in the House of Commons for his work for the National Buildings Record. A Royal Commission on the Ancient monuments of England had been set up in 1908 to study and record the subject. At the height of the 1940 Blitz it was realised many unrecorded architectural treasures were being destroyed. Official photographers were sent to towns of interest including Lewes. Visits were made in 1942, and on four occasions in 1943, a team was in action on the day of the January bombing raid, producing some spectacular pictures of the aftermath. The camera lens captured, probably unintentionally, pictures of wartime structures that escaped the attentions of the censor. These included the School Hill pillbox, the Cliffe Bridge anti-tank blocks and emergency water tanks including the one in the High Street.

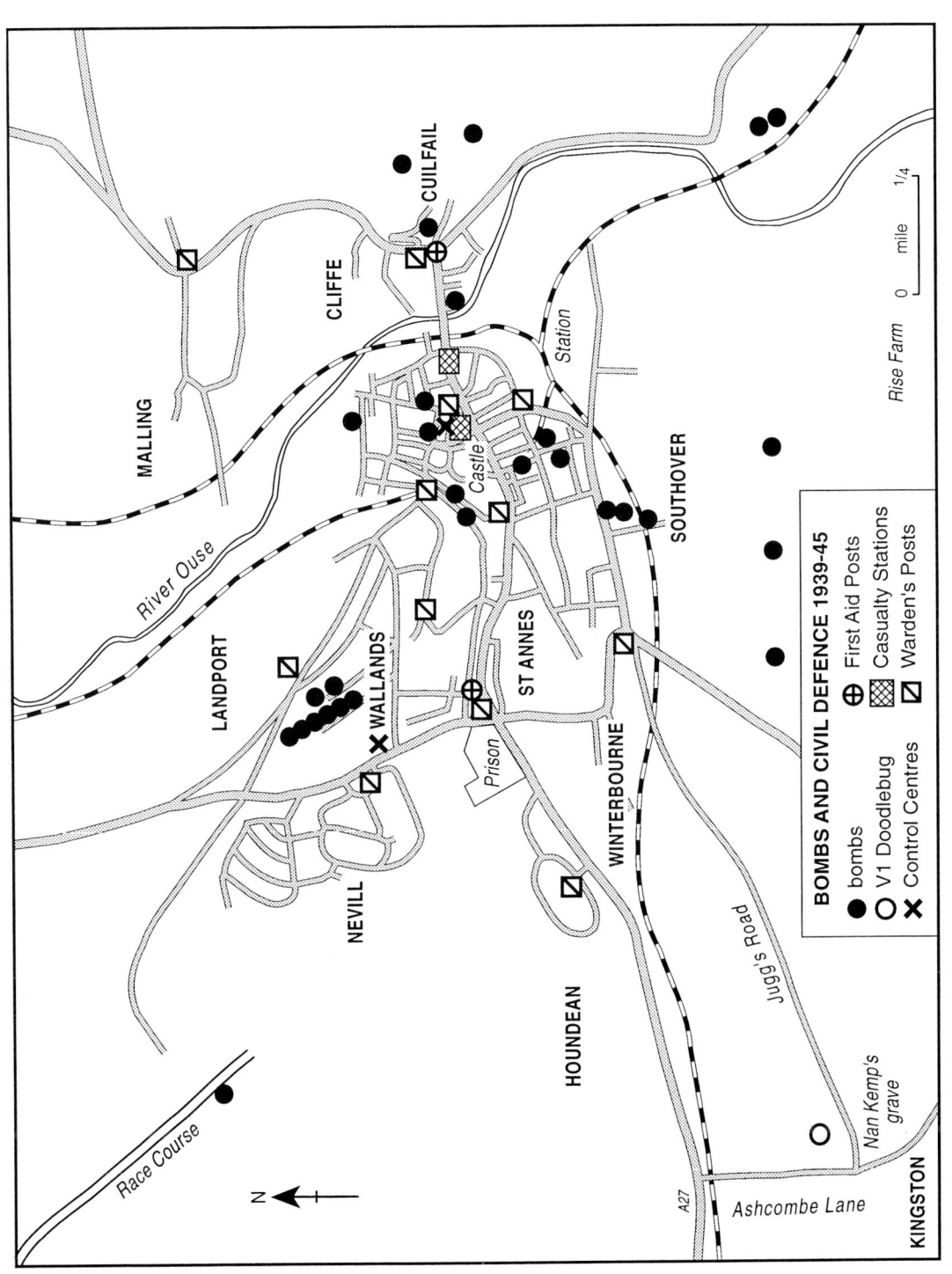

Map by Susan Rowland

10. The 16th Sussex Home Guard

On 9th April 1940 the tempo of the war took a sudden upturn with the German invasion of Denmark and Norway. Anglo-French intervention ended in failure with the evacuation of southern Norway on 3rd May, and Narvik on 12th June. Mr Neville Chamberlain, the Prime Minister, was challenged in Parliament on 7th May but won a vote of confidence on his conduct of the war by resorting to party support. Three days later Hitler's Blitzkreig descended on the Low Countries and France. On the same day Mr Chamberlain resigned and Mr Winston Churchill formed a coalition government. Mr Chamberlain, terminally ill, died on 2nd November 1940. One week after the attack on France, on 17th May the Secretary of State for War, Mr Anthony Eden, broadcast an appeal at 9.00 pm asking for able bodied men between the ages of 18 and 65, not already engaged on National Service, to enrol in The Local Defence Volunteers (LDV). They would be provided with uniforms and arms and would, with the regular forces, defend the localities in which they lived.

Local Defence Volunteers

LDV Enrolment took place at Police Stations. Even before Mr Eden had finished his appeal the Police Station in West Street received the first volunteers. This was repeated at police houses in the surrounding villages to such an extent that the few enrolment forms issued were soon used up. Resourceful officers resorted to using carbon papers to type out forms six at a time or to using charge register sheets, beat reports and other Police forms as substitutes. The forms required personal details, nationality, occupation, availability for duty by day or night and details of military experience including use of firearms. Many volunteers who were licensed holders of firearms offered these for service as well. The enrolling Police Officer was required to vouch for the applicants.

LDV Pelham House 31-5-1940   *Sussex Express*

In the Lewes area nearly 1,000 men had enrolled by the end of June. Initially the No 1 Platoon was under the command of Major G B Beard of *Sunnyside* Rotten Row and consisted of 254 men. Those joining came from all walks of life, A R Hall, Chauffeur, The Cottage, Rotten Row; F H Coote, Outfitter, High Street; T H Gebbie, Dentist, St Anne's Terrace; M Herriot, Hotelier, *Shelleys;* F Holford, Publican, *White Hart Shades*; W J Hoyle, Bookseller, Southover; A Kidgell,

Caretaker, Old Naval Prison; W G Pelham, Newsagent and Confectioner, St John's Terrace. The surrounding villages raised sections of men that later merged into company strength. Chailey, Cooksbridge, Falmer, Firle, Glynde, Ringmer. The unit from villages south of the town was called Brookside. Peacehaven, Newhaven and Seaford all had units under the Lewes commander. Initially the British Legion Club and the Naval Prison were used as Headquarters.

The first Commanding Officer of the Lewes LDV was Colonel H Powell Edwards of *Oditune Place* Plumpton. Those were the days of the LDV armbands, few rifles and very little ammunition but plenty of enthusiasm. Enemy parachute troops constituted a real threat so it is not surprising that these volunteers were dubbed "Parashots". Nearer the truth than realised was the less flattering title "Last Ditch Volunteers". Until requisitioned by the army the Golf Clubhouse on Cliffe Hill was used as an observation post. Patrols of the Downs, guard duties on road blocks at the entrances to the town, Cliffe Bridge, the Waterworks, Gas and Electricity works were the routine. Drill and later when weapons and ammunition became available, target practice at Oxteddle Bottom Range at Southerham or at the indoor small bore range in the Naval Prison.

LDV Enrolment at 30th June 1940

Beddingham	25	Chailey	46	Ditchling	117
Denton	38	E. Chiltington	18	Falmer & Stanmer	38
Firle	68	Glynde	46	Iford	18
Kingston	28	Lewes	655	Lewes Cavalry	55
Newhaven	128	Newick	25	Offham & Cooksbridge	80
Peacehaven	129	Piddinghoe	27	Plumpton	58
Ringmer	123	Rodmell	33	Seaford	387
Streat	21	Telscombe Cliffs	29	Telscombe Village	8

Mr Eden's call for volunteers had overwhelmed the administration. The Lewes unit was first called "E" Company with sub-units in the villages taking the title of Platoon but these were some misnomers as the numbers involved were so large that the army establishment of 150 men for a company and 40 for a platoon was exceeded. The Territorial Army Association that had a long experience of managing volunteer units took on much of the supply and administrative work. The original structure was Police and County Council related so it followed that Sussex was divided into two zones east and west, later these were unified under Colonel E J W Pike as Zone Commander, with headquarters at Newick. One important early change made by Mr Churchill, who disliked the term LDV was, that from 23rd July 1940, the organisation would be known as the Home Guard. The first officers in charge of units were Lt Col B Whiteman Lewes, Brig Gen The Hon A F V Russell CMG MVO Newick, Capt C Cosworth Chailey, Maj G Braddock Plumpton, Capt D Glass Ringmer, Capt The Hon Cecil Firle, Capt H W Styles Brookside with Newhaven and Peacehaven, Maj T de B Barwell Seaford and Capt J Sturgis Hamsey.

Detailed accounts of the Brookside Platoon follow the events in Lewes and elsewhere in "E" company. Brookside one of the largest platoons, commanded by Capt Styles, amounted to 250 men. They received their first 100 P14 rifles and 1,000 rounds of ammunition at Newhaven Police Station on 19th May 1940. These rifles were part of a consignment of one million negotiated by Mr Churchill from United States. This was part of the leased West Indian Bases agreement. The rifles were of 0.300 calibre, smaller than the standard British army Lee-Enfield rifle at 0.303. These P14s rifles had a red band painted on the stock of the rifle and all the cartridges had a red painted base to avoid jamming with incorrect ammunition. The shortage of weapons meant that only the night patrols could be armed. The remaining rifles being issued to those most likely to be called out in an emergency, the rest armed themselves with whatever weapons they could find. An era of pitchforks, pikes and pick handles had arrived. Bottles with petrol, phosphorous and rag wicks were improvised for the famed "Molotov Cocktail". Storage of weapons also had to be arranged. A lock up garage in Abinger Place was used to store some of the rifles and a shed behind the *Black Horse Hotel* held detonators and phosphorous grenades. The brick store at the corner of the Castle bowling green is referred to in official records as a bomb store but the exact nature of the contents was not recorded.

The Home Guard

It was accepted that the Home Guard in its early days could not defeat the Germans in a set piece battle but could do much to delay the enemy's timetable. A knowledge of the local countryside and c-operation with the regular forces would achieve much. In the summer of 1940 the 5th Battalion of The Duke of Cornwall's Light Infantry commanded by Col Sir J Pole Carey which covered the coast between Brighton and Eastbourne, came to value the help and knowledge of the local volunteers. Later Canadians on training exercises were often surprised by the appearance of Home Guardsmen who, using their local knowledge, crept up on them unawares. Many eyebrows were raised, once uniforms began appearing, at the medal ribbons worn by some 1914-18 veterans who formed such a large part of the strength bringing with them a wealth of experience and discipline. When sections were not on patrol, they would meet twice a week, Tuesdays and Thursdays, for one and a half-hour's training. These arrangements meant that platoon officers would be on duty most nights of the week.

Mrs R Hedger
Lt Colonel H W Styles' insignia and unit flashes

A company headquarters was formed in Lewes. The County Council provided four rooms in the Surveyor's department. Mr W Mitchell of the Shell Oil Company was appointed Adjutant. Captain L Downey ex-Sussex Yeomanry took on the job of Quartermaster with Mr W C Jeal a solicitor's clerk as an assistant. Towards the end of 1940 Col Powell Edwards retired through ill health, his place was taken by Capt Styles. Col Edwards who had formed "E" Company, covering 200 square miles of the County had worked tirelessly founding and organising the unit. Capt G Janson a Rodmell farmer took over the Brookside Platoon.

By now weapons were becoming available but in small quantities. The police whose help had been requested and readily given, collected up shotguns, these were test fired and those that survived were handed over with a supply of cartridges. These were supplemented with Thompson sub-machine guns and as the ammunition position improved some range target practice was allowed. Until this time cartridges were to be used for operational purposes only. Army fatigues or denims comprised the first uniform to be issued, these trousers and battledress blouses were designed to be worn over ordinary uniform and always looked untidy and baggy. These together with a forage cap and LDV armband, later changed to Home Guard, sufficed until late 1941. Army style serge battledress and trousers, black leather gaiters, army boots, steel helmets, greatcoats, service box respirators, gas capes, haversacks, ammunition pouches and a weapon for every man were finally achieved by the end of 1942.

Organisational change continued to take place, "E" company of the Home Guard became the 16th Battalion of the Sussex Home Guard with correctly sized companies and platoons. A battalion would normally have 750 officers and men, of four rifle companies of 145 men, each of three platoons with a strength of 40. There would be additional officers and men for both Battalion and Company headquarters. The 16th Sussex area was large enough to support a double strength establishment. Lewes, Peacehaven, Newhaven, Seaford, Brookside, Ringmer and the Ditchling companies incorporated platoons from Glynde, Firle, Offham, Cooksbridge, Newick and Chailey. They were all proud to wear the Royal Sussex Regiment's cap badge. A khaki cloth shoulder title proclaimed Home Guard in yellow and a square patch bore the legend "16 SX" in black.

The Lewes "Cossacks" I Wycherley on the gray 1941 *Sussex Express*

Lewes had been a racing training centre with eight stables. It also had a strong hunting following. Both sports had been curtailed by the war so there were plenty of under employed riders and horses. A Cavalry section with 52 members was formed to patrol the Downs, these soon gained the title "The Lewes Cossacks" names such as T Masson, F Rees, A W Dalgety, The Rev Ensell and I Wycherley all found mounts in this unit. The Headquarters were at Hope in the Valley Stables. An important post was the Racecourse grandstand where a bar was still operational. In May 1943 the women's auxiliary was formed to undertake intelligence, communications, clerical and catering duties. This reached a strength of 44 by the stand down in December 1944. Despite repeated applications they were refused permission to wear uniform.

Recommendation for promotion to commissioned rank was by gazetting in the same way as army officers. Names were submitted for approval by battalion commanders to a promotion board. The status and authority of Home Guard officers in relation to Army officers were ill defined. Initially Home Guard officers were regarded as junior to Army officers of any rank. Generally young Army officers accorded due respect to the older Home Guard officer who would usually have had considerable First World War experience. Finally the War Office decided that Home Guard officers would be junior to the same regular army rank.

Kingston first aid team 1943 *R Hedger Sussex Express*

In the winter of 1941-2 the 1st Canadian Division came to Sussex relieving the British units holding the coast. The Canadians were frequently moved and this meant that combined training was frequently interrupted with new schemes of additional wiring and trench digging being carried out. Lt Col Styles, always mindful of the requirement for his men to follow their full-time occupations, arranged that no man should go on a dusk to dawn patrol more than once a week. Unless there were exceptional states of readiness requiring it, patrolling, in the worst weather of the winter was curtailed and "In-lying piquets" were manned instead. The Battalion HQ was established at 31 High Street, the Chailey RDC offices. "A" Company had its headquarters at the old Naval Prison with platoons stationed at the following locations, No 1 platoon 34 King Henry's Road, No 2 Mill House Juggs Lane, No 3 *The Swan Inn* Wardens' Post,

No 4 *Snowdrop Inn* and Golf Clubhouse, No 5 *Grey House* Malling Street and Warden's Post, No 6 *The Forge* Falmer, No 7 Hamsey Place, and No 8 The Civil Prison. Other companies were "B" at Seaford, "C" at Newhaven and "D" at Ringmer.

By September 1940 the East Sussex Zone had 26 companies in 11 battalions and West Sussex had six battalions together amounting to 35,000 men. Besides the Post Office unit with a county-wide strength of 1,400 men there were 3,600 in the Southern Railway Battalion. By 1942 the total numbers of the Home Guard in the whole of Sussex had reached 37,746 men. The 16th Sussex (Lewes) Battalion like many other were short by 1,000 of its establishment of 2,500 men.

Cup Grenade launchers Convent Field 21-5-1943 *R Hedger Sussex Express*

Functional Units

These were composed of men who served in units related to their employers and the need to give specific protection employing their specialised knowledge. The Southdown Bus Company's employees were formed into the 12th Sussex (Southdown) Transport Company, 36 men enrolling from the Seaford garage. Post Office workers, both postal and telecommunications, were enrolled in the 11th Sussex (39th GPO) Battalion. Lewes provided 7 men, Newhaven 4 and Seaford 15. The 25th Sussex (Southern Railway) Battalion enrolled over 173 men at Lewes in "J" Company. Newhaven provided another 123 recruits, Seaford 51, Cooksbridge 14 and Glynde 23. Such were the numbers employed on the railway and their patriotism. There was an element of togetherness reminiscent of the "Pals" units of the First War when staffs of the two electrical supply companies formed sections. Eastwood's Cement works had its own section and so did County Council employees.

Action Stations

The Lewes town defence map gives dispositions, shaded in red, of the Home Guard upon it going into action. There were certain posts to be manned and duties undertaken by the unit. Post No 1, was by *The Chalkpit Inn* where evidence of an excavated area for a machine gun post still exists just north of the entrance to the car park. Post No 2, was at the Racecourse grandstand. Post No 3, covered a large area around the Prison crossroads and included the observation post (OP) in the southern boundary wall of the Prison facing along the Brighton Road. This embrasure in the flint wall was supported by angle iron and remains to this day. Evidence of the rifle pit behind the wall has gone. Post No 4, was at the junction of Ashcombe Lane and Juggs Lane. No 6, at The Waterworks by the Kingston Road railway bridge. Post No 7, The Cockshut near the tennis club. Post No 8 at the *Snowdrop Inn*, with No 9 at the Golf Clubhouse. No 11 was at Malling Hill. There were also OPs at Juggs Lane (two), and another was at the bottom of Hill Road with a view over Landport. The eastern approaches were covered by an OP near The Long Barrow looking over Malling towards Ringmer. Another with a southerly view perched precariously on the steep hill-side below the last house *Southdown Cottage* No 23, Chapel Hill. These observation posts were dug into the ground with corrugated iron shuttering and wooden strutting. The spoil was piled up round them for protection and covered with displaced turf which provided natural concealment. They contained minimal emergency rations and two wire mesh bunks for the off watch men. No 19 Platoon had two more at Hamsey Place and Hamsey Farm. The units of the 16th Sussex would have also been responsible for the blocking of the Old Hamsey River Bridge carrying the Uckfield railway. The 25th Sussex would have carried out similar duties in respect of Southerham railway bridge and Every's bridge that took the Uckfield railway over the Ouse near the site of the Phoenix Causeway.

The 25th Sussex (SR) "J" company had 24 men stationed at both ends of the London railway tunnel, at the White Hill portal and at its station exit. The footbridge at Cabbage Path was also covered. In the goods yard 12 men were posted, Every's Bridge had 12 men, the north end of the shunting yards opposite the Gasworks 11 men, Southerham bridge 12 men, and the south end of the shunting yards opposite the disused chalkpit in South Street 11 men. The Railway Station was "J" company's headquarters garrisoned by a reserve of 64 men.

"A" Company, 16th Sussex Home Guard dispositions for defence of the town were: -

No 1 Platoon	Posts Nos 1 & 2	*Chalkpit Inn* & Race Hill Grandstand
No 2 Platoon	Posts Nos 3 & 4	Western Road & Kingston Ridge
No 3 Platoon	Posts Nos 5, 6 & 7	Juggs Lane, Kingston Road Railway Bridge & Tennis Club Cockshut
No 4 Platoon	Posts 8 & 9	Golf Club & *Snowdrop Inn*
No 5 Platoon	Posts 10 & 11	Mill Road & Longbarrow OP
HQ Coy	Post 12	Old Naval Prison

The Home Guard progressively became a potent defence force, well equipped, well trained and well motivated towards its role. This gave so many World War One veterans a chance to don uniform with a purpose and re-learn old skills as well as new ones. It would relieve to a significant degree the need for the army to deploy many men for home defence. Competition for labour became more severe as the war continued and the less interesting Civil Defence services were becoming starved of members. It was decided to form a Civil Defence platoon within the Home Guard to help civil defence whenever their other duties allowed. It reflects well on the equipment of the Home Guard that of the 106 armed men who formed this special unit, all had personal weapons 20 of them being automatic, usually Sten guns. Pictorial evidence shows the 16th Sussex armoury to include five Vickers heavy machine guns, EY rifle cup grenade launchers, a two pounder anti-tank gun, Northover projectors and spigot mortars. By 1943 the unit was at peak efficiency with a plentiful supply of grenades and small arms ammunition. Frequent exercises with the regular army, itself training for the invasion of Europe, helped to bring this about. A third birthday parade and demonstration in the Convent Field in May 1943 was watched by 2,000 spectators. Despite the amount of live ammunition used, there are no recorded deaths or injuries in the Lewes Home Guard units. These did occur, at a Brickwork's in Horam on 10th October 1941 when a Home Guard Sergeant was killed and four army officers injured in a mortar bomb explosion. One week later two members of the Haywards Heath Battalion were killed at Slaugham during live ammunition practice. The Commonwealth War Graves Commission records just one member of the 16th Battalion dying while on duty, Lance Corporal Raymond Goode aged 63 of Seaford, on 6th May 1944, from natural causes.

The voluntary nature of Home Guard duties ceased, and a stricter military discipline was instituted. From December 1941 men could be directed into the Home Guard and at the same time the option for members to resign at 14 days' notice was withdrawn. In November of the same year a member of the Haywards Heath Battalion was brought before a Field General Court Martial on a charge of striking an officer. The charge was eventually withdrawn because of doubts about whether he was on duty at the time of the offence, and to the authenticity of his signature on an enrolment form. In October 1942 a Lewes Home Guard was fined £5 with 18 shillings costs for being absent from duty without good cause. In March the following year a member of the 11th Post Office Battalion was before the court for absence from duty having missed four parades. His defence was that besides his full time job he was also working as a rat catcher. He had not been issued with a rifle nor had he received any training in its use, both points denied by unit officers. The case was dismissed.

The Auxiliary Units

From the earliest days of the Home Guard separate units evolved known as the Auxiliary Units. Each unit was small in numbers, specially and secretly trained at Highworth near Swindon in the arts of self defence, radio operation, sabotage, intelligence gathering and survival. Their principle job was to stay behind if an area was overrun by German forces and report on all matters of interest to the defending army. Active operations were not necessarily planned as this would draw attention to their presence and almost certainly lead to their elimination. They wore Home Guard uniform but would not participate in regular Home Guard duties. They were all required to sign a declaration of confidentiality under The Official Secrets Act.

Women's Auxiliary 21st May 1943   R Hedger *Sussex Express*

The seven strong Lewes patrol was one of the twenty-one in Sussex and included among its members Mr C Cannon, of Harper and Eade, Mr C Gearing, of Muddells the Undertakers, Mr Dick Giles, Chief Cashier, Barclays Bank, Mr P Bridgman, Monumental Mason, Mr Herbert Baker, Chemist and Mr Ken Day of the grocery shop in New Road. Features of the activities of these groups were hideaways concealed in woodlands or on the Downs. One such was located near the Red Lion Pond at Beddingham manned by Mr William Owen, Steward of the Firle estate, Mr Eric Brickell of Iford and two other farmers. Mr George Cook of Cooksbridge, Mr Tom Smith and Mr Jack Harman, farmer of Offham, had their operational post in Coombe Plantation behind Coombe House. Mr Bill Webber, a market gardener of Firle carried out his duties, as part of a four-man patrol, in a post in a wooded area high above the village. It was connected by a field telephone to two observation posts. Some small stocks of weapons and explosives with iron rations were kept in the posts. The construction was carried out by Royal Engineers using wood strutting and corrugated iron shuttering. The posts were buried to a depth of ten feet and were equipped with two bunks. Mr Harmer observed that after a night's occupancy the air was heavy and one went off duty with a thick head. The secretiveness of this undercover operation was epitomised by the choice of a dormouse in red on a khaki ground as a unit badge.

The area headquarters for these units were at Tottington Manor, Small Dole on the Brighton Henfield road. Many men in these units who were trained at Highworth in Somerset were issued with handbooks with far from innocent instructions. A printed cover headed The Countryman's Diary 1939 with a fictitious advertisement for Highworth's Fertilizers that said "Do their stuff unseen until results are obtained". A further Auxiliary Force connection with Lewes has been recorded. That was with Miss Beatrice Temple who was Mayor of the town in 1972-3. Miss Temple served during the war as a Senior Commandant in the ATS (Auxiliary Territorial Service) in charge of radio communications with the auxiliary units. The nearest radio control centre to which the Lewes auxiliaries would have reported was Heathfield Park where the 55th British Divisional headquarters were located. None of the three local operational posts had radios.

Vickers Guns Convent Field 21-5-1943 *R Hedger Sussex Express*

In November 1994 a reunion of the surviving Auxiliaries took place at Tottington Manor. It was only to be expected that with such a secret organisation it was the first time that most of them had met. The meeting provided an explanation of the workings of the radio network. Parallel to the patrols a small number of radio "Hams" had been recruited and provided with radio sets by the Royal Corps of Signals. These radio telephony sets were simple to use, powered by six volt accumulators, and fitted into a wooden casing measuring fifteen by five by six inches. They operated on ultra high frequency using the abandoned pre-war BBC Alexandra Palace television wavelength. The maximum range of fifty miles would have prevented German eavesdropping from France but the system would have been vulnerable if an invasion had occurred. Aerials were concealed under tree bark and among branches. Little information survives of the identity of the Lewes radio operator but he was thought to have been a local Doctor. This local operator would send information to an Army signal section whose task it was to monitor several civilian contacts and then relay the messages to Miss Temple's unit at Heathfield.

Stand Down

The Home Guard, its main duty done, with the campaign in Europe appearing to be progressing successfully, was officially stood down on 28th October 1944 with a farewell parade to All Saint's Church at 10.30 am on Sunday 26th November 1944. A march past the County Hall in the rain where the salute was taken by their CO was followed by sandwiches and beer served at the old Naval Prison. Three weeks later the German offensive in the Ardennes underlined the fact that the war in Europe was far from over.

In February 1945 a local Branch of the British Legion, implementing national rules, advised members of the Home Guard that, unless qualifying under previous membership of the forces, they would not be eligible for membership. This provoked a storm of protest bringing forth some ill judged comments about "Call up dodgers" finding a refuge in the Home Guard, a charge often levelled as well at full-time members of the NFS. Both organisations would accept men who were under age or medically unfit for military service. Lt Col H W Styles, the Home Guard Commander, was also President of the local British Legion Branch and resigned his presidency in protest at the ruling. After so much dedicated service it was a great pity for the Home Guard to end on a sour note.

The last word is best left to Lt Col Styles who reminded the critics that during the course of its existence 1,400 men had served of which 512 had been called up for service with the forces, taking with them the benefits of significant military training received in the Home Guard. During the life of the unit it had received stores and equipment to the value of £40,000. Very little being lost or written off. More equipment was handed in than issued Probably this difference is explained by items "Borrowed" from sympathetic army units stationed in the area. Cap badges, which in the early days had been in short supply, were kept as souvenirs whilst many would find the caps, greatcoats, boots and gaiters which they were allowed to keep would be useful as working clothes, with clothes rationing still in force. Each man received a certificate of appreciation from King George VI for his services.

11. Fortress Lewes

Between 30th May and 4th June 1940 the British Expeditionary Force was evacuated from Dunkirk and on 18th June British forces withdrew from Cherbourg. By 25th June France had capitulated. The German forces now occupied the Channel coast and Lewes was in the front line. As an anti-invasion measure new Defence Regulations were announced. Defence Regulation 18b empowered the detention of aliens who were then sent to the Isle of Man for internment. German males had been interned from September 1939. On 31st May, 18 local women and girls of German or Austrian origin were arrested and sent for internment. On the same day an Italian chef employed at *Shelleys Hotel* was fined for being out after the 8.00 pm curfew for aliens. By 22nd June, with Italy's entry into the war, the chef would also be on his way to the Isle of Man. Quoting Mr Winston Churchill on 18th June 1940 "What General Weygand called the Battle for France is now over. I expect The Battle of Britain is about to begin".

Local Defences

Local Defence Volunteers (LDV) manned the road blocks that had been set up on roads leading into the town and here travellers were stopped and required to produce their identity cards. Unless you lived within the restricted area, 10 miles of the coast, or had genuine reasons for entry you would be turned back and reported for possible prosecution. The road blocks were at Mill Road in Malling Street, *The Snowdrop Inn* South Street, *The Chalkpit Inn* on the Offham Road, Kingston Road by the Stanley Turner Ground and at the top of Falmer Hill. To begin with the blocks were constructed of old carts, lorries or County Council road repair trailers arranged in chicane fashion. Later massive concrete blocks were constructed four feet square and five feet high finished with a pyramidal top, each block was anchored by a substantial below ground stub. To close the gap concrete cone shaped "Dragons Teeth" which could be manhandled into position were used. Some of these remain at the Cliffe Corner Car Park as bollards. For some years after the war one of the concrete blocks remained at *The Snowdrop*. To avoid helping an invading enemy all road direction signs were removed and place names had to be obliterated on buildings and signs. This was not entirely effective as Morrish the drapers at the corner of Fisher Street had a sign that included the word "Lewes". This had been repainted so often that even after covering with paint the word still stood out in relief. Unwittingly the Town Council continued to post notices outside the Town Hall headed Borough of Lewes until prompted to desist by the "Lewes Rouser" column in the Sussex Express.

Falmer Hill road block 1940 *Brighton & Hove Herald*

The East Sussex County Council organised parties of volunteers to dig trenches on the Downs to foil gliders carrying airborne German troops landing. Manual efforts were supplemented by mechanical drainlayers to speed up the defences. Luftwaffe aerial photographs, taken in August 1940 and captured in 1945 by the American Army, show the progress of these works on the Race Hill and near "The Squares", a series of pathways through thick scrub possibly the remains of an old field system to the west. Flatter farmland nearer the rivers was obstructed with steel scaffold poles with wire cables tensioned between them.

Anti-tank block Snowdrop Inn 1950 *H Windless*

Pillboxes

The War Office selected a number of sites for fixed defences or pillboxes. Contractors were given six weeks to complete the works most of which were priced at £200. The usual thickness of concrete was eighteen inches, the demand for wooden shuttering used to hold the concrete in position while setting was so great that wood was reserved for the inside. A single course of brickwork was used for the outside shuttering. This was left in position on completion but was not an integral part of the construction. At the end of the War landowners were given the option of retaining the structures and receiving £10 or having the pillboxes removed.

Several close to Lewes remain. At Rise Farm a type 22, hexagonal pillbox, 10 feet wide and 7 feet high survives. Near Swanborough a type 22 and by the Brooks next to the London Railway line a type 24 rhomboid shaped pillboxes exist to this day. This latter pillbox was camouflaged as a signal box. At the Pells by Pelham Terrace one was disguised as a cafe with toilets. The one at Swanborough looked like a roadside tea room with a verandah. The Rise Farm pillbox appeared as an extra haystack. Most of the disguises were flimsy constructions of wood framing, canvas and chicken wire and sufficed to mislead aerial photography. The Prison had two pillboxes both type 22, one at the main entrance sited to fire down Western Road with the outside painted to match the knapped flint boundary wall. The other pillbox covered Spital Road and was set into the bank close to the site of the present electricity transformer. A 1947 photograph shows this pillbox still in position but the one at the prison gate had gone leaving just a chalk scar. Riverside sites were used for other pillboxes. One was located near the New Recreation Ground south of the present Willeys Bridge. This was blown up by the army before site redevelopment in May 1961. A postcard view by Judge's of Hastings taken in 1954 of the Ouse at South Street shows a pillbox in the meadows across the river from the entrance to the Cement Works now the Cliffe Industrial Estate. Consternation was caused in 1940 when the army chose a site at the Outfall works immediately over the main 21inch outfall pipe for another pillbox. Construction was completed despite the protests. Most would have been manned by eight men with three light machine guns.

Cliffe Bridge was given special protection, on the west side three large concrete blocks were built one on each side on the pavement with a third centrally placed. They were approximately two feet wide, six feet high and from a five-foot base tapered to three feet at the top, each had slots to take steel girders that would completely prevent the passage of vehicles or tanks. Although there was a lamp on a wooden post in the middle of the road and the edges of the blocks were painted white, the scarring of the sides confirmed the number of vehicle contacts, one of which ended fatally. The bridge was prepared for demolition with two depth charges being dug into chambers deep in the western abutment.

Rise Farm pill box 1940, builders and disguise *Colin Thompsett*

To cover the exit from the bridge a pillbox was sited in the entrance to the Goods Yard behind the fence next to the Old Tabernacle Church. This pillbox was blown up in October 1946, the demolition was not without incident, pieces of concrete were hurled into Cliffe High Street damaging some parked vehicles. This was attributed to poor construction with defective concrete. By far the most unusual pillbox was the one built on the lower part of School Hill immediately below the porticoed doorway of number 212, Broughton's Ladies School and extending to cover the adjacent window of No 213. This one a type 28 was 8' 6" high, 8' 0" wide and 21' 0" long. It occupied the pavement and the small area behind the railings, and it abutted the property extending to the kerb. It had one large embrasure facing Cliffe Bridge and was designed to hold a 2-pounder anti tank gun and three light machine guns. It would be garrisoned by ten men. This pillbox was painted to resemble the buildings and even in a top quality photograph it is easily missed at first glance. It was a great nuisance to residents especially in the blackout and no regrets were expressed when it was dismantled with pneumatic drills in September 1944.

Rise Farm pill box 1994 *R A Elliston*

To the left of the bicycle a camouflaged anti-tank pill box covers Cliffe Bridge   *RCHME Crown Copyright*

Pipe Mines and Fougasse Sites

Other means of defence against the invader were installed. At Baydean south of Iford Farm on the A26 a pair of pipe mines was buried full width under the road. These were lengths of pipe four inches in diameter packed with explosive and connected to a detonator. This was fired manually by wire from an adjacent slit trench on the approach of an enemy vehicle or tank. Closer to Lewes at *The Chalkpit Inn* and the Mill Road Malling check points Fougasse devices were placed. Like the pipe mines they needed to be sited at a point where the road is banked at the side so that a disabled vehicle blocks the way forward. In April 1994 the remains of one with part of its charge intact were discovered at the side of the road in Ashcombe Lane just west of Kingston Ridge. A Fougasse was made of forty gallon oil drums filled with waste oil and fitted with an explosive igniter charge fired from a slit trench. The drums two feet wide and three feet tall were buried sideways into the roadside bank. A four-inch drain pipe was let into the upper side to vent the drum allowing the ignited oil to pour rapidly onto the road. An installation comprised of two drums about 15 yards apart. Where possible both sides of the road would be equipped. Mr George Baxter, now of Shoreham, then a youthful member of the Lewes LDV, helped install those at Ashcombe Lane where two sets of four were placed either side of the Juggs Lane cross roads.

The River Crossings

Cliffe Bridge with anti-tank blocks on the right April 1943 *RCHME Crown Copyright*

A river is a natural defensive line, an obstacle to attackers but a possible hindrance to defenders. The key to the situation is the control of the bridges. The Ouse crossings at Newhaven, Southease, Southerham railway bridge, Lewes Cliffe, Hamsey and Barcombe were, except Southerham, of relatively flimsy construction and quite unsuited to heavy, military traffic such as tanks. Plans had been made to deny their use to a German invader but alternative arrangements had to be made to ensure the unhindered passage of the defending British troops. A first step was decking over the spaces between the rails on the Southerham railway bridge. This was followed by the construction in 1940 at Southease of a Hamilton box girder bridge by the army. In 1943 this was replaced 100 yards upstream by a Bailey Bridge. The construction was part of a class 40 (40 tons capacity) route installed by the 53rd Divisional Engineers based in Maidstone. Bailey bridges were assembled from preformed panels but required a level launching site. The flood banks at the riverside were brought up to level by using chalk spoil excavated by the Canadian Tunnelling Companies working on HMS *Forward* at South Heighton. This was an underground bunker for the Naval Control of the Newhaven port. On completion a test was arranged with twenty Churchill tanks provided by Canadians stationed at Seaford. One tank broke down on the way, the other nineteen reached Southease and crossed the new Bailey bridge to the satisfaction of the assembled senior officers. The tanks made a safe return to Seaford. The disabled tank had been repaired by its crew and then went on to complete its mission. The inspecting Officers and

Military Police had left the site by the time the latecomer arrived. Without directions it went over the old swing bridge turned and retired by the same route. Despite a two-ton maximum weight limit the bridge survived the thirty-eight-ton tank. The deck planking of the bridge still shows the scars of the encounter to this day. The skewed railway level crossing gates also were often damaged by tanks and other army vehicles using the military bridge over the river.

Other Bailey bridges were installed in 1943. One connected Soap Factory Lane in Malling Street with Bridgman's Wharf in Eastgate Street, to the south of the present Phoenix Causeway. Immediately after crossing the river the traffic passed through a timber store shed before exiting by the rear entrance to Every's Ironworks yard. This bridge bore a notice "For Military Traffic Only" and provided an important alternative to Cliffe Bridge. Another appeared further up the river near the humped backed bridge at Hamsey close to the old barge turn round. At Barcombe Mills in 1941 a military box girder bridge had replaced three old weak brick bridges that crossed river meanderings, but to do so a new road had to be built. This work was undertaken by Royal Engineers who used regular deliveries of train loads of brick rubble from blitzed London buildings to make the road above the riverside fields. This in turn was replaced by a Bailey bridge in 1943.

Hamilton Bridge Southease 1940 IWM H12002 CrownCopyright

An excavation undertaken in 1940 remains a mystery to this day. Through the late summer and autumn excavations took place high up on the downland above the Malling Coombe. The site was on the face of southern slope and as the chalk spoil was visible from School Hill it was not a well-kept secret. More than one youthful observer managed to visit the tunnels and the descriptions tally, two parallel tunnels running inwards slightly inclined downwards joining about thirty yards in. No one saw anything warlike stored there nor other evidence of occupation. One piece of documentary evidence is recorded as having been received by the secretary of the Lewes Golf Club and that was a letter from a Royal Army Service Corps unit stationed at Preston Barracks Brighton in July 1940 asking permission to use the road up the Clubhouse for military traffic.

The Invasion Threat

Following Hitler's "Last Appeal to Reason" speech on 19th July 1940 and its British rejection, on the 22nd Operation "Sealion," the German invasion of England, was planned for mid-September.

Lewes, as an important road and rail junction, would have been an objective for the German 9th Army that had planned to land two Infantry divisions and a Mountain division between Hastings and Brighton to secure a bridgehead 15 miles deep. A second wave of two Panzer and two motorised divisions was to follow. Kent, Sussex and Surrey were regarded as the most threatened areas. For the defence there were three divisions, the 1st and 45th British and a New Zealand Division plus a Motor Machine Gun Brigade and one other Infantry Brigade. Planning was of the highest order but there was a woeful shortage of artillery and tanks most of which had been lost in France. The shortage of artillery was evident when a troop of 18 pounder field guns of World War One vintage with wooden spoked iron rimmed wheels complete with ammunition limbers of the same era was observed noisily speeding from Station Approach into Lansdown Place in August 1940. They were of the kind reserved for the firing of ceremonial salutes but were, on this occasion, towed by fifteen hundredweight army trucks instead of horses.

The Government issued a leaflet to every householder under the title of "What to do if The Invader Comes", its message was clear. Do not spread rumours, stay put unless told to evacuate by the military, observe and report any unusual activity to the authorities, if parachutists land do not give them information, hide maps, bicycles and food. Do not block roads unless ordered to do so by the military, ensure that your vehicle is immobilised and petrol is not available to the enemy. All information would be given locally and not by the wireless. Following the congestion on continental roads during the German Bliztkreig, which hampered the movement of Allied troops, the Government instituted a "Stay Put" policy for civilians unless it was a military necessity to evacuate a town following a German invasion.

Fleeing the Invaders

Contingency plans were devised to deal with any necessary movement of populations. In the first instance Lewes might have been a reception area for the inhabitants of Newhaven and Seaford displaced from their homes during an invasion. The cinemas, church halls and schools were earmarked for this purpose. The plans also provided for an exodus of the residents of Lewes but these did not consider the possibility of refugees from the coast. Civilian assembly points (CAPs) were designated to the north of the town and all such sites were the subject of military approval. It was reasoned that the best way of keeping refugees off the road would be to provide them with some shelter, food and water. Residents from east of the river would go in the direction of Glyndebourne and Gote Farm Ringmer. Those from the west would go to Offham, Barcombe Newick and Chailey to destinations such as Ketche's Farm Sheffield Park, The Ades Chailey, Brookhouse Farm East Chiltington and Barcombe Council School, Plumpton Racecourse, and just outside the town's defences, Brown's Farm, at Landport. Field kitchens would be provided and latrines dug, all able-bodied men would be required to help with these tasks. An earlier instruction envisaged that most refugee traffic would be westwards and certain roads would be reserved exclusively for military traffic unless a mass panic exodus occurred. The roads from the Prison to Newhaven, the Prison to Chailey, Brighton to Uckfield and Lewes to Polegate would all have designated crossing points. These would allow civilian traffic to pass. Army maps were marked with black arrows for traffic moving to the scene of fighting and red for traffic moving away. Any unauthorised vehicles would be driven off the road into the nearest field, immobilised, the tyres deflated, and if necessary the vehicle burnt. The Police who were to play a major role in controlling the refugees would have been issued with sidearms but were very doubtful if they could exercise effective control in an invasion situation.

Lewes Nodal Point Type "A"

Lewes was designated a type A "Nodal Point" capable of holding out for six days. Type B nodal points were only required to hold out for three days. In case of the town being cut off from London and Regional Headquarters at Tunbridge Wells a Triumvirate was set up to run the town under military direction. The three were the Mayor Ald Crisp, with Ald Hoyles as Deputy, Superintendent Hopper of the Police and the Commanding Officer of the Home Guard Lieutenant Colonel Styles. All information to the population would be given by loudspeaker van and by special grey notice boards at points round the town. The defended area would be the whole of the built up area within the Borough boundary except the Houndean Rise area and the new houses at Malling Hill, Malling Villas and Mill Road. It was estimated that 300 persons would need to be evacuated from these clearance areas and brought into the town. This measure was ostensibly to give clear fields of fire for the defenders. An enemy attack which penetrated the defences of the town would be countered by a withdrawal to an area designated as "The Keep". This was bounded by Brook Street, the river frontage, the railway line behind Friars Walk, Lansdown Place, Southover Road, Keere Street, New Road, St John's Terrace and St John's Hill.

Code names abounded in the June 1941 top secret "War Book". Lewes was "Brussels" Uckfield was "Winnipeg", "Texas" concealed East Grinstead. Brighton was "Sydney" and Newhaven "Burma" while Haywards Heath was "Lisbon". The rivers received the same treatment, the Ouse became "Jupiter", the Cuckmere was known as "Dehli" and the Adur as "Mars". Enemy airborne landings were designated "Migration" and those from the sea "Mitre", weather conditions for them were graded as (one) suitable, (two) possible, (three) unsuitable. The code "Bugbear" meant that an invasion was imminent and the Home Guard was to be mustered, "Bouncer" meant that an invasion was expected and was

PRISONERS DEMONSTRATE FROM LEWES GAOL ROOF

Type 22 pill box at the Prison *Sussex Daily News*

used before "Bugbear". There were two other states "Stand To" a state of readiness and "Normal". Attack codes were also designated "DR" a destructive raid by sea and or air, "SG" a smash and grab seaborne raid, "AS" meant armed sabotage and "SS" secret sabotage or pilfering. There were codes for the categories of demolition of factories and other installations ranging from "A" disastrous for the course of the war, "B" for secret apparatus," C" loss serious but not disastrous and "D" local or limited effect if lost. Most of the listed establishments were in the Brighton area such as Allen West, CVA Machine Tools, The London Nameplate Co Xylo Works and the Capstan Engineering Co. At Newhaven the Military Plotting Room at HMS *Forward* South Heighton was declared to be vulnerable and in Lewes the RAF Special Communications Centre at the telephone exchange was listed as category "D". The kerosene (paraffin oil) stocks at Martin's Garage at the Cliffe were also earmarked for destruction.

The War Book

A "War Book" was arranged on "Domesday" lines listing the quantities and locations of essential supplies, the strengths and locations of Civil Defence and Home Guard units. On reflection when the relative strengths of the defences of the town are balanced against the weight of a German attack, a more pessimistic description of the War Book might have been "Doomsday Book". A Canadian unit stationed in the area recorded that the axis of a German attack on the town could have been from the north. With the town dominated by the high ground of both Cliffe Hill and the Race Hill it could not have held out for long once these positions had been secured by an invading force.

Welfare provision for up to 1,600 persons was planned, these included replacement of lost identity cards, ration and pension books, fares to relatives' homes, repairs to houses, and limited financial help in cases of loss. A mobile WVS canteen organised by Mrs M G F Geering of North Street would help with preliminary feeding arrangements. Mrs Sudell, Voluntary Services Organiser, for the County Council co-ordinated the welfare arrangements. Unorganised refugees from the coastal areas would need larger scale dining facilities. These were at the Girls' County School 200 diners, Mountfield Road Schools 200, the Tabernacle Church Hall (Riverside Centre) 100, Forester's Hall, Station Street 100, Salvation Army Hall, St John Street and St Mary's Hall, Highdown Road 50 each. For part of the war the County Council stored three mobile field kitchens at the Isolation Hospital in Nevill Road. No account survives of their intended use.

At The Avenue Children's Home six 16 gallon boilers had been installed in a garden shed, with a capacity for 200 meals. A further 200 meals would be provided from the Mountfield Road School kitchen and 700 meals from Pouchlands Hospital Chailey. A specimen recipe for 150 persons is recorded. "Take 20 tins of vegetable soup and 10 tins of baked beans and add to two gallons of boiling water stirring constantly. When nearly to the boil again, add five three-pound tins of meat loaf diced into one inch cubes and boil for five minutes, reduce the fire and serve each person with a portion containing three pieces of meat". For the first three days of an emergency no charge would be made but after that the meals would be sold at cost. Emergency stocks of food were held in Findlater Mackie's wine cellar next to the Corn Exchange, Shelleys Stables, Messrs Brooke and Prudencio's Mineral Water factory in Malling Street, Moppetts Stores Priory Street and Philcox's stores in the High Street. The Home Guard would be expected to use emergency ration packs on a scale of one pack for five men for the first 48 hours. After that the army would be responsible for feeding them. The Housewives' Service had 380 people who were willing to open their homes in an emergency.

There were 12,000 persons in the Borough living in 3,750 houses. It was calculated that there were 3,692 spare habitable rooms each capable of accommodating one person.

Water supplies were carefully identified both for drinking and for fire fighting. Most of the reservoirs and the pumping station were outside the defended area. Residents would be given six hours' notice to fill all available baths and buckets. After that main water would be cut off. Boreholes were listed at Cuilfail, the Phoenix Ironworks, Pells Baths, the Grammar School for Boys' Mountfield Road, the outfall works, and Mann's Dye works Friars Walk. Wells were at Beards Brewery, Kenwards Nursery Southover, and Bell Lane recreation groumd. Seven transportable tanks were located at the Waterworks and filling points for these would be at reservoirs at Juggs Lane, Western Road, No 3 reservoir at the Race Hill, Highdown Road and South Way. Stocks of chlorine and bleach for purifying the water would be kept on both sides of the river. The estimated population and garrison of 15,700 could consume 80,000 gallons daily. Water would be rationed to two gallons per person per day. At the Western Road reservoir two hundredweights of bleach for disinfection purposes were stored. The Pells Baths would provide half a million gallons and the Grammar School swimming pool another 60,000 gallons.

The sewerage arrangements were similarly detailed. The outfall works although near the perimeter would continue to function as long as they were held. Apart from some elevated areas of the town that might manage by gravity, most of the low lying parts of the town's system depended on electricity for pumping. It was anticipated that supplies would be cut and therefore WCs. could not be used. All foul waste would have to be collected up and buried. Two sites were reserved, the outfall works and Baxter's Field. Stocks of petrol were identified at Every's Iron Works 500 gallons, Caffyn's Malling Street 5,000 gallons, and Lewes Motors 1,500 gallons. The British Petroleum installation next to the Corporation Yard remained empty and unused. The Police also kept lists of tractors, plant and tools. They provided an out of town motor messenger service in case of disruption of the telephone system and as a back up Sergeant Bristow at the West Street Headquarters maintained a carrier pigeon loft. An alternative Police HQ was located at *Saxonbury* Kingston Road. The War Book contained details of Civil Defence, Fire Service, Gas Decontamination, Casualty Treatment and Doctors who were named as A E Cawston, W R Dunstan, D Galbaith, M L Irvine, Eileen Nugent, H Rice, C G Sinclair, W Stoors and R S Tooth. No provision was made by the Army for dealing with casualties. This would be left to civilian resources.

An Army Garrison figure of 800 soldiers was noted, the actual units would vary according to postings, examples in 1941 being the 6th Field Regiment Royal Canadian Artillery and the Fusiliers Mont Royal. In 1943 another Canadian Unit was the South Saskatchewan Regiment and at other times British units such as the 1st/4th South Lancashire Regiment formed the garrison. By November 1942 the reality of a German invasion had receded and instructions were issued to cease capital works construction on the defences of Nodal points. Despite this, as late as June 1943 proposals were put forward, that should an Invasion take place the majority of Civil Defence ambulances would be withdrawn to back areas so that they might be used to transport military and civilian wounded. This produced such an outcry about the effect this would have on the morale of the Civil Defence service and the population that it was very quickly dropped. Within a year the only invasion in the minds of the townsfolk would be the Allied Invasion of Europe.

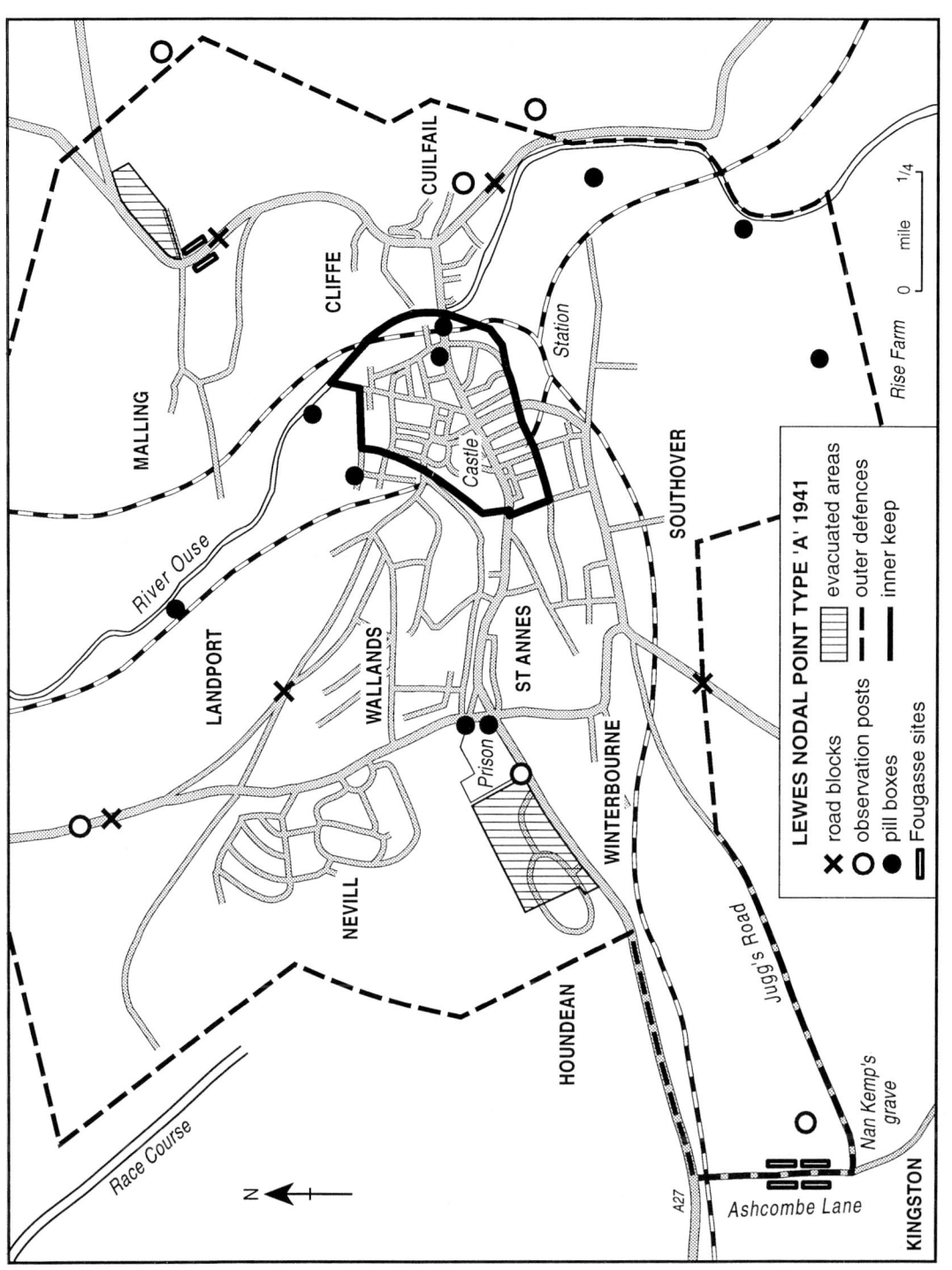

Map by Susan Rowland

12. Garrison Town

An unnatural quietness descended on the town following the recall of reservists to the colours and the embodiment of the Territorial Army in the last week of August 1939. Lewes had already seen many of its men of twenty years of age leave, called up under the Military Service Act in May 1939. The town's role in respect to accommodating the army may be divided into four phases closely linked to the progress of the war.

The first phase up to the time of Dunkirk was that of housing, basic training and a transit area for units going to France. After the French capitulation the town acquired front line status as part of the heavily defended invasion area, as far as the scarce resources of Southern Command would allow. This phase continued while Britain stood alone, with the influx of troops of the Canadian Army making its presence felt in many ways. There followed a time of change to a more offensive stance with the Downland being taken over for training areas with live firing ranges and the mounting of the Dieppe Raid. Finally for a year from mid 1943 a rising tide of military activity took place until D-day 6th June 1944 after which the military presence declined as more units moved again to France.

Soldiers were billeted in private houses with families for which the householder was paid, and if board was provided, extra food rations could be drawn, although most of the soldiers were fed by the army. Unoccupied accommodation was requisitioned ranging from the newly completed flats owned by the Council in Priory Street to larger houses such as School Hill House and Lewes House.

1st/4th South Lancs Dispatch Riders Albion House   *Mr & Mrs P Horrocks*

Albion House, Dr Cawston's home and surgery, at the corner of Albion Street and School Hill and No 8 Albion Street were also commandeered. These houses were unfurnished when taken over but were equipped by the army to minimum standards, camp beds, thin mattresses, grey army blankets, trestle tables and forms. Food was eaten from mess tins, bed linen and floor coverings were rarely provided. Cooking utensils and fuel including coal for heating were on issue but fire wood was not. The army habit of scrounging made up the deficiency of fire lighting wood. If discarded wooden packing cases were hard to find, it is not surprising that wooden parts of buildings deemed to be expendable were consumed for this purpose. This activity contributed much to the dilapidation of property occupied by the army.

The old Naval Prison, vacated by the Territorial Army, was pressed into service as was the Mountfield Road drill hall that housed the men of the Royal Artillery. Astley House Stables in Spital Road, now the site of the Police clothing stores, became the home for a time of part of the 1st/4th South Lancs Regiment. Mountfield House by the railway bridge in Mountfield Road was also taken over and used initially by an army dental unit, later it was used by the 1st Canadian divisional reception centre. Part of Caffyn's garage in Malling Street was taken over and Rugg's garage Station Street, now Caburn Court, was used to house a Light Aid Detachment of the REME. Such a unit would undertake first line repairs to equipment and vehicles and it would have comprised fourteen men and a breakdown lorry. The army's use of these premises meant that the basement air raid shelter was no longer available to the public.

Entertainments

1,200 PETITION FOR SUNDAY CINEMA OPENING

Lewes Controversy

About 1,200 signatures accompanied a petition in favour of the Sunday opening of Lewes cinemas, which has been sent to the Town Clerk (Mr. C. W. Stephenson) by the management of the Odeon Theatre, Lewes.

A burning issue of 5th April 1940 — *Sussex Express*

Entertainment for the off duty troops and their welfare was a problem. The town had little to offer, with just two cinemas that did not open on Sundays. There were occasional public dances and Whist Drives, several societies and sports clubs catered for specialist interests but this usually involved membership. Army life is highly mobile so those diversions held little appeal for the majority who might have to move on at a moment's notice. About thirty public houses in the town plied their trade during the war years and their popularity with the soldiers often contributed to the shortage of essential supplies and to some of the unruly behaviour that occasionally ended in Court appearances. The licensed opening hours, a legacy from the first war of Noon until 2.00 pm and 6.00 pm until 10.30 pm, was especially vexatious to the Commonwealth soldiers. For those with the money, time and access to unit transport, Brighton was the Mecca. Sixteen Cinemas, all open on Sundays, the Hippodrome and Grand Variety Theatres, the Theatre Royal and the Imperial Theatre, the SS Brighton Ice Rink, Sherry's Dance Hall, the Regent Dance Hall and the Dome Dancing and innumerable public houses were for many the unattainable. While a good train service operated throughout the war, bus services were restricted from 1942 starting at 1.00 pm on Sundays and permit holders, usually war workers only being allowed on the buses after 9.00 pm on both weekdays and Sundays.

Today Public Library facilities are readily available but in the war years soldiers would have had difficulty in getting the two ratepayer guarantors for tickets to the County Library at Southdown House St Anne's Crescent or at the Borough Library in the Fitzroy Building. An expensive alternative would have been either The Q Library in the Cliffe or Boots' The Chemists Library, both of which would have required punitive deposits from transitory soldiers. This need was met by gifts of books by donors such as Lady Boughey of Malling House and the Sussex County Forces Welfare Association that provided besides books, radios, indoor games and toilet articles for servicemen.

The Service Canteens

In November 1939 a squad of RAMC recruits still in civilian clothes and with civilian respirators were quartered in Albion House. Major Stuart, their Commanding Officer, asked the local British Red Cross to help with basic first aid and nursing training. Miss Adkin, BRCS Sussex 48 detachment Commandant, gave permission for Mrs M Geering its Quartermaster and her assistant Mrs T Masson to give the necessary help. Bed making, temperature taking, bandaging, and the care of injured men formed part of the training given. Major Stuart then had the idea of setting up a recreation room for the men. He again turned to Mrs Geering and her assistant for help. They found a dilapidated annexe to be available in the garden of Albion House and this was pressed into use. An appeal to local residents soon produced the required linoleum for the floor, carpets, cutlery, crockery, and dishes. The Canteen, opened on 1st April 1940. The local Food Office identified it as "The Soldiers Recreation Room and Canteen". Within a month the RAMC left the town and there were just a few members of the Royal Artillery in the town whose needs were met by the YMCA in Westgate Street.

J & S Geering Sussex Express
Mrs M Geering centre in uniform and staff of Albion House Canteen 1945

The Red Cross helpers who served at the Canteen in the early days brought in their own milk, tea and sugar and besides serving kept the rooms clean. In August 1940 Captain Locky, of The Queen's Royal Regiment, asked if his men could use the canteen, so it was business as usual. Those were days of the Battle of Britain followed by the London Blitz. The Queen's and other units remained until December 1940 when the 1st Canadian Division arrived. Tea and other supplies that had been available on Food Office licence now became subject to stricter controls. The Ministry of Food decreed that all independent canteens must either amalgamate with recognised bodies or close. Mrs Geering, who had earlier turned down an offer from the Canadian Red Shield Organisation to support the canteen, approached Mrs M Lister the Lewes WVS Centre Organiser offering her the canteen as a going concern.

The following day Lady Egerton of the WVS agreed to the proposal asking Mrs Geering to continue with her good work.

By November 1942 the provision of sleeping accommodation for servicemen on leave or on long passes became an urgent necessity. Many men had taken to sleeping rough in air raid shelters or on public benches. The YMCA was full most nights. Following a resident's letter to the local newspaper, Mrs Geering decided to do something to improve matters. So with a friend she approached the WVS HQ having already found some available accommodation in Albion House. The rooms had been damaged as the result of army occupation. The WVS decided to undertake the task itself and by March 1943 the first WVS residential Hostel for troops was opened. On 1st April 1943 the canteen moved into the main house from the garden annexe that it had occupied since 1940. The average number of men served in the canteen at this period was around 600 each day, rising just before D-day in 1944 when 993 were served on a Sunday. Numbers declined after that and by October only a few men were served each day. The rundown continued into 1945 with the canteen closing on 14th September. The building was used for a time after that as a training centre for hostel workers who were to go to South East Asia Command.

This account of the Albion Street Canteen was kept by Mrs Geering which furnished many surprising highlights. In the early days with her husband, a well-known signwriter in the town, she toured outlying camps with a van serving refreshments to troops in isolated places. The van had been provided by voluntary funding. In the year ending April 1944, 116,124 hot drinks, 75,472 light teas, 88,858 suppers, 2,201 breakfasts and 4,038 dinners had been served at the canteen. Accurate record keeping was essential in order to get supplies of rationed goods. In June 1942 the Food Control Committee disputed and investigated the number of meals served at the Albion Street Canteen. The figure claimed was a fifth of the total reached in 1943. Nothing more was heard of the official challenge, proof indeed if it was ever needed of the volunteers' efforts.

The opening hours were from 9.00 am to 10.00 pm with the staff of three on duty during the day and four each evening. All, save a paid cook from September 1943, were from an unpaid pool of over 30 volunteers.

Ald Crisp visits the Westgate Street Canteen March 1940   *Sussex Express*

Each month a small profit was paid into the Hostel account, that by 1945 amounted to over £1,000. The minute book throws light on some of the problems encountered. The canteen and hostel were run as separate operations and it is recorded that each would have its own coal cellar with separate locks. From October 1943 a member of the Military Police or Special Constabulary would be on duty at closing time. Obviously difficulties had occurred. Christmas Day 1943 saw the canteen open as usual with free drinks to all the troops. A year later so few troops were left in the town that the canteen closed for Christmas. The bathroom of the hostel had its own rules, men were allowed until 10.00 am, after that it was for ladies only. When the hostel opened Lewes was proud to record that it was the first WVS hostel of its type in Sussex.

On 15th March 1940 the Mayor Ald Crisp opened a canteen for the forces at the Christian Alliance for Women and Girls in Westgate Street. This became known as the YMCA canteen and its opening was headlined in the Sussex Express "From Women Only to Men Only". The Mayor undertook to provide a piano. Besides light refreshments the canteen would provide billiards, table tennis, darts and the use of baths. It was found necessary to report a month later that the recreational facilities would be limited to chess and draughts when the canteen opened on Sundays. This report was made under the shadow of the debate in the town on the Sunday opening of cinemas. In January 1943 the Westgate YMCA Canteen moved to the first floor of 62 High Street, its pillared doorway through which so many servicemen passed, remains there to this day. The move enabled the YMCA to increase its hostel accommodation for servicemen in Westgate Street and the opportunity was taken to transfer the operation of the canteen to the WVS. The new canteen was equipped with a billiard room and a quiet room. British servicemen were not the only customers as on occasions German Prisoners of War from camps near Rodmell and Southease were served. The hostel held servicemen from all countries. One United States serviceman lost £17 while sleeping there, which resulted in two Commandos being prosecuted and returned to their original unit in disgrace.

WVS Mobile canteens Southover House 16th January 1942 *Sussex Express*

Figures for the year ending September 1944 show that the High Street Canteen and the Westgate Street Hostel provided hot drinks 20,004, snack meals 131,977, main meals 30,450, breakfasts 3,598, and 6,907 nights' accommodation. From the last figure it may be deduced that the Hostel had about twenty beds and about 50 per cent of guests slept in and missed their breakfasts!

The Cinemas

The first request for seven day opening of Cinemas from 7.00 pm to 10.00 pm was made in March 1940 by Lieutenant Colonel Gary Hill of 181st Field Ambulance RAMC. Councils could decide by local bylaws if cinemas might open on Sundays or recourse could be made to the Defence Regulations to permit this. The Lord's Day Observance Society always challenged any such Sunday opening application from cinema proprietors. Good Fridays and Christmas Day were the other occasions when cinemas in the town closed. The Odeon was for the proposal and Mr R Briggs manager of the Cinema de Luxe was against, observing that it did not say much for the army if they required a daily dose of films. The Rev Kenneth Rawlings came out in favour of the Sunday opening.

In October 1940 a Sunday Concert at the Cinema de Luxe for the troops was a "Sell Out" and would be repeated with under 16s being admitted. This took place in December with free admission but with a collection for comforts for the troops. Max Miller, the Brighton born variety star, brought two shows to Lewes on Sundays in 1940, one at the de Luxe on 9th June for the forces, the other from the Brighton Hippodrome to the Odeon on 8th November for the forces and Civil Defence workers. By January 1941 the Council had voted by sixteen votes to five to allow Sunday Cinema openings as a war-time measure only. A suggestion that HM Forces be admitted free and the other takings given to charities was turned down. The Council was empowered to demand a levy from Cinema owners who opened on Sundays, the proceeds being given to charities. The Odeon was required to pay £25 and the Cinema de Luxe £15. These sums were increased to £90 and £50 respectively in 1942. The Cinema opening arrangements required annual licensing and one provision restricted the working hours of employees from 2.15 pm until 9.00 pm and not more than six days out of any seven. Mr Briggs decided, despite the Odeon opening on Christmas Day 1943, to close the de Luxe to give his employees a day off.

The two Lewes cinemas followed the traditional programme of screening a twice weekly change of programme on Mondays and Thursdays with, once Sunday opening was allowed, a special Sunday programme consisting usually of older films. Economic considerations dictated the choice of older films for Sundays. These films were cheaper to rent which offset the enforced charity levy placed on the cinemas. The cinemas afforded a three-hour escape from reality. They were warm, although smoke filled, and the only reminder of war was an occasional message flashed on the screen over the film to say that the air raid sirens had sounded. The cheapest seat would be 6d (2½ pence) and the dearest 2s:3d (12 pence) in the balcony at the Cinema de Luxe on School Hill with slightly higher prices at the more modern and comfortable Odeon in the Cliffe.

Queues would wait outside the Cinema de Luxe and, with more popular films, the thirty yards long Odeon arcade would be full of waiting patrons. The programmes ran continuously from 2.30 pm until 10.00 pm and one entered when a seat became free. The programmes would consist of a main film lasting about ninety minutes, a supporting picture of an hour, plus a newsreel with a trailer of the next week's films and some local advertising. Audiences at the Odeon would have enjoyed Judy Garland in "The Wizard of Oz" in 1940. The following year Tyrone Power starred in the "Mark of Zorro" also at the Odeon. "Mrs Miniver" with Greer Garson and Gregory Peck was shown at the de Luxe in 1943 and "The Road to Morocco" with Bing Crosby, Bob Hope and Dorothy Lamour in 1944. In 1945 the Cinema de Luxe screened "Up in Arms" with Danny

Kaye and Dinah Shore and the Odeon was showing "For whom the Bells Toll" again featuring Gregory Peck. Films were of two classifications, "U" suitable for all ages and "A" for adults or children with adults. Many were the devices employed by the under sixteens to gain admission to the forbidden "A" films. Children were catered for by a Saturday afternoon showing of selected films at the Cinema de Luxe at 3d per head. At 6d a child a Saturday morning's entertainment of similar kind plus an episode of a serial could be enjoyed in the Mickey Mouse Club at the Odeon.

Council Sports facilities, namely bowls, tennis, putting and swimming, had always closed on Sundays in peacetime but the demands of war caused change in an unplanned way. As a wartime measure the Pells baths opened on alternate Sunday afternoons from 2.00 pm until 9.30 pm. One hot Sunday afternoon in May 1944 the Pells Bath was closed. Many would-be swimmers arrived to find the bath gate locked. A group of soldiers led the way and climbed over the wall followed closely by younger agile residents. After a telephone call to a councillor, Mr Bell, the Bathkeeper, was sent for to open the gates allowing over 200 swimmers to enjoy themselves that day. By June complaints were also made about the Convent Field and the Bowling Greens being shut due to insufficient staff being available to supervise them seven days a week. Quite early in the war another of the town's recreational features had been lost when the Stanley Turner Recreation Ground was abandoned to cattle grazing.

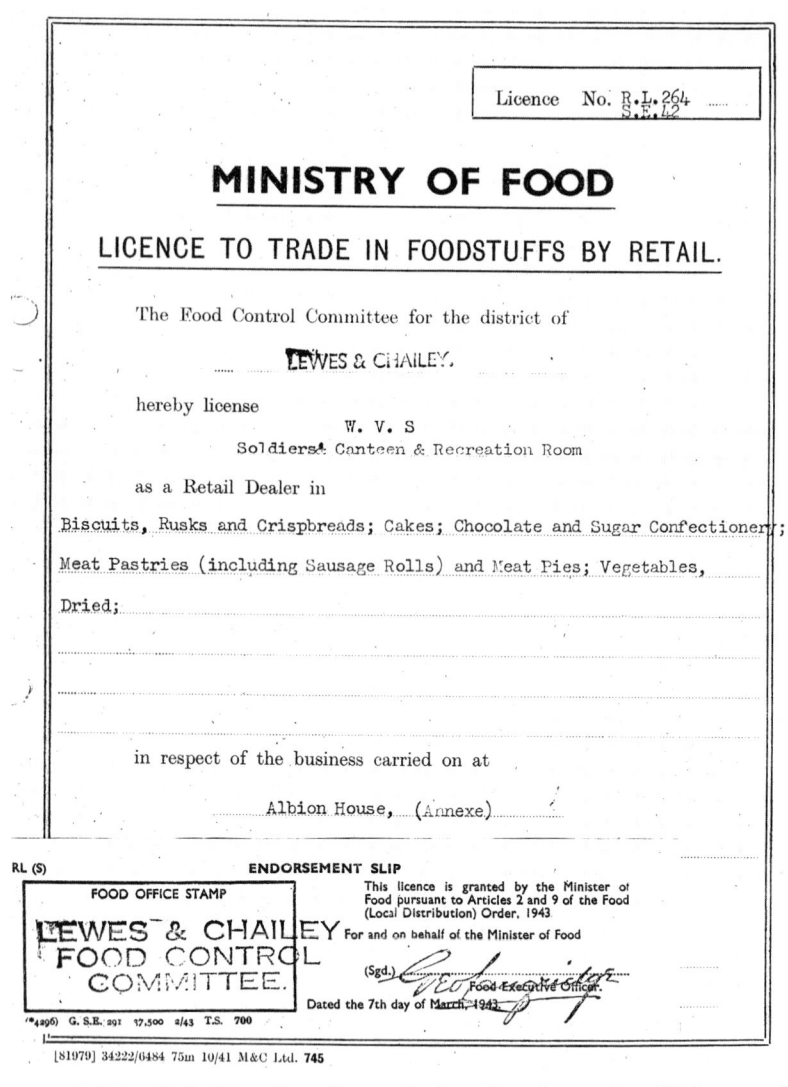

Legend is a powerful inspiration and doubtless some local soldiery discovered the Prince Regent's reputed exploit of driving a carriage down Keere Street. On 11th July 1943 it was revealed that the feat had been repeated with the modern equivalent. An army Jeep had been coaxed past the lamp standard at the top and in fourwheel drive had made a safe descent.

Wartime Weddings

It was inevitable with so many young men of the town away in the services and the influx of just as many if not more young men of the forces that cupid's arrows should still find targets. It might be supposed that there could have been an increase in the number of marriages in the town during the war years. However a count of those reported in the local newspapers shows an expected increase in service weddings and a corresponding decline in civilian weddings. The decline towards the end of the war probably reflects the decline in the numbers of available young men due to the call up and military postings abroad.

Marriages reported in Lewes 1938-45

Year	Civilian	Service	Total
1938	42	1	43
1939	34	2	36
1940	35	19	54
1941	12	40	52
1942	12	42	54
1943	6	26	32
1944	5	21	26
1945	2	33	35

These figures may not give the complete picture as not all weddings were reported in the local papers and a number of Lewes men and women were married away from the town. It does reflect to a degree on the fortunes of war with peaks coinciding with the presence of large numbers of troops in the area. Brides found their grooms among the Canadian soldiers, the first Canadian wedding in Lewes taking place in October 1941. There were to follow New Zealand, Dutch, American and Rhodesian bridegrooms and British servicemen. There were also many weddings between service couples. Girls in the services had to cope with special problems, they would not have had clothing coupons for wedding dresses, so if they wished to have a white wedding the problem was solved for them by the Women's Voluntary Service which ran a wedding gown loan service. Food rationing affected wedding receptions, limiting the type and variety of food that could be served. Many saved precious rations for weeks for the occasion.

Wedding cakes also took on camouflage. An artilleryman's bride managed to secure a fruit cake with a layer of marzipan but icing was out of the question. Clark's Bread Company ran a loan service of white decorated cardboard "Caps", returnable, to cover the cake to resemble icing. Austerity was a feature of the wedding of Miss Camilla Boughey daughter of Sir George Boughey of Malling House when she married Lieutenant Robert Barclay at South Malling Church in January 1941. The bride carried a small bouquet of violets but there were no bridesmaids or special wedding clothes. No formal reception was held as the family were still mourning the loss of the bride's brother in France in August 1940.

In 1943, because of the number of Canadian servicemen's marriages in Sussex, two special clubs were set up, one in Queen's Road Brighton and the other in Chichester. These Princess Alice Clubs were under the patronage of Countess Alice, the wife of the Earl of Athlone, the Governor

General of Canada. The objects of the clubs were to provide support for the wives, some of whom were to become bereaved and to prepare all of them for the new life they would lead when they arrived in Canada after the war, when they would be members of a group of 33,000 wives accompanied by 17,000 children who would cross the Atlantic.

At the end of the war the overseas soldiers were returned home ahead of their brides who

Lewes A.R.P. Officer's Son Married

SERGT. NEVILLE SAINS AND MISS ALICE HOPE

3rd July 1943 at St Thomas à Beckett Cliffe Sgt Neville Sains and Miss Alice Hope   *Sussex Express*

followed in late 1945 and 1946. Some found the adjustment difficult in a new country, and not up to their expectations as correspondence in the Sussex Express revealed in late 1946. Most settled down and it was estimated that about sixty war brides and children left the Lewes area for Canada. The traffic was not all one way as a Mr Chiasson, a Canadian soldier with a local bride, decided to return to England and set up in business as a shoemender at "The Lewes Shoe Hospital" in a World War One army hut on the bank on the east side of Nevill Road near the present day entrance to the Wallands School. He remained there until the school was built. After that he conducted his business from School Hill and then Market Street.

English soldiers posted to Lewes also found their brides in the town. Private P Horrocks of the 1st/4th South Lancs Regiment and Private C Palmer of the No 4 Commando were two who returned after the war and settled in the town. Not all the wartime romances ended in weddings in Lewes. In April 1942 the local papers carried a report of the wedding of Leading Aircraftman Ronald Heavens of 8 The Course to Miss Agnes Perrot in the Pro Cathedral Calgary, Alberta, Canada, with Leading Aircraftman T Geering of Green Wall acting as his best man.

13. The Military

Military stationing in wartime is always a matter of secrecy and the frequency with which movements are made renders it difficult to make an accurate account. Situation reports and location statements, which were updated daily, that have survived, have many red ink alterations, and, to fox the historian, each one is headed with the words "Copy No -- Secret, destroy the previous issue". Before 1939 Lewes was located in the Eastern Command Area with headquarters at Hounslow Middlesex, its sign being a white Bulldog on guard on a black background. From June 1941 the South Eastern Command was formed for the Sussex, Surrey and Kent military or corps districts, with headquarters near Reigate. This formation used a roaring defiant Tiger's head for its badge and as a Command survived to the end of the war. The Sussex and Surrey district headquarters was, from 1943, located at Haywards Heath. Its badge, a black Timber Wolf, open mouthed, with a bright red tongue on a pale green oval, commemorated the 1st Canadian Corps which had defended the area since early 1941. Many of the Lewes Home Guard, particularly the Cavalry Section, wore this badge. The Canadian Corps had a Sussex Martlet on a green circle as a corps badge.

Location statements generally listed only the headquarters of formations and not the billets of its smaller units. Orders, communications and post would all follow down the correct channels. In the early days of the war it is possible to deduce the units located in and around Lewes from newspaper reports and advertisements. The "SS Brighton" Ice Rink advertised ice hockey matches and named the Canadian Army unit team names. On the 5th April 1940 the 3rd Field Regiment Royal Canadian Artillery would play the winners of another match between the Royal Canadian Regiment and the 3rd Canadian Infantry Brigade. Later less specific team names such as Medics versus Gunners would appear. Court appearances gave details of the unit of the offender. Coroners' inquests identified the unit where accidental deaths had occurred, and gave the location of the inquest and the name of the coroner. Later, in the interests of security, Courts would still give the name but would describe the defendants as an English or overseas soldier. Inquests, apart from the briefest detail of the circumstance of the death, gave no other detail apart from the name of the deceased. Sometimes the only documentary evidence of an establishment comes from a coroner's inquest. On the 8th March 1946 an inquiry into a fatal fall from a lorry revealed that an Army ammunition depot had been established at The Broyle Ringmer. It is now an ESCC site. This store also held furniture, barbed wire, pickets, camouflage netting and uniforms.

Army units consist of fighting troops in infantry battalions of 600 officers and men and armoured regiments of 61 tanks. In greater numbers would be the troops of all the supporting arms, the Engineers, Artillery, Ordnance, and Service Corps. There were also independent units and specialists such as Commandos. The fighting troops were organised into brigades of three battalions of infantry, or in the case of tanks an armoured brigade of three tank regiments of 193 tanks. These in turn were combined in larger fighting units comprising all arms, known as divisions. An armoured division might have strength of 21,000 officers and men, an Infantry Division 17,000. Two or more divisions would constitute a corps with its own headquarters. British infantry regiments might have several numbered battalions serving in different divisions. Canadian Infantry were in regiments which were all of battalion strength. Representatives of many of these formations were to be found in the town either on or off duty, the shoulder titles of which will evoke memories for some readers.

The 1940 Invasion Threat

Until June 1940, with the bulk of formed units in France as the British Expeditionary Force, the town provided a home for units in training and there was no perceived requirement for home defence. With the German invasion of the Low Countries all this changed abruptly with the formation of the LDV subsequently known as the Home Guard. On the 5th June 1940 the only formed divisions in the country were the 51st Highland Division, the 52nd Lowland Division and the 1st Canadian Division. The 3rd British Division was being reconstituted after Dunkirk and amounted to 4,500 men under Major General B L Montgomery. A reinforcement of France led to the loss of the 51st Division at St Valèry-en-Caux, but the order for the 1st Canadian and 3rd British Divisions to go to France was countermanded at the eleventh hour. To counter the German Invasion threat in 1940 the War Office had XII Corps comprising the 1st and 45th British Divisions and the New Zealand Division. The 29th Brigade Group and the 1st Motor Machine Gun Brigade covered Sussex, Surrey and Kent. The 8th Devons and the 4th/5th Duke of Cornwall's Light Infantry of the 45th division were based in the area between Lewes and the coast. The Queen's Regiment which provided the guard for the Messerschmit that crashed in Houndean Bottom, were housed in Southover Manor School, they were part of the 1st London Division. Another aircraft guard for the Junkers 88 which came down at Court House Farm Barcombe on 9th September 1940 was provided by the Argyll and Sutherland Highlanders. In reserve in Surrey was VII Corps consisting of the 1st Armoured Division, the 1st Canadian Division and the 1st Army Tank Brigade.

The Canadians

From October 1940 five brigades of the 1st and 2nd Canadian divisions, now identified as VII Corps, took turns in strengthening and manning the coastal defences of Sussex from Newhaven to Worthing. The Canadian army headquarters were at Headley Grange, Leatherhead with an advanced headquarters at Worth Abbey, Crawley, and divisional headquarters at Staplefield Court, Haywards Heath. The 1st Canadian division remained in Sussex until April 1943 when it left to take part in the landings on Sicily. In September 1941 the 38th (Welsh) and the 55th (West Lancs) divisions were established as forward divisions for Sussex. Lewes was within the 55th division's area, that had a divisional boundary which approximated the zero meridian line from Telscombe through Offham northwards. The 38th west of the line and the 55th to the east. These defensive arrangements continued for two years. With an ever more efficient Home Guard and with the advent of the Normandy landings the 38th Division was posted to Hampshire in October 1943, the 55th Division being posted to Northern Ireland in January 1944. From 5th June 1943 the 55th divisional headquarters was at Heathfield Park with its 164th brigade headquarters in Firle Park. Part of this unit was the 1st/4th South Lancs which found many billets in Lewes. The other two brigades of this division had headquarters at Dicker House for the 165th and Mountfield for the 119th.

The Canadians based in and around Lewes formed a significant part of the forces engaged on the Dieppe raid, many sailing from Newhaven. The Fusilliers Mont Royal, The South Saskatchewan Regiment and, although based at Seaford, the 14th Calgary Tanks were all well remembered in the town. There was much heartache when the survivors returned on 19th August 1942. Canadian soldiers were also to play a significant role two years later in Normandy when the 3rd Canadian infantry division formed part of the D-day assault. The 2nd and 4th divisions left Sussex for the Dover area in April 1944, crossing to Normandy in the first and last weeks of July respectively, taking with them familiar regimental names such as the Argyll and Sutherland Highlanders of Canada (Princess Louise's) and the Lake Superior Regiment.

May 1942 found the 1st Canadian Forward Battery in the Manor House School, Southover High Street, with the 6th Canadian Forward Battery at Preston House, Firle. The South Saskatchewan regiment was occupying Firle Place. Uckfield House became the HQ for 1st Canadian Infantry Brigade in January 1943. *The Delves,* Ringmer housed the 6th Canadian Infantry Brigade signals section. Firle Park provided a home for 2nd Canadian Field Regiment Royal Canadian Artillery with B battery at Glynde Place and C Battery at West Firle.

Lewes received its first Canadians at Christmas 1940 with the arrival of elements of the 2nd Canadian Infantry Division, the Black Watch (Royal Highland Regiment of Canada). The Royal Regiment of Canada later relieved them with the bulk of the battalion being stationed in Brighton with "D" company

Royal Engineers Museum
Royal Engineers build a downland tank road

in Lewes. Mr Jack Poolton of Ontario remembers his number 16 platoon being housed in *School Hill House.* One of his unit's duties was guarding the petrol station at Newmarket on the Brighton Road with the guard room in a nearby bungalow. His unit had come to England for coastal defence duties after a spell in Iceland. The mobility of units is emphasised by his stationing in several points in Sussex from Winchelsea to Littlehampton. His regiment left Littlehampton for the Dieppe raid on 21st August 1942, where he was captured, spending the rest of the war in German prisoner of war camps.

The Garrison Engineer and Chief of Works' departments for the Sussex sub-district were installed in Southover Grange. On 28th January 1943 the Carleton and York Regiment, based locally, were assigned to help the Lewes Civil Defence in the event of a heavy air raid. A week earlier the West Nova Scotia Regiment had helped during the raid on Lewes. Both were units of the Canadian 1st Division's 3rd Brigade. The 5th Anti-Aircraft Brigade 465 Heavy AA battery was located at Northease Farm and Glynde Chalk Pit, while the 338th Searchlight unit was based in Coombe Place, Offham. Earlier in the war the 450th Company of the 70th Sussex Searchlight Regiment Royal Artillery had been based in a field between Paygate Corner and Glyndebourne. The unit had mobilised at Highcroft Drill Hall Dyke Road, Brighton and eventually made their way in darkness to the site, asking for directions on the way at a house named *Little Heaven.* They remained at Paygate until June 1940 when they moved to *Leonardslee* near Cowfold.

By April 1943 the Princess Patricia's Canadian Light Infantry were in Sunshine House, Belgrave Road, Seaford. The Newlands School, Seaford was where the Seaforths of Canada were based. School Hill House was also used by the Royal Canadian Artillery whilst the South Saskatchewan Regiment used 8 Albion Street for billets. Distinguished visitors took up residence in Southover Manor School in November 1944. They were the No 1 Special Service Brigade, Lord Lovat's Commandos. Earlier the same year the 9th Mobile Bath unit had been stationed at Hyde Manor, Kingston and 23rd Kinema Section in *Barons Down*, Brighton Road.

The South Downs Training Areas

"Wild West" Scenes In Crowded Lewes Streets

Stock and Animals from Balsdean Farm entraining for Yorkshire 18-5-1942   *Sussex Express*

Sussex had managed to find a home for a garrison of about 70,000 soldiers but more was to be needed. With so many raw recruits, both British and Canadian units needed training areas. It was natural for the army to turn to the South Downs which, apart from a few farms and livestock, were virtually uninhabited. Accordingly in 1941 requisitioning orders were served on owners and tenants. The Downs were divided into eight areas from east to west, Beachy Head to Seaford Head area No 1, Alfriston to Iford area No 2, Southease to Woodingdean area No 3. The Lewes Racecourse, Ditchling Beacon to Stanmer area No 4, Devils Dyke to the Old Dyke railway was area No 5, beyond which lay area No 8. Areas Nos 6 and 7 were in West Sussex. Cliffe Hill and Malling Down do not appear to be have been separately numbered. These areas were wired off with two strands of barbed wire on chestnut stakes. At all points of entry, both paths and tracks, red triangular signs were fixed bearing the legend "WD (War Department) No entry Military area". Lewes became accustomed to the deep rattle of Bren guns, the crack of mortars and the sharper bark of field artillery in action. A knife rack barbed wire barrier was placed across the entrance of the motor roads leading to the Race Hill and an armed sentry stationed whenever training and firing was taking place. All save the main roads through the Downs were closed.

In 1941 a tank training area had been established at Seaford Head with a concrete access road from the A259. Later the Canadian School of Artillery was based there. The Downs above Alfriston was the impact area for artillery shells fired from guns deployed either at Wilmington or on Cliffe Hill, which had been used for this purpose from October. On such occasions a sentry would be posted above Iford and red warning flags flown on Firle Beacon and in Firle Park. On every occasion when live ammunition was used a direct telephone line was set up from a point on the range to the nearest police station, from the Old Forge at Falmer or Woodingdean crossroads, in the case of area No 4 Ditchling-Stanmer, to Lewes. On more than one occasion either the army failed to set up the link or there was a technical breakdown in the communication equipment.

Kerbside memorial at Pelham Terrace to Clifford Kenyon 1st/4th South Lancs Regiment (p39) *T Whittington*

The army had to surmount several problems connected with Downland use. A number of high voltage power lines of the national grid traversed the training areas and these had to be avoided. Much of the land was used for water catchment which meant that not only had water installations to be protected but that temporary toilet arrangements for large numbers of men had to be organised with strict attention to the prevention of contamination of the ground water. Trespassers were frequently caught by the army within the training area, even when live ammunition was being used. They were detained with the minimum of force, handed over to the civil police and a court appearance inevitably followed, often, in addition to a fine for being in a prohibited area, a further fine was levied for failing to produce an identity card when apprehended. Poachers in search of rabbits to supplement wartime rations, mushroom pickers, blackberry gatherers and even a group of lady horse riders were examples of some of the transgressors. Some hikers in June 1943 staying in Ovingdean managed to reach Newmarket before being caught by

C Squadron of the 43rd Reconnaissance Regt, who were based at Astley House stables. Cattle were found grazing at Ashcombe during 3" mortar practice in July 1943. Children were an additional hazard in the training areas. Seven from Brighton wandered into the Newmarket Hill area in March 1944 and found a No 69 Bakelite Grenade and started to unscrew it. The resulting explosion injured five of the seven, one losing a hand and one requiring treatment at the Queen Victoria Hospital East Grinstead. The 4th Battalion Welsh Guards in training at the time gave first aid.

Standing orders regarding the use of the ranges forbade all firing on Saturdays and Sundays and at night with live ammunition. The list of permitted weapons included .303 calibre rifles, pistols, machine carbines, 7.92 BESA guns, 2, 3 and 4 inch mortars, Piat mortars, 25pdr field guns, 4.5 and 5.5 gun-howitzers, pack howitzers as well as 75 and 155 mm field guns all with high explosive charges. No firing was allowed from moving vehicles. A range officer with a minimum of twelve months' commissioned experience supervised live firing. He would be suitably equipped with maps and overlays for the weapons fired and could determine safe direction for firing and observe the fall of shot. All blinds (unexploded shells) were to be marked for disposal, any damage was to be reported to the WD Land Agent and Valuer at Preston Barracks, Brighton and any shells falling outside the range were the subject of enquiry by the Corps Commander, Royal Artillery. A 500 yard safety zone was allowed for on the range templates. An army radio van was stationed near the police telephone link and would relay information to and from the range officer's radio van. Depending on the scale of the exercises, either a medical orderly or medical officer with an ambulance would be in attendance.

Stanmer Village had been totally evacuated in May 1942 and given over to the army. The houses in the village were used for battle training with an order issued for roofs, doors and windows to be left undamaged. This went largely unheeded and some of the houses were ruined by "Mouseholing" a battle technique in which soldiers progress from house to house by blowing holes in walls and ceilings usually with grenades. The church and graveyard was placed out of bounds. Lewes witnessed an unusual scene at this time when one of Mr Dalgety's Farms at Balsdean was evacuated. All the farm implements, goods, chattels and livestock were brought by the army through the High Street via School Hill to the cattle dock in the goods yard for loading on a train for Yorkshire.

Friendly Fire

"Friendly Fire" is a modern term but it describes accurately the overshoots which occurred from the training ranges and from other less well identified sources. In October, Colonel Roland Gwynne of Folkington Manor, remonstrated with an artillery unit firing from Wilmington Common, the firing continued despite the protest. Lieutenant Colonel Powell Edwards of *Oditune Place,* Plumpton had more to complain about when seven large calibre artillery shells fell close to his home in March 1944. In January 1943 several shells landed near Plumpton Church close to the footpath from Wales Farm to the Agricultural College. More landed on the tennis court of Colonel Churchill Hales' house *The Laines*. The following February the Agricultural College experienced some more near misses and 95mm shells also fell in Old Rectory Fields Westmeston. For some residents of Plumpton things might have been worse as on 17th May 1944 a stray shell hit the *Half Moon* Public House. Some damage occurred but normal service at the bar continued.

On 14th May 1944 at 1600 hours a shell was heard coming from a southerly direction and it landed on the south side of the "Chalky Road" (Prince Edward Road Causeway) allotments. It exploded injuring a man, a part-time fireman who worked for Chandlers, who was with his two children, working his allotment. The children were uninjured and Dr L Langford, Deputy County Medical Officer of Health, who was close by, rendered first aid and the man was taken to the Victoria Hospital where he recovered. The police contacted the Canadian School of Artillery at Seaford and the radio control vans at Woodingdean, establishing that the missile was a 25 pounder shell. In view of its destructive force all four had a narrow escape.

Again in 1943 the 43rd Divisional Artillery, firing towards the Alfriston range, from the Lewes Golf Course injured a man working on the roof of a bungalow, at Bishopstone with shrapnel penetrating a car parked nearby. On 8th August 1943 an explosion occurred outside 35 Eridge Green Landport, leaving a two foot diameter two inch deep crater, the explosion breaking windows at number 8. Senior air raid warden Dusart reported a similar incident at the rear of 8 Prince Edward's Road and War Reserve Constable Ridley reported a woman with a leg injury. At around the same time, 2200 hours, Air raid warden Fuller found a crater on the tennis court in the Paddock and windows broken in No 20 Paddock Road with shrapnel embedded in the opposite wall. An enquiry by 5th Canadian Light Anti-Aircraft Regiment took place and an order was issued that no more Bofors shells were to be fired across the town. On 14th April 1944 Mr Harold Snaith received head injuries, from which he recovered, when a 2-inch smoke mortar penetrated the roof of the cowshed in which he was working at Ranscombe Farm, South Malling.

On 20th January 1945 a 3-inch calibre artillery shell was found at the side of Malling Street 50 yards north of the *Prince of Wales.* In July twenty British aircraft cannon shells penetrated the windows of 28 Malling Street. Some ordnance came and departed in a less spectacular way. In February 1944 a 25 pounder smoke shell was found in a field at Southover farmed by Mr Robinson of Ifield. The shell was collected by the 96th Field Regt RA. The fate of a Schmorley-Piat bomb found in a ditch near the Waterworks is unknown. In January 1944 a 13 year old boy hit an army missile, which he had found on the Downs near Ditchling, with a chopper. As a result he was injured on the face, arms, legs and lost the sight of one eye. Two children playing near the pillbox at the Spital-Nevill Road junction in May 1945 found some phosphorous bombs. The boy and girl were both injured in an explosion and required hospital treatment. A case before the Lewes Juvenile Court concerned five schoolboys who had gained access to a military store, the padlock of which was broken, rolled paper tubes had been filled with cordite and these homemade fireworks were let off in a train taking the children home from Lewes. Fortunately there were no serious injuries, some girls however complained that their hair was singed. The police recovered Verey lights, and smoke grenades from a shed at the home of one of the boys. A probation order was subsequently made by the court.

Range directives regarding small arms firing required that the aiming points should be low in the valleys and targets if used must be set below the crests of hills. The village of Kingston was subjected to a fusillade of bullets from the 1st Leicester's firing from Kingston Farm. The following month Sir Amherst Selby-Bigge had the windows of Kingston Manor broken from the same cause. Twice in July 1944 Housedean Farm was damaged by machine gun fire from Loose Bottom. The Argyll and Sutherland Highlanders of Canada were in training at the time. Court Farm, Falmer was hit by fire from Newmarket Hill, the line of fire was supposed to be Rottingdean to Lewes. In May 1944 the Toronto Scottish were engaged in 4-inch mortar practice when a projectile hit Ashcombe Farm. The 4th Devon's and the 5th Manchester's firing Sten guns near Ditchling scored hits with 0.38 calibre bullets on the home of Mrs S Ralli at *Old Middleton,* Westmeston. Intentional detonations of blinds caused further damage to buildings at Drew's Farm, Wales Farm and Fallbrook at Plumpton. Sir Stephen Demetriades experienced some near misses with shells in October 1943 at *Middleton,* Westmeston.

To the south-east of Lewes, in February 1944, machine gun and mortar fire from Itford Hill was misdirected and fell on Swanborough and Iford Farms. The 8th battalion of the Middlesex regiment that was stationed at *Mill House* Rodmell were responsible. At the end of March shells fired from Balsdean fell astride the Lewes-Brighton road cutting the railway telephone lines near Falmer. In April 1944 Brigdens Farm, Ranscombe Lane and Comps Farm, Beddingham received a number of shells falling short fired from Caburn to the Alfriston range. The next month a "Blind" 25 pounder shell landed on *Little Dene* injuring cattle and damaging a cottage. Even the police going about their lawful duties were not always safe. An officer detailed to make an inspection of a Flying Bomb crater near the Brighton road heard gunfire. No certificate detailing usage of the range that day had been received by the police, nor had the telephone link from the Old Forge at Falmer to Lewes Police station been established. It was discovered that the 8th Canadian Light Anti-Aircraft Regiment had decided to carry out a practice shoot without informing anyone.

A potentially disastrous accident happened at Newhaven at 5.00 am on 22nd November 1944 when a British barge loaded with 180 tons of high explosive broke away from its tug in heavy seas. It drifted on to the shore under the cliffs to the west of the town where it struck a land mine and exploded. Almost every house in Newhaven suffered the effects of blast but there was only one death, a sailor killed by a falling wall. Lewes rescue and repair squads were called into help at Newhaven with repairs although Lewes also received some damage to shop windows. The shock and noise of the explosion were heard more than twelve miles away. Lewes Town Council received £82 from the Newhaven Urban District Council for services rendered in connection with this incident and a further £1,200 from the War Damage Commission.

Military Traffic and Exercises

Military traffic through the town was a regular feature of wartime life, both in convoy and single vehicles. Often they would halt and tracked carriers if stopped on a hill would be angled into the kerb. When starting from this position a shower of sparks and granite chips would fly up from the kerbstones. For many years Station Street kerbstones bore these marks. Walls often were demolished, *Brookside* in Southover was the subject of a compensation claim for £6 from the Corporation for repairing a wall, so too were claims for a number of lamp standards, the one by St Anne's Church that fell victim to a tank was valued at £6.50. A run back incident with a tank in East Street is said to have demolished part of Bridgman's the monumental masons at the bottom of East Street but post-war photographs do not show evidence of repairs. A troop of Canadian Churchill Tanks caught a kerbside bicycle at St Anne's Terrace, Western Road, the first flipped it in the air the next delivered a final crushing blow. This caused much amusement to the tank crews. It might be said in their defence that a tank under way took a distance to stop. The result was yet another claim for the Assistant Adjutant General's department in London. Another instance of a tracked vehicle going out of control on a metalled road happened when a Bren Gun Carrier crossing Cliffe bridge managed to lose its grip and ended in the Bazaar at 4 Cliffe High Street.

The police received many requests from military units passing through the town in convoy for the traffic lights to be turned off at the Library Corner and at Fisher Street. Whenever possible this was done, but often a military motorcycle dispatch rider with the convoy would take up point duty at road junctions. Military control of traffic was not without hazard. On 27th October 1943 a convoy proceeding past Library Corner to Brighton against the traffic lights hit a pram containing two evacuee children. Although the pram was knocked over and the children thrown on to to the road they and the nursery nurses from Glyndebourne escaped serious injury. Later charges of driving without due care and attention were brought. Other road accidents that ended fatally are described in the Misadventure chapter.

Sussex Express

US Army lorry halts to allow NFS contingent to pass Station Street 1943

Large scale exercises were carried out by British and Canadian troops sometimes involving the local Home Guard units as well. These exercises were originally designed to counter a possible German invasion but later they were in preparation for the "Second Front" or D-day landings. An exercise took place on 3rd August 1942 near the site of the Battle of Lewes when the 3rd Canadian Infantry Brigade comprising the Royal 22e (Deuxieme) Regiment, the Carleton and York and the West Nova Scotia Regiments with the 14th Armoured Regiment (The Calgary Tanks) undertook field exercises under live artillery fire. Exercise "Spartan" took place over a period of four days in March 1943 with ten divisions of Canadian and British troops participating. It was designed to test the breakout capabilities of the Canadians after a landing in France and took place over a wide area from Sussex to Berkshire.

D-day June 1944

Concrete hards had been constructed at Bishopstone Tide Mills and on the west side of Newhaven Harbour at the site of the present Marina for embarkation of troops and tanks for the Dieppe Raid. These now came into use again for D-day. Lewes was astride two roads that fed men and vehicles into the port before and after 6th June 1944. Holding Camps had been established in Stanmer Park area 1j, Bineham Wood on the Lewes to Newick Road area 1x, Sutton Hall Barcombe area 1o, Firle Park area 1k and Middleton Westmeston area 1g. The orders establishing these camps were made under the Regulated areas order (No 2) 1944 and signed by the Lieutenant General Schreiber GOC South Eastern Command. These became the sealed camps before D-day. Hyde Manor at Kingston was designated as an alternative marshalling area for vehicles. Newhaven and Shoreham had been grouped together by the Admiralty orders issued in December 1943 because of tidal conditions. They would accommodate one squadron of Landing craft tanks (LCT) between the two ports with attendant Landing craft infantry (LCI) berthing only at Newhaven. The port could deal with four medium coasters, three LCTs and one LCI at a time with 19 vessel movements in twenty-four hours with a capacity of 1,800 soldiers per lift. The movement tables for D-day plus three, show that in the morning 17 LCI (large) lifted the 4th Lincoln's, 1st/4th King's Own Yorkshire Light Infantry and the Hallamshires in all 1,600 men for Gold Beach. These soldiers had come from Pakefield, Lowestoft and Hopton. In the afternoon the 204th Pioneer Company and 185 Coy Military Police embarked for Gold Beach, these had come from Walton on the Naze, Essex and Lingfield, Surrey. The 86th General Hospital from Luton also left for Sword Beach and the 81st General Hospital from Leighton Buzzard for Gold Beach. The 50th Pioneers who had been based at St Leonards also were on board. A footnote showed that the 4th Lincoln's took with them 333 folding airborne bicycles!

D-day plus five saw 1,800 infantrymen of the 1st Tyneside Scottish and the 10th and 11th battalions of the Durham Light Infantry embark for Gold Beach, they had come from Thetford. The totals for the day to Gold and Juno Beaches were 4,500 men. Also in the lift were stores, maintenance, petrol supply and pioneer units. All the units moved on these two days had been held in a secure area j Stanmer Park or area x Bineham Wood near Chailey where on average the stay would be four days. The Hallamshire battalion of the York and Lancaster Regiment record in their history the greetings they received from the inhabitants of Lewes as they passed through the town on their way to Newhaven. They had come by rail to Newick from East Anglia. Troop carrying lorries were usually routed through the town via Beddingham to Newhaven, other transport taking the road through Rodmell. Both roads had at intervals fire points of fire extinguishers and buckets of sand. Firle Lime works on the east side of the Beddingham road was used as an ammunition dump for the naval vessels at Newhaven and in a loop of the river near Piddinghoe trots of landing craft had been moored under camouflaged netting for some weeks before D-day.

Anti-aircraft protection was provided by United States gunners at Iford and Piddinghoe. The traffic was two way with movement orders specifying that about 2,000 men of the 6th Airborne Division would be brought back on D-day plus 3 and 700 glider pilots from the D-day airborne landings would return on D-day plus 7 via Newhaven on their way to Larkhill Camp Fargo. Commandos were to be dispatched to Petworth, escaped British prisoners of war were to be sent onwards to the Great Central Hotel, Marylebone, London. "Evadees" the name given to downed airmen who avoided capture, and certain civilian categories returned to Newhaven would have special security arrangements made for them. Personnel landed by air sea rescue services would go to Cowley Barracks Oxford, uninjured RAF personnel were sent to Bognor. The landing craft often brought back wounded soldiers, some of whom were sent to the Royal Sussex County Hospital at Brighton. A dressing station had been set up on the West Quay at Newhaven and the secure areas including the one at Cooksbridge now became available for reception of men transferred back from Normandy.

Late May 1944 remains in the memory of many Lewes residents who had witnessed a great build up of troops, equipment, vehicles and tanks parked wherever cover was available especially under trees and as suddenly as they had arrived so just as quickly they had disappeared. All was clear by mid-morning on 6th June when the news of the D-day landings was released. Lewes had helped in many other ways. The ground floor garage in Southover House, home of the County Surveyor's Department, had been taken over as a vehicle waterproofing centre some weeks before. The Stanley Turner recreation ground and pavilion had been used as a laager for convoys for overnight stops and as a bath centre for the troops.

Blackout shutters at Woolmore's shop also protect against blast damage	*RCHME Crown Copyright*

An important contribution to the war effort and the training of troops for D-day was undertaken by Mr C Bell, the Bath's Superintendent, who taught many servicemen including members of No 4 Commando to swim.

The military presence in the town now declined and although the training areas on the Downs would be in active use until the end of the war few residents expected that the war still had another fourteen months to run of bitter and costly fighting before Germany and eventually Japan surrendered.

****

14. Misadventure

A significant loss of life to both civilians and service personnel occurred in and around Lewes due to war activities other than enemy action. War memorials to service men and women throughout the land and in Canada record names of those lost through accident and illness and those due to enemy action. The Lewes war memorial is no exception. His Majesty's Coroner for East Sussex was Doctor E F Hoare, Barrister at Law, of *Hill Bungalow,* Kingston Ridge. It was his task to inquire into all deaths of unnatural causes where normal medical certification was inappropriate. Such enquiries might lead to an inquest often with a jury present but on occasion without. Inquest reports would appear in the local papers. On at least one occasion an inquest into the deaths of five soldiers was held but no report appeared in the press. Today this would be labelled a "Coverup" but in 1943 publicity would have been regarded as prejudicial to the public interest. Reports in the early days of the war gave the victim's unit name but not its location, later reports would be more guarded stating a "Soldier or an Overseas Soldier" and his name. Inquests were usually held in the Forester's Hall, the *Royal Oak Hotel* in Station Street, or in the Crown Court if available. The Sussex Police maintained records of incidents involving servicemen or the public who suffered injury or death due to war activity. Details of units given provide a clue to the stationing of troops within the area.

The Misfortunes of War

1939

September 8th Five days after the outbreak of war and his arrival from London an evacuee schoolboy was killed when he fell over the cliffs at Seaford.

September 15th William Knight, of Mill Path Ringmer, aged 42 was knocked from his cycle and killed. His cycle had a front light and a reflector but no rear light that had become compulsory with the blackout regulations.

1940

May 16th Dispatch Rider Gunner Albert Henry Walter Coombs, of Greatham Hants, 276th Battery 69th Anti-Tank Regiment Royal Artillery part of the 45th Division, hit a Greengrocer's van on the Lewes-Chailey Road and died following an operation in The Victoria Hospital.

June 13th A man depressed by the possibility of a German invasion killed himself with a shotgun.

July 5th Private Joseph William Carter aged 27, of Farringdon Berkshire, in 4th/5th battalion of the Duke of Cornwall's Light Infantry part of the 45th Division, died after an accidental discharge of a rifle. Another soldier going off duty unloaded his weapon and placed the bullets in his pocket. For an unexplained reason the rifle went off and the bullet entered the cookhouse where the victim was working. After the incident it was discovered that there was a bullet missing from the ammunition clip in the off duty man's pocket. It was presumed to have been left in the breech of the rifle and to have caused the fatal wound. Doctor Irvine certified that the man was dead on arrival at The Victoria Hospital.

August 6th Ian Francis Desmond Mather, a member of the New Zealand Forces died after being run down on the Lewes-East Grinstead Road.

October 4th A guardroom disturbance occurred when a Provost Corporal George Brown was shot dead when he tried to arrest a drunken soldier armed with a rifle.

October 7th Trooper Andrew Morgan was killed after a rifle had been cocked by another Trooper and laid against a chair in the billet. A third member of the unit, the 2nd Lothian and Border Yeomanry, Royal Armoured Corps attached to the 47th (London) Division, accidentally kicked the loaded weapon that discharged itself killing instantly Trooper Morgan of Edinburgh. The Coroner observed that this was the fifth accidental shooting death he had inquired into. There were unfortunately to be more.

October 12th A ration and supply party of four members of the RASC sent from Hurst Green to Brighton combined business with pleasure. On the return journey they became lost and were redirected when they reached East Grinstead. Early the next morning a farm labourer on his way to work, found Driver Richard Walter Ennis, lying in the road at Stoneham between Lewes and Uckfield, with serious injuries. Witnesses said that the victim, who was pronounced dead on arrival at the Victoria Hospital, was one of the men who had been asleep in the back of the lorry at the start of the return journey. It was presumed that he became unwell and fell out over the tailboard.

November 2nd Private Andrew Nisbet McGrow, of Glasgow, an Argyle and Sutherland Highlander, a passenger in an army lorry travelling eastward in Cliffe High Street in the early hours of a Saturday morning, was killed when the lorry struck the anti-tank obstructions on the western side of the bridge. An illuminated bollard in the centre of the road and white painting of the obstruction failed to prevent the accident. The roadway narrowed to nine feet at the point of impact. Another member of the battalion was seriously injured in the accident. The report in the interests of security omitted the word anti-tank confining itself to "An Obstruction." The unit to which he belonged had in September provided the armed guards for the Junkers 88 that had crashed at Court House Farm Barcombe.

November 6th Thomas Edward Ford, aged 51 a cowman, of Earwig Cottages died in The Victoria Hospital. He was cycling on the Lewes-Uckfield Road when he was overtaken by an RASC lorry, the driver of which gave the cyclist five feet clearance but had seen him wobbling after being overtaken. Police evidence showed that the cyclist's pedal had hit the verge causing him to fall off and hit his head.

November 22nd Mrs Anne Clements, aged 73, was returning by bus after a visit to the cinema, alighted from the bus in the blackout at St. Anne's Crescent and crossing the road behind it stepped into the path of a car coming in the opposite direction. She died of injuries in the Victoria Hospital.

1941

January 24th Henry Hope, aged 53, an employee of the Town Council had left his home in St Nicholas' Lane after dark at 8.15 pm on the previous Monday evening, his route took him past the rear entrance to Rugg's Station Street Garage that led to a basement. This basement had been converted into an air raid shelter with the entrance protected by a wall of sandbags fourteen inches thick and six feet high which had the misfortune to collapse as he passed by burying him under one and a half tons of sand. A soldier sitting in a truck parked on nearby waste ground heard a rustling sound as the sandbags collapsed at 9.00 pm and ran to get help from ARP members and the Police. A doctor called to the scene pronounced life to be extinct. Sandbags used in great numbers in the early days of the war for protection against blast and bomb splinters, were made of jute that rotted under damp conditions leaving sandbag walls in a dangerous condition, many such walls were replaced with bagged concrete.

The Cliffe Corner Tank Accident

March 21st The 44th Royal Tank Regiment part of the 1st Army Tank Brigade was stationed in Stanmer Park. Five of the 26 ton Matilda tanks, two troops less one tank, had been ordered to go on a training exercise at the Seaford Head Tank Training area. These were the days before tank transporting low loaders were commonplace, so the tanks went on their own tracks from Stanmer through Lewes, negotiating the obstacles on Cliffe Bridge, with six inches to spare on either side, before turning right into South Street at 3.00 pm.

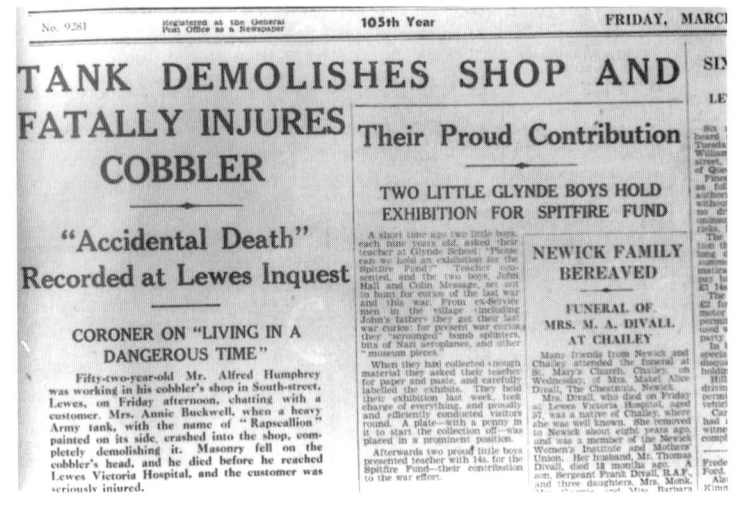

Sussex Express Headline Friday 21st March 1941

Tank turning is achieved by braking the inside track of the turning circle and driving forward slowly with external track of the turning circle. On rough ground this presents no problem but shiny metalled road surfaces offer little adhesion for tank tracks and a skid is always possible. With the weight involved momentum once gained is difficult to stop. Four of the five tanks made the turn satisfactorily but the last, named Rapscallion, driven by Trooper James Webber, slid round on locked tracks hitting and damaging a baker's van parked just in South Street. The baker sitting in his van was shaken but unhurt. The tank continued in its circular path, its tracks gouging out the granite kerbstones, the marks are still visible today. The tank by now almost faced the direction from which it had come. The rear of the tank slid sideways into Rushbridge's Yard that contained a small row of cottages and a wooden shed attached to No 4 South Street owned by the Corporation and rented out to 52 year old Edward Humphrey, a shoemender from Brighton, who lodged on Chapel Hill. The frail construction of the shed was reduced to matchwood and rubble in moments. A customer, Mrs Annie Buckwell, sustained serious leg injuries and was removed to the Victoria hospital. Mr Humphrey was also taken to the hospital but was pronounced dead on arrival by Doctor Eileen Nugent. A serious escape of gas occurred but prompt action by the Lewes Gas Company averted the risk of an explosion.

At the inquest Mr Elgar Geering, owner of the Antiques Shop, gave evidence and War Reserve Constable Gates gave measurements and said that the officer in charge of the tanks refused to identify the unit or the type of tank involved. A Treasury Solicitor was also present. Soon after the accident on 23rd April the unit left for North Africa, the tank commander, Sergeant Walter Grainger from Stafford, was later killed in action in Egypt in January 1942 and buried at Halfaya Sollum. Trooper Webber, from Taunton, the driver was injured and died in captivity in Italy in July 1942 and was buried at Casserta near Naples. The third member of the tank crew was wireless operator gunner Trooper Herbert Whiteman.

44th Royal Tank Regiment Matildas from Stanmer at Seaford Head 1941 *IWM H8032 Crown Copyright*

Immediately after the accident the tank was parked facing up Malling Street. Over the years fable has overtaken fact. The small car park site next to St. Thomas' church in the Cliffe has been wrongly identified as the site of the tank crash. Shaw's Corner Stores and adjoining Watford's Butchers shop were both demolished as part of a pre-war road improvement scheme in September 1938. In May 1941 the Council received £58 compensation from the War Office for the destruction of the shed. Mr Humphrey was an Air Raid Warden at Post No 2 at Cliffe Corner.

May 9th Privates Charles Clifford Morris, aged 24, of Winsford Cheshire, and Edward Appleton aged, 27 of Warrington Lancs, both members of 2nd/4th Battalion South Lancs Regiment part of the 55th (West Lancashire) Infantry Division, were killed when their 15 hundredweight army truck overturned when negotiating a narrow gateway and rolled over on a steep slope. The East Sussex News, a broadsheet local newspaper, which amalgamated with the Sussex Express and County Herald in July 1941, carried a full report of the inquest including the names of two local farm workers who saw the accident and helped at the scene. Mr Cyril Furmidge, who now lives in Malling Street, was able to locate the accident spot as the track leading from Southerham Farm to the rifle butts at Oxteddle Bottom.

May 30th An evacuee aged three from London died by drowning in a swimming pool at Glynde.

June 2nd Sub-Conductor Stanley Smith, Royal Army Ordnance Corps attached to HQ 55th Division, aged 36, of Horwood Bucks, was killed at 10.45 pm at the Glynde turnoff on the A27 on Whit Monday when riding a motorcycle towards Lewes. He had just overtaken an army lorry when he hit, head on, an army car travelling in the direction of Eastbourne.

June 27th Barcombe Railway Station Goods Yard was the scene of considerable military railway traffic with the reception of wagon loads of brick rubble from blitzed buildings in London. This was unloaded by soldiers and used by Royal Engineers in making up the new road to the military bridge to replace the three weak brick bridges over the river meanderings at this point. At 5.00 pm the previous Saturday a rake of 12 trucks of rubble had been left in the sidings. On the Monday following a goods train arrived to collect the empty trucks. A series of shunting operations followed involving detaching the engine of the collecting train, drawing forward the trucks still to be emptied to get at the empties at the rear of the siding. To the railway staff this was a familiar procedure. The RE officer in charge blew a whistle for the soldiers to stand clear as the engine set back, it buffered up and as with loose coupled wagons the impact was transmitted into movement throughout the rake of wagons. Private Thomas Francis Knowles, aged 24, of the 2nd/4th South Lancs Regiment of Ashton on Sale, Cheshire was caught between the last wagon and the siding buffers receiving injuries from which he died after admission to the Victoria Hospital.

September 1st Gunner George Lawrence, aged 25, of 346th Field Battery of the 87th Field Regiment Royal Artillery from Bristol was dead on arrival at the Victoria Hospital having suffered gunshot wounds to the head while in the Guard Tent at Glynde Place. He is buried in Lewes Cemetery.

December 26th A Private soldier of the Seaforth Highlanders of Canada, the 1st Canadian Infantry Division from Calgary Alberta, aged 44, shot himself in a fit of depression on Boxing Day.

1942

January 6th Nine Canadian Soldiers of the West Nova Scotia Regiment of the 1st Canadian Infantry Division that had spent sometime in and around the Lewes area travelled to Shoreham to practise opposed river crossings in assault boats. The river Adur is tidal, fast flowing and wide at Shoreham. The men were in full kit with weapons and as they approached the distant bank "Thunderflash" rockets were thrown at them as part of the exercise, this caused movement in the boat, which overturned throwing all the occupants into the water, three managed to reach the bank but six were swept away and drowned despite Major F B Courtney's efforts, who jumped into the water, to save them. Lance Corporal William MacClean, and Privates H R McDonald, E G Melanson, Joss Ellis Gaudet, aged 20, of Belleview Cove Digby County, a farm labourer from Nova Scotia, H T Forasworth, and S A Jaccques were the victims.

February 20th Miss Betty James, of Lewes, engaged in operating a chaff cutting machine as part of her Land Army duties on a farm at Blackboys, became entrapped in the machinery and despite emergency treatment at the scene by a Doctor died later in hospital. Her name is on the Lewes War Memorial.

February 24th James Lowson a Canadian Tank crew member lost his life when a tank on hill climbing exercises overturned.

March 1st The South Saskatchewans were under canvas in Firle Park at this time, Private H A Blanchard, failed to make the correct response to a sentry's challege and was immediately shot dead. No public report of this accident was made.

March 3rd Miss Margaret Walker, aged 22, of Sheffield Park one of three young ladies cycling abreast was hit by an overtaking army lorry and killed.

March 7th Trooper Nelson Bird, from Carlisle, an army Dispatch Rider, skidded on a patch of mud on the Brighton road at Ashcombe. Witnesses said that he had just overtaken an army car travelling from Lewes and hit an army lorry that was coming from Brighton.

March 19th Trooper Herbert William Martin, from Thornton Heath, lost his life when another tank on hill climbing exercises crested the summit and then ran back before overturning.

March 20th A carbon copy of the 4th October 1940 Provost Corporal's death occurred. A case at the Sussex Assizes heard how a Military Policeman, Peter Michael Boyle, was shot dead with a revolver when attempting to arrest a drunken Canadian who had resented being challenged at the unit's guardroom. The accused received two years' sentence in prison.

April 3rd Private Paul Carpentier, 2nd Division Ammunition Company Royal Canadian Army Service Corps, aged 22, from Dalahousie Ontario, was riding a motorcycle on traffic control duties with a Canadian army convoy of vehicles travelling east in the High Street towards Cliffe Bridge when he was thrown off his machine by an army lorry and received fatal injuries.

May 22nd "Russian Roulette" ended fatally when Canadian Soldier Russell Harry Brightwell, aged 23, of the the Regina Rifle Regiment part of the 3rd Canadian Infantry Division, of Moose Jaw Saskatchewan, was killed when "Larking About" with a comrade the previous Saturday. The deceased was sitting on a bed, a revolver that had been fired once and was assumed to be empty lay on the floor. The challenge was to see who could draw the fastest and fire. Brightwell was shot through the heart and died immediately. An officer told the inquest that both men were dispatch riders and had been issued with revolvers. They were under orders to always keep the revolvers loaded.

May 22nd William Arthur Piper, aged 79, was walking in South Street Chailey at 6.10 pm when without warning he turned and crossed the road into the path of an oncoming motorcycle ridden by Matthew Torbitt Kennedy of the Canadian Army. Mr Piper according to witnesses seemed to hesitate as he crossed the road, he was rendered unconscious and died later in the Victoria Hospital from a fractured skull.

July 17th Three Canadian soldiers who had been to Lewes in search of entertainment in the public houses of the town. They managed to miss unit transport back to camp and set out to walk back to Firle Park. The trio were seen later by a Canadian Provost Sergeant at Cliffe Corner heading back into town. Two of the three made it back to camp. The next morning the body of Rifleman Alphonse Louis Eugene Ducharme, of the Royal Winnipeg Rifles part of the 3rd Canadian Infantry Division, aged 32, was recovered from the Ouse near Eastwood's Cement Works. At the inquest evidence was heard to the effect that on the way home there had been an altercation. The survivors were unable to give any clear account of exactly what had happened. The deceased had drowned but the abrasions that were found on the head may have occurred after he had fallen in the water. Verdict accidental death.

July 18th Trooper William Greenaway, aged 36, from Dagenham Essex, a member of the 23rd Hussars, was killed in an army tank when it turned over and rolled fourteen feet down a steep bank. Few details were given in the interests of security. It is now known that the unit was part of the 11th Armoured Division based at Plumpton Racecourse.

August 17th Two burials in the Lewes Cemetery in war graves tell but just part of a tragedy, Corporal Thomas Barradell, aged 23 and Private John Walker, aged 21, both from Derbyshire and serving in the 2nd/5th Battalion of The Sherwood Foresters (Notts and Derby) Regiment, of the 46th Infantry Division, were buried on the same day. They lost their lives in a training accident on the Downs that also claimed the lives of two other members of the battalion, Sergeant Ernest Harris, of Nottingham and Corporal Louis George Busselton, of Derby. During live ammunition practice with a trench mortar, a round fell short among the men and exploded with tragic results.

August 21st An accident occurred on a "Road near Lewes" when a Bren Gun Carrier travelling at 20 mph suffered a broken offside track. An NCO at the inquest said that he saw the carrier veer from the near side of the road to the off side where it hit a bank and overturned throwing the crew of three out. Private William Alec Parker, of the 2nd/4th Battalion of the Hampshire Regiment, 46th Infantry Division, the driver of the carrier, received injuries that proved fatal. Medical evidence was given by Doctor Eileen Nugent. An officer of the unit vouched for the satisfactory state of the vehicle and concluded that the breakage of the track was due to a manufacturing fault. Official records show that the road was the lower Racecourse Road.

October 2nd Viscount Wolmer, aged 30, Farm owner and Captain of B Company 2nd/4th Battalion Hampshire Regiment of the 46th Infantry Division, heir to The Earl of Selborne of Bradshot Hall, Blackmoor, Hants and Private John McKinley, of the same unit, of Ash Surrey, lost their lives during field exercises. They were advancing under an artillery barrage firing live ammunition when a shell fell short.

October 9th Lance Bombardier Reginald Douglas Smith, 224th Battery, 94th (Dorset and Hampshire Yeomanry) Field Regiment Royal Artillery, aged 26, of Dorchester was one of seven soldiers standing in an army lorry that overturned while travelling off the road and was pinned underneath the vehicle, receiving fatal injuries.

October 10th A Ringmer woman, aged 76, was knocked down while she was walking in New Road Ringmer. A Canadian army dispatch rider Gunner Hammond was travelling from Glyndebourne and was witnessed to wobble shortly before the accident. The lady who was seen walking with her daughter in the centre of the road received injuries from which she died in the Victoria Hospital. The rider was convicted of driving without due care. His speed being estimated at over 50 mph. He was fined £5 plus costs.

November 9th Lance Corporal James Bradburn, of Pendleton Lancs, a member of the 59th Reconnaissance Regiment was killed when a 15 cwt truck in which he was travelling on a downland track, skidded on a bend, hit a fence post and overturned throwing him out and pinning him under the vehicle.

November 9th Bombardier Harold Rothman Holden, of Atherton, was one of thirteen men in a 3-ton lorry passing a parked van in a narrow street in Alfriston. The canvas cover of the lorry supported on a steel framework caught the overhang of one of the houses. The collision severely damaged the steel frame, causing the deceased severe head and internal injuries, from which he died later in Hurstwood Park Hospital.

November 26th A bizarre accident with a trench mortar claimed the lives of two Canadian soldiers, Theodule Pinet and Donat Carmier. After they fired the mortar the projectile hit a wire fence and rebounded back on them exploding just 30 yards from the firing position.

1943

Jan 11th Molly Lipscombe, aged 9, received fatal injuries after cycling into the back of a van at Station Road Plumpton that had stopped suddenly. At the inquest it was revealed that the van driver had been following an army dispatch rider motorcyclist and had seen something fall from him into the road. The van driver stopped to retrieve the object and the accident happened. The object dropped was the dispatch rider's service revolver.

April 24th Reginald William Newman, from Winnipeg, Manitoba and Robert Ross Brogden, a farmer from Cartwright Manitoba, of the Princess Patricia's Canadian Light Infantry a unit of the 1st Canadian Infantry Division were fatally injured, dying later in the Princess Alice Hospital Eastbourne, by a round falling short during exercises with live ammunition practice using trench mortars. Doctor Hoare conducted the inquest. Although based in Lewes his jurisdiction extended from Hove to Rye.

May 6th Harry Bernard Grant, of the North Nova Scotia Highlanders part of the 3rd Canadian Infantry Division, from Stewiacke County, Colchester, Nova Scotia, died during a friendly wrestling match, after a heavy meal, from inhalation of vomit.

May 6th Leslie Mason, also from the North Nova Scotia Highlanders of Canada, accidentally killed himself with a bullet fired from a Tommy gun (Thompson submachine gun)

May 14th Miss Edith Gander, aged 17, employed on a dairy round for the Lewes Co-operative Society was knocked down and killed by an army lorry, part of a military convoy, while she was delivering milk in South Street. Earlier on 20th January she had a narrow escape by diving under the counter in the Co-operative confectionery shop in West Street, where she was then working, when the bombs demolished a house opposite and blew in the shop windows. The family had suffered tragedy three years earlier when Edith's younger sister had been fatally burned. Edith put out the flames with her bare hands but her sister died later in hospital.

June 6th George McGeary, of the Pioneer Corps, died after an altercation with a Canadian soldier in a Public House at Seaford. As medical evidence at the inquest revealed a contributory medical cause for the man's death, the Canadian was not required to face charges.

July 16th Private Melvin Sorensen, aged 21, of the 45th General Transport Company Royal Canadian Army Service Corps, a motorcycle Dispatch rider from Paddock Wood, Saskatchewan, was marshalling a westbound army convoy on the Offham Road at 8.30 pm. It had reached a point about 100 yards east of Offham when he pulled out from behind the last vehicle in the convoy and met a car travelling in the opposite direction driven by Colonel Powell Edwards. The motorcyclist braked and skidded on an oil patch on the road sustaining injuries that proved fatal, dying the next day in Hurstwood Park Hospital.

August 17th A Bren Gun Carrier accident on Chailey Common claimed the life of Trooper James Douglas Edgcombe, aged 19, of the 55th Independent Squadron Reconnaissance Corps attached to the 55th (West Lancashire) Division of Ruislip Middlesex, who died in Hurstwood Park Hospital. The carrier overturned on a slope that had been safely traversed on many previous occasions.

August 20th George Tappenden, a Rolling Stock Superintendent for Brighton Corporation Trolley Buses, who had married the previous day, was walking with friends from Cooksbridge, where he was staying, to Offham. On the way he was struck from behind by an army lorry and was dead on admission to the Victoria Hospital.

August 20th Captain Ian Grant Gibson, 4th Battalion of The Welch Regiment, part of the 53rd Infantry Division, stationed at Faversham was killed in an incident on the Downs at Ashcombe near Lewes on 12th August. A Hawkins anti-tank grenade, an oval tin 4x3x2 inches bound with wire and containing one and half pounds of high explosive, had been thrown in a training exercise and had exploded. As the officer approached the site of the explosion with three other men a second explosion occurred killing him instantly and injuring the other men. After this accident the army issued an order regarding blind (unexploded) Hawkins grenades. The order stated that due to uncertainties with the fuse an unexploded grenade must be left for fifteen minutes instead of five before it was approached for examination. Captain Gibson is buried in Lewes Cemetery and is commemorated on the Lewes war memorial.

September 3rd Trooper Harry George Walker, of the 29th Armoured Reconnaissance Regiment (South Alberta Regiment) 4th Canadian Armoured Division, aged 31, of Salt Prairie Manitoba, was engaged in practice firing of a trench mortar when a freak accident occurred. The first rounds had been fired satisfactorily when the order was given to shorten the range, this entailed using a screw adjustment to bring the mortar barrel nearer to vertical The next round fired hit a tree branch overhanging the firing position that detonated the projectile. Shrapnel from the exploding shell rained down on the firing position with one steel splinter penetrating the man's steel helmet killing him instantly.

September 9th Gunner Charles N-------- with a friend, both Canadians, who had been over indulging until closing time on the previous Saturday were found on a road in East Sussex with multiple injuries having both been run over. No vehicle military or civilian could be found that might have been involved. The friend survived but despite multiple blood transfusions Gunner "N" died 36 hours later.

September 29th An inquest held without a jury and to which the press were not admitted, the only report survives in Police Files deposited with the East Sussex Record Office. Members of the 1st/5th Battalion of the Welch Regiment were undergoing battle training on the Downs to the west of Lewes in Training area No 4. They were part of the 160th Infantry Brigade of the 53rd Infantry Division stationed near Rye. Twenty-five pounder field guns had been deployed on The Gallops above Spital Road. The battle conditions being practised required troops to advance behind a creeping artillery barrage using live ammunition. The accident happened 1 mile from Streat Hill Farm near Horseshoe Plantation. A 25 pounder shell falling short exploded killing four men outright from No 8 platoon and injuring five more. The men were Private Frederick Anster, Private Walter Evans, Private Henry John Wright, aged 23, Private Reginald Richard Stanger, aged, 26, all members of A company. Private Cyril William Brown McCullam, died on 4th October in the Victoria Hospital. It is estimated that the safe survival distance for men to be from an exploding 25 pounder shell was 250 yards.

1944

January 7th Sergeant Reginald Donald Adgey, one of two motorcyclists riding towards Ringmer, was seen by Mrs Carlson, a widow of 86 years, who saw the accident from the window of her home at 4 Malling Down. It transpired that his footrest hit the kerb and in turn the rider hit a lamp post he was taken to the Victoria Hospital and later transferred to Hurstwood Park Hospital where he died.

March 2nd Lance Corporal Thomas Earl South, 69th General Transport Company Royal Canadian Army Service Corps, one of two army motorcyclists travelling towards Firle skidded on the road by the *Fox Inn* at Southerham. He was taken to the Victoria Hospital and then transferred to Hurstwood Park Hospital where he died.

March 10th Edward Hurst, of Leicester, an NFS driver was killed when his van overturned on the Uckfield to Lewes Road. The van clipped the verge after being overtaken by an army lorry and then turned over four times. This man's death is one of the three recorded in The Commonwealth War Graves List of Civilians killed in Lewes as a result of War Operations. One of the others was nine year old Stanley Johnson killed in the air raid of 20th January 1943. The other was Joseph Crawley, aged 77, of 14 Eastgate Street, who also had an address in Abbey Street Bermondsey. From the death certificate it seems that he was injured in a raid on London, evacuated to Lewes where he succumbed, enemy action being listed 1b, a contributory rather than the principle cause of death on 26th February 1941.

March 17th Private James Edward Cleaver, Royal Canadian Armoured Corps aged 27, of Oak River Manitoba, was directing traffic past a disabled tank when another tank approached and signalled to pass. As it did so it skidded crushing Private Cleaver and injuring three other soldiers. An Army Medical Officer who attended the scene pronounced the man to be dead.

April 18th Fusilier John Williams, 6th Battalion The Royal Welch Fusiliers, 53rd Infantry Division, aged 39, of Blaenau Festiniog, the driver of an army Jeep at Firle conveying mock casualties as part of an exercise, died when his vehicle skidded and hit the nearside verge and then overturned. It was reported at the inquest that despite the Jeep having cross country tyres it had also been fitted with wheel chains. While being practical for muddy off road conditions chains were totally unsuitable for use on a smooth metalled road.

May 5th Stanley Hills, aged 13, died in the Victoria Hospital after receiving head injuries falling from the military Bailey Bridge between Soap Factory Lane Malling Street and Bridgman's Wharf. He was playing on the bridge at the time contrary to notices displayed that the bridge was for military traffic only. The tide was out and it was believed that he hit his head on an underwater obstruction.

May 12th Mrs Emma Waghorne, aged 78, a retired prison officer evacuated from London, was injured by a Bren Gun Carrier that mounted the kerb in the bottleneck by the Masonic Hall. The carrier had been attempting to pass a three-ton army lorry travelling in the other direction to Brighton. Mrs Waghorne's leg was fractured and she died later in the Victoria Hospital.

May 27th Sergeant Alvin John Braden, aged 26, of the 18th Armoured Car Regiment (12th Manitoba Dragoons) 2nd Canadian Corps, from Salt Prairie, Portage La Ferry, Manitoba died after being hit over the head in a public house in Seaford. Forty witnesses were interviewed but there was no satisfactory outcome of the investigations and a verdict of misadventure was returned.

June 16th Two soldiers were killed at Ringmer in a road accident. Gunner Walter John Abbott, aged 24, 8th Light Anti-Aircraft Regiment Royal Canadian Artillery from Rice Lea Saskatchewan and Sergeant Eric Sidney George Watts, aged 26, Royal Army Service Corps of Isleworth Middlesex. The previous Sunday, 11th June, an offside to offside collision occurred between a three-ton army lorry and a 15-hundredweight army truck. Both vehicles turned over one on its side the other upside down.

June 25th Miss Kate Collins was killed at Broyleside Ringmer when she was hit by a French army motorcyclist who sustained a broken arm in the accident.

July 28th Five Commonwealth soldiers were killed while unloading ammunition from a lorry before placing it in a pit on the Downs near Ditchling for destruction. A controlled explosion was planned with an electrical detonator. It was assumed that all the percussion detonators had been removed from the condemned ordnance but this was not so and the fatal explosion was the result. Staff Sergeant William Able Finkle, HQ 4th Armoured Brigade Company Royal Canadian Electrical and Mechanical Engineers, Sergeant Andrew Bernard McCann, aged 29, Royal Canadian Army Service Corps (RCASC) of Eganville Ontario, Lance Corporal Victor Childs, Private Ernest Purdy, aged 24, of the 4th Armoured Brigade RCASC, Private Luhy Carbrie O'Cleary, aged 44, of the 10th Infantry Brigade Company RCASC, all lost their lives.

August 4th John Trigwell, of Ringmer, aged 12, died while playing in Bridgwick Chalkpit at the side of the Lewes-Ringmer Road. It would appear that he had found the nosecap of a 25 pounder artillery shell and on throwing it against a piece of concrete an explosion occurred. He received fatal injuries from the resulting splinters. A brother who was with him was unhurt and ran home to give the alarm. The previous day the boy had been warned about playing with "Thunderflashes".

Of the 86 deaths attributed to war activity other than due to enemy action within a six-mile radius of the town 67 were service personnel and 19 were civilians. These totals do not include the 29 United States servicemen killed in the Dakota Crash at Newmarket. Fatalities listed include, 8 due to firearms, 23 to ordnance, 36 due to vehicles, 8 under off road conditions and 7 with tanks or tracked carriers being involved. In all the reports referred to above the first date is the report date and where known the date of death is given separately. Ten of the accidents involved army motorcyclists resulting in the deaths of four other road users and six motorcyclists. Canadian soldiers who died in England because of an accident, illness or war wounds are buried at Brookwood Military Cemetery, Surrey. Some Canadians irreverently referred to Brookwood as a motorcycle dispatch rider's holding camp, such was the number of road accidents involving men on these duties.

Doctor Hoare and his wife narrowly escaped becoming one of his own statistics when during the blackout at 7.00 pm on the night of 31st October 1941, his car left the road and ended up overturned in a field on the road between Chailey and Lewes. The couple escaped with a severe shaking and the car was eventually recovered and repaired by Martin's Garage.

****

15. The War Effort

Lewes was an administrative centre and market town and had little industry to support a total war but nonetheless it gave of its very best. The town provided support to a farming community with its agricultural implement makers and ironmongers. Service industries such as building, motor engineering and sawmilling served town and country. The Southern Railway company was one of the larger employers in the town with over 200 employees. This emphasised the importance of the town as a railway junction with six routes radiating from the station. Eastwood's Cement works in South Street was a large employer and its products were of war significance. Every's Phoenix Ironworks with its cast iron foundry, brassfoundry and steel fabrication facilities was of prime importance employing well over 300 workers and as the war progressed many of them would be women.

War workers at Culverwell's 1942 *Rex Carter*

Culverwell's produced, among other items, trailers for the County War Agricultural executive, while Every's produced hand grenade cases in cast iron for Mills bombs. Later in the war Bailey bridge panels and landing craft parts would also be turned out in quantity. Despite scrap metal drives the huge pile of scrap iron that had been a feature of the work's yard before the war, grew ever smaller. Martin's Garage carried out lathework, turning fusecaps for shells. They also undertook fettling of tank brake shoes produced at Every's. At the end of the war a display was placed in the Gas Company's window during July 1945 organised by the National Savings Committee showing examples of war work by firms of the town. Among the exhibits were chemicals from Courtin and Warner of Bell Lane, Admiralty canvas coal bags, hammocks, fenders for boats, and kitbags made in the Prison, a variety of wood products from Turners of 35 High Street, including wheel boxes, ladders, and barrel staves. Every's exhibited cast iron sea mine sinkers. Eastwood's supplied cement for the D-day Mulberry harbours. Everett's manufactured hypodermic syringes and needles at their factory now called "The Old Needlemaker's" in West Street but many will remember its earlier existence as Broad's Candle factory. Wickerwork baskets for projectiles, rubble clearance, suction hose strainers, panniers, hampers and baskets for parachuted air drops also featured, some of which would have been made by Mr Thomas Ide, a blind basket maker of St Martin's Lane, who had come to the town with a group of blind evacuees from Croydon.

National Service

National Service required the registration of all men and women of certain age groups. Initially The Military Service Act had enabled men of 20 years to be called up. This was later extended as the war progressed so that by December 1941 men aged 18 and a half to 51 were liable for service. Unmarried women from 20 to 30 years could be called up for service in the women's forces or directed into full-time Civil Defence duties. In areas where the Home Guard was under strength men between the ages of 18 and 55 could be directed to do up to 48 hours' duty and training per month. Public announcements in the newspapers would give the arrangements for registration for National Service of young men reaching the required age, which by 1944 was 17 years and eight months, with call up following by their eighteenth birthday. In the early days of the war a recruiting office opened in a shop on School Hill.

Lewes registrants would attend at the Labour Exchange located in the old Central Boys' School in Southover Road, where their details would be recorded and the individual's preference for service noted. The Navy and RAF were the most difficult to enter. Some weeks later they would be called for medical examination that would be conducted at the Oddfellows Hall, Queen's Road, Brighton. In due course, if fit, enlistment papers and a travel warrant would follow giving the new recruit a week or so to report. The 1941 Census of population was abandoned because of the war but the 1931 count showed that Lewes had a population of about 12,000. Taking the age groups liable for service this population produced a maximum total of about 2,800 men and 800 women. Both totals of availability would be reduced by those in essential occupations, by medical unfitness and by a handful of those with conscientious objections. The Sussex Express carried a regular feature each week of photographs of local men and women who had joined up and it was estimated that 1,500 men and women from the town served with the fighting forces.

Comforts for the troops became a local cottage industry with women's groups knitting, collecting books, toiletries and cigarettes. The Mayoress, Mrs H J Turquand, Ald Crisp's daughter, started a comforts' fund for the services and by May 1940 had raised £56. Later in 1942 it was reported that she had organised a working party that had met

A weekly Sussex Express feature

each week in the Council Chamber since the start of the war. Two hundred and sixty names were given in by January 1940 of men in the services who wished to receive parcels of cigarettes from the Mayoress's fund. By mid 1942 it had supplied 3,300 items to the forces including 562 to the crew of HMS *Lewes*, 80 babies' layettes for the wives of servicemen and evacuees and answered an SOS from the Royal Sussex County Hospital Brighton for bandages.

From April 1941 it would be possible to obtain airgraph forms from the post office to send letters to service men in the Middle and Far East. The forms were 11 x 8 inches, writing was allowed on one side only as they were microphotographed for transit and enlarged to half size at the receiving end, it was a two-way service that was rapid and inexpensive.

Taking the national figures made available at the end of the war by the Ministry of Information a town the size of Lewes would have a population distribution as follows :-

Men and women called up for military service	1,200
Those engaged in industry and Civil Defence	1,785
Those engaged in public services, utilities and distribution	3,060
Housewives, students and invalids	2,550
Those too young or above age for service	3,315

Using the same figures applied to service personnel who became fatal casualties (4.5%) a population of 12,000 would sustain 57 killed or missing and 40 prisoners of war (3.4%). As the War Memorial contains 126 names, over twice the national average, either a higher proportion of those enlisted were in the Navy and Air Force where casualties were higher or the population sample is too small which leads to inaccurate numerical conclusions. A comparison with Brighton, population 147,000, and a similar method of commemorating its war dead to that of Lewes shows its recorded total of 864 to be nearer the expected national average of 660 casualties.

The Lewes Territorials

The Lewes company of the **5th Cinque Ports** battalion of the Royal Sussex Regiment mustered at the Mountfield Road Drill Hall on Friday 1st September 1939. Together with the 2nd and 4th battalions of the Regiment and the 4th battalion of the Buffs, East Kent Regiment they formed the 133rd Infantry Brigade, a first line Territorial unit. With other brigades they comprised the infantry for the 44th (Home Counties) Division from September 1939 until December 1942. In October of that year they were converted to lorried infantry.

The division went to France on the 8th April 1940 and took part in the defence of Amiens in the battles of St Omer-La Basse. They were then evacuated from France on 30th May 1940. After a period of re-fitting and training the units embarked on 31st May 1943 for the Middle East Theatre taking the long route round the Cape of Good Hope arriving in Egypt at the end of July 1943. Their arrival provided much needed reinforcement for the newly appointed General Montgomery and enabled the defensive position at El Alamein to be stabilised, blocking General Rommel's dash for the Nile.

They took part in the battle of Alam-el-Halfa from 30th August to 8th September. The 5th Royal Sussex was attached to the 8th and later the 10th Armoured divisions at this time. The Battle of El Alamein from 23rd October to 4th November 1942 was their last major engagement. After that the division ceased to exist and its component units were sent to other formations. The Royal Sussex became part of Paiforce whose duty was to protect Palestine, and guard Iraq and Iran with their oil fields and the overland supply route to Russia.

The 210th Field Company Royal Engineers raised in 1920 with men from Lewes, Newhaven and Seaford was based at at the old Naval Prison. It was part of the divisional engineer component of the 44th division. On mustering in September 1939 it was found that the company was, in common with the companies from the other Sussex towns, too large to fit the army organisation and was divided, a duplicate unit, the 264th Field Company, being formed.

The 210th moved to Dorset on embodiment and sailed from Southampton to France on 3rd April 1940. When the German forces invaded Belgium the unit undertook bridge demolition on the River Escaut but by the 21st May the company had reached Knocke and commenced digging trench lines. Two days later the unit withdrew to Dunkirk. Those who reached the port were evacuated by the 31st May, many were at this time captured by the enemy.

The unit regrouped at Oxford and became part of the 12th Corps Engineers. There followed a period of defence construction in the north-east. The next year 1941 was spent in training and defence work construction in East Kent. Gourock was the departure port the following year on 29th May when the troops sailed for North Africa landing at Suez on 21st July. Work on the Nile delta defences followed and subsequently the unit played its part in the battles of Alam-el-Halfa and El Alamein, undertaking significant mine laying and mine clearance duties.

The next theatre of operation was Sicily from 5th August to November 1943. A return to England then took place in December 1943 for the D-day invasion and they landed in Normandy on D-day plus 2. Bridge building and mine clearance took the men from Normandy to Belgium, Holland and Germany by the end of the war. The 210th Field company ceased to exist in 1946.

One of the first tasks of the duplicate **264th Field Company** was for three weeks to provide a guard for vulnerable points at Newhaven. Training at Gravesend and Chatham followed. As the Field company which served the 12th (Eastern) division they took part in the campaign in France from 22nd April to 7th June 1940. During this period the men built roads, camps and drainage systems. On 18th May the unit entrained for Amiens. Ahead another train with men of the 2nd/7th Royal Sussex was bombed. By the 23rd they were on a train bound for Le Mans. On 4th June they left for Caen and Cherbourg landing at Southampton from the steamer *Duke of Argyle*.

After refitting the unit moved to Mayfield carrying out defensive works during 1940. The following year they were located in the west country helping to clear bomb damage in Plymouth. In November 1942 the unit set sail for Algiers. Bridge building, road making and mine clearance were the duties undertaken. The unit continued its service in Italy, the Yugoslav island of Vis, and then after a further spell in Italy journeyed to the Western Europe Theatre for duty in Belgium Holland and Germany. In December 1945 the unit was disbanded.

The 159th Heavy Battery Royal Artillery Regiment were also based in the old Naval Prison. They had been formed in 1920 from the Kent and Sussex Heavy Brigade. It was called up at the time of the Munich Crisis spending ten days on station at Dover. Mobilisation for the Second World War took place on the 24th August 1939. The orders were received in the late afternoon but by midnight the same night they were on action stations at Dover. The unit identity changed during the war but it took an active part in many of the actions in protecting coastal convoys and firing against the German guns at Cap Gris Nez. The unit provided a large number of men for Field Regiments during the war. One section was sent to Newhaven to assist the Navy in the operation of the examination service, the surveillance of neutral vessels possibly carrying forbidden items to German ports. Following Dunkirk the battery received a visit from HM King George VI, with a party of Commonwealth Prime Ministers and Lord Ironside, Chief of the Imperial General Staff.

Prisoners of War

Statistically about 45 servicemen from Lewes probably became Prisoners of War. Those in Italian hands or German camps fared reasonably well once they began receiving regular Red Cross food parcels. Captives of the Japanese suffered a great deal and one family, after a long wait, heard that their relative was "safe" in Japanese hands. Eventually they were to mourn his loss through starvation and disease. The Japanese only began to allow communication and deliveries of food parcels once the tide of events had turned against them. Even after the war had ended the Japanese could not produce lists of all the prisoners that they had captured.

LEWES PRISONER OF WAR

This photograph from a German prisoner of war camp has been received by Mrs. Sandles, of 3, Brook-street, Lewes, from her son, Pte. Alfred Sandles, who is on the extreme right of the front row. There may be other local men in the group.

An exchange of British and German prisoners considered unfit for further fighting took place in September 1944 when Corporal F Morris, captured at St Valery in 1940 who had been in Oflag 7c in Bavaria, and Driver Hall, of Lancaster Street, who had been captured at Knightsbridge near

Tobruk in 1941 came home in October 1944, the first of the three exchanges that took place during the war. German prisoners in this country were returned on the *SS Gripsholm* a Swedish vessel that had brought the British men from Gothenburg. In February 1945 Driver Jennings of The Royal Engineers was released and came home. He had been captured at Dunkirk. In April Private H W Wickham returned home. He had been captured in Tunisia in 1942 and escaped from his camp when the guards ran away after hearing the guns of the American Army advancing into Germany. All the captives had reason to be grateful for the Red Cross food parcels that were sent out at the rate of one per man per week. Next-of-kin parcels could be sent once a quarter, these were strictly controlled and had to be re-packed by the Red Cross to ensure British and German prohibited articles had been excluded. The censor had to be passed and a credit made to the next-of-kin of clothing coupons. An allowance of forty coupons per parcel was made.

Red Cross funds were augmented by Ald Crisp organising a football match at the Dripping Pan on the 9th November 1941 between his own XI and a side from Brighton and Hove Albion that included some Arsenal players. One young observer remembers the Bren guns on anti-aircraft tripods at the four corners of the ground but would prefer to forget the score. The Mayor's side lost five-nil.

A Prisoner's Tale

Flight Sergeant F E Hall, a wireless operator air gunner in 207 squadron of the Royal Air Force, was shot down on his twenty-fifth birthday 7th September 1942. He was part of the crew of a Manchester bomber flying from Waddington in Lincolnshire on a raid to Berlin. The maximum bomb load would amount to 4,000 pounds. On that night their 4,000 pound load contained the largest bomb produced at that time a 2,000 pounder known as a "Cookie".

Over Holland the plane was attacked by German nightfighters and an engine set on fire. The bomb load was ditched on a searchlight which had been troublesome. The crippled plane made for home losing height all the time eventually crashing in the North sea near the Frisian Islands. The crew took to their inflatable dinghy and paddled ashore where they were captured and removed to Amsterdam gaol.

At the family home *Beverley* in Houndean Rise, the news arrived that their son was missing on operations. The Sussex Express of 12th September 1941 carried the news of his loss, mentioning his wife formerly Miss Joan Lusted. The wedding had taken place at St Anne's Church just six months previously in April. The reception was held at Holloway's restaurant. It was celebrated with a wartime cardboard cake cover instead of icing. The best man, also from 207 squadron, was to lose his life on the first 1,000 bomber raid on Cologne on 30th May 1942.

After interrogation in Frankfurt, Sergeant Hall progressed through a succession of six German prison camps, Silesia near the Czech border, Poland, East Prussia and finally Fallingbostel 150 miles south-west of Hanover. He made his escape from a forced march column of 1,000 prisoners which had been kept on the move during the closing stages of the war. They had been kept midway between the Russian and Anglo-American lines to be used as bargaining counters during armistice negotiations.

The escape was made before the column crossed the Elbe. A guard complete with dog was bribed to ignore the escape bid and Sergeant Hall and a fellow prisoner walked westward through both German and Allied lines to freedom. An American Dakota aircraft brought them back to England. He had lost five stone in weight so a month's stay in hospital before being sent on leave with double ration cards was ordered for the escapee. He was back in Lewes in time for the Mayor's reception at the Grange on Wednesday 16th May 1945.

Sergeant Hall had a special briefing before flying duties. He had been given a code and a contact to write to with intelligence, in the unlikely event of being shot down. Normal prisoners' letters were used with innocuous phrases, Mr Eric Parrish of Wightman and Parrish was the recipient and each time he received a letter it was sent on without delay to the Air Ministry for decoding.

It was a surprise to Mr F E Hall to learn in 1994 that his name was on the Lewes War Memorial as missing believed killed.

Bevin Boys

The dependence of Lewes on coal is best shown by the needs of the town's gasworks in Morris Road. It used 240 tons of Yorkshire coking coal per week. This meant a transfer of 24 railway wagon loads by road from the goods yard in the Cliffe. Before the war it had a stockpile for 12-14 weeks' consumption. After the end of the war in 1946 it had enough for one week. The waterworks in 1942 had a stock of 272 tons and by the same date in 1946 it had 20 tons left, enough for six weeks' pumping. By July 1943 national coal supplies were threatened by a shortage of workers and increased demands, so men aged from 18 to 25 were directed into the mines. These men earned themselves the title of "Bevin Boys" after the then Minister of Labour Mr Ernest Bevin. The direction was achieved by balloting each monthly intake for the forces and by offering those registering the choice of the mines or the armed services.

Local headlines were made in June 1944 when four young men were reported as leaving for the coal mines with preliminary training at Annersley followed by posting to Chesterfield. Robert Martin-Cramp a Compositor, Army Cadet and member of St John's Church Choir of Sun Street, Kenneth Bridgman, articled Chartered Accountant with Frank and Co, of Garden Street, Stanley Parsons of 1 Abinger Place also an Army Cadet, who hoped to go into the army and who worked for Mr Moller of Brinkhurst's Stores, Fisher Street and Albert Pollard full-time National Fire Service man. All the four men were disappointed at not being chosen for the fighting services but accepted the ballot result with resignation. Gerald Harmer also of Sun Street, a friend of Robert Martin-Cramp, working in an aircraft factory "Somewhere in the south-east", became an "Optant" and chose to become a Bevin Boy to do his National Service.

Women at War

This short section underlines the fact that the women of Lewes wholeheartedly engaged in all the activities of a town at war and their contribution is recorded in full throughout the text. They bore the brunt of coping with rationing, shortages, looking after evacuees, caring for families and in addition undertaking work outside the home. Many had their menfolk away in the forces causing anxieties for their safe return that sometimes unhappily was not to be.

Local headlines brought to public attention an unsatisfactory state of affairs regarding the direction of married women into essential work done on a local basis. It became known in October 1943 that some married women had been sent to work in the homes of the well-to-do in the Wallands area to carry out domestic duties. Protests were made and the Labour Exchange said that there was so little war work in the town that to comply with the direction of labour order they had "advised" the women to take the unfilled domestic vacancies. It was later agreed with the area office at Brighton that the women were under no compulsion to accept such direction and there the matter rested. Women were needed to replace men who had been called up and to meet the need for an enlarged workforce. One in twelve jobs previously done by men was undertaken by women. In May 1941 a team of women repainted Lewes Railway Station. Conductresses became a familiar sight on Southdown buses, postwomen and delivery women became part of the street scene.

Women at work Lewes Station 30-5-41 Sussex Express

The Women's Institute (W I) was forced to abandon their accustomed meeting place in St Anne's Parish Room as it had been taken over for a first aid post and met in wartime in the Forester's Hall Station Street. Comforts of knitted garments were one of the many activities which they excelled in. The record book shows a recipe for an eggless cake in January 1940. Topical talks featured the work of the women's ambulance service and the distribution of bean, tomato and onion seeds sent from the USA under the auspices of Mrs Roosevelt, the President's wife. The minutes noted that the Chairlady, Miss Lee, was called away on 16th September 1942 due to an air raid warning. She was fulfilling her Civil Defence obligations. In 1943 the WI adopted the crew of a high speed air sea rescue launch based at Newhaven. Later that year the minutes lament the difficulty of providing cakes for the meetings due to the effects of rationing. In January 1944 they were pleased to record a letter of thanks from a rescue launch crew at Newhaven for the comforts sent while three months later they were invited by the Chailey RDC to a lecture on a new type of German incendiary bomb. By July 1944 there was a call for photographs of members' relatives in the forces to be used in connection with the National Savings "Salute The Soldier Week".

Agriculture

Lewes became closely associated with The Women's Land Army (WLA) founded in September 1939 with Lady Denman of Balcombe Place, Sussex as the Honorary Director, a post which she had held in the First War. Recruits came forward but acceptance by farmers was slow, suspicious of their capabilities. Farm workers often had reserved status protecting them from being called up. With their male workers protected, many farmers saw little need for the women, but later in the war their attitude was to change and they glad to have the help of the WLA. Four weeks' basic training on a farm with board and ten shillings pay was the girls' introduction to farm life. Later Plumpton Agricultural College, founded in 1926, ran courses for the WLA training over 4,500 during the war.

Lewes became the nearest entertainment centre and in October 1942 a Hostel for the WLA was set up at 26 Lansdown Place. It was open seven days a week from 2.30 until 9.00 pm. The girls started with a modest social life at the Hostel with a party for girls only. Later they felt

Women's Land Army in training at Plumpton *Sussex Daily News*

confident enough to hold public dances, a very successful one at All Saints' Parish Rooms in January 1943 followed by another the next year in February 1944 at The Forester's Hall in Station Street. A strong darts team managed to force the local Home Guard to a draw at Lansdown Place but succumbed to the team from the *Station Inn* Barcombe. Opinions varied about the uniform of brown cord breeches, brown shoes, green pullover, khaki shirt and felt hat. The girls probably being not too enthusiastic but the soldiers who thronged the town found the girls had a very acceptable American Western appearance.

Much of the work was physically demanding, some farmers were more considerate employers than others. Often Land Girls had poor accommodation and were worked almost as slaves. Their placements were controlled by the County War Agricultural Executive that carried out government agricultural policies. The local offices were in the High Street, 59 (Westminster Bank) 110 (St Anne's Rectory) 203 and 208, Winterborne Lodge Brighton Road, and Rotten Row House. In addition there was a machinery and repair depot in Malling Street and a hostel at Rodmell.

Women's Land Army "Salute the Soldier Week" July 1944   *Mrs B Fletcher Sussex Express*

The WLA members were numbered like service personnel but received wages as decided by National Wages Councils of 37 shillings and sixpence per week out of which they paid for their keep in hostels or on farms where they worked. At the end of the war these arrangements worked against them when the government refused them a service gratuity because they had received the going rate for the job. It produced great bitterness and led to Lady Denman resigning in protest. In the end it was agreed that grants towards continuing agricultural education would be made and a donation was made to the WLA Benevolent Fund that stood at £175,000, all raised by the girls' own efforts. For a time in May 1944 an empty gown shop at 81 High Street was used by the WLA as a charity shop to support the Benevolent Fund used to help cases of hardship and the Educational Bursaries. It had a target of £3,500.

If proof was needed of the size of the contribution to food production, a parade was held in October 1945 when 1,000 Land Girls from East Sussex marched through the town to an inspection in the Dripping Pan. As a final insult, the girls on demobilisation were allowed to keep very little of their uniform. A greatcoat, a shirt and a pair of shoes, and as one put it was hardly sufficient in which to walk down the street in. No wonder they took on themselves the title the "Green Cinderellas". The need for the WLA continued after the war with a dance being held in May 1946 to help a recruiting drive.

The Lewes Outfall works in Ham Lane made its own contribution to war production by growing eleven tons of flax per annum. Food production and harvesting in particular made significant demands on the available labour. Advertisements advised farmers how to contact the army to get help with harvesting. In September 1942 selected prisoners at Lewes Gaol would be allowed out to help on the land. In the summer of 1943 The County Boys' School was proud of its hay making achievement of a ten-ton stack made entirely by hand including the carting. By September 1943 Italian Prisoners of War, now re-designated "Co-operators" as their country had asked for an Armistice in August 1943, were working on farms but this brought its problems as they were transported to the farms in coaches and to conserve petrol the coaches remained at the farms during the working day. Questions were asked why were the drivers were standing about all day doing nothing, the question remained unanswered. There was undoubtedly resentment by the populace at large about the conditions the Italians enjoyed. They were allowed out un-escorted on Sundays to go to Mass with a three-mile limit imposed but no fraternization was allowed. The Sussex County Magazine revealed that farmers were complaining that prisoners of war were receiving twice the civilian food ration.

Employment Protection

Men and women called to the services were guaranteed their jobs back when they were demobilised. This had its snags, called up as boys they returned as men to their old jobs and boys' rates of pay. Some employers, mainly public services, made up the conscripted employees' pay. The East Sussex County Council did this from the outset but Lewes Council where frugality had always been the watchword refused to do this at first, but relented by November 1940, when pay was made up to 80% less service pay. A long running battle over schoolteachers' pay erupted in June 1941 when four members of the Education committee resigned because the Council refused to implement the Burnham award. The frequent resignations of teachers from Mountfield Road School had nothing to do with the grade two scales paid whereas elsewhere the same post would be grade three, so the Council claimed. By January 1943 the Council decided, by the casting vote of the Mayor, that it would pay a war bonus to its teachers and clerical employees. The bill for which would be £2,500 a year. By the end of 1943 the Council agreed to a teachers' cost of living award without dissent, by May 1944 the House of Lords ruled that the Council must make up the pay of its staff on active service. The Council succeeded in having the last word when they decided not to pay the bonus to members of staff who left their employ.

These arrangements were not universally popular in the town as many employees of private businesses received only their service pay. Finally in April 1945 it was agreed that national pay scales should apply to Lewes Council employees. The obduracy of the Council would surface again in the British Restaurant controversy. Some workers at Every's Ironworks felt disadvantaged. It had never allowed union membership but with the death of Mr J Every in October 1941, at the age of 84, and with the need for a maximum war effort the management conceded to union membership among its employees. This however did not mean that union rates of pay would be forthcoming, consequently a lady welder was dismissed after a difference of opinion with the manager about being paid twenty pence per hour instead of the union rate of twenty-two pence. The Council could be equally resolute when dealing with trades unions. A retired employee who had been employed to supervise the New Recreation ground at the Pells at ten shillings per week was dismissed after a union applied, in March 1942, for the post to be a properly paid job. In future supervision would be limited to regular inspections for hazards that would be undertaken by a Council officer.

National Savings

Paying for the war required sacrifices of overseas investments and significant reductions in personal spending. The public were exhorted to invest in National Savings. Special campaigns were mounted throughout the war to boost savings. The first in 1940 was "The Spitfire Fund", which hoped to raise the cost of an eight-gun fighter plane that had helped to win the Battle of Britain. Prisoners in the gaol sent twelve shillings from their pocket money towards the fund. The cost of a Spitfire was set at £5,000. In the event the fund closed in September and despite two donations from the USA it managed to reach only £3,542. It was the only savings campaign in which the town failed to reach its target, but in total £100,000 had been raised since the outbreak of war.

In 1941 the savings drive was spearheaded by a "War Weapons Week" between the 17th and 24th May. An illustrated programme was produced and children were particularly involved by asking them to look out for 30,000 leaflets that were to be dropped by an RAF plane piloted by Flight Lieutenant Alan Griffiths, one of the sons of the Rural Dean Canon E Griffiths. Some leaflets would carry signatures of local residents and if the finder presented the leaflet to the signatory the finder would receive a Savings Certificate. One such leaflet was found by a County School girl who claimed the reward from Mr Walton proprietor of the *White Hart*. The leaflet carried a price list of weapons ranging from a pistol at £4 to a medium tank at £15,000. The week's target was to be £100,000, The Sussex Express would run a darts tournament, but the editorial column took exception to the snobbery attached to a dance in connection with the week's

---

Leaflet Raid

Leaflets have been signed by the following :—

Alderman Major T. SUTTON	Mr. F. H. COOTE
Mr. H. W. WALTON	Mr. PHILIP TURNER INMAN
Mrs. WALTON	Messrs. J. C. H. MARTIN & Co. LTD.
Mr. P. JOY	
Mr. W. F. C. MCWALTER	Messrs. J. C. H. MARTIN & Co. LTD.
Mr. R. O. DALLAWAY	
Mr. C. T. BUTLER	Messrs. J. C. H. MARTIN & Co. LTD.
Mr. LIONEL G. URIDGE	
Messrs. ALBION RUSSELL & Co.	Miss T. F. STEAD
Mr. M. R. HERIOT	Colonel B. WHITEMAN
Mr. M. G. MORRIS	Miss E. HARVEY SMITH
Rev. H. M. HARRIES	Miss N. HARVEY SMITH
Mr. P. HAINES	Mrs. DAVID GRIFFITHS
Mr. F. NEWINGTON	Rev. E. GRIFFITHS
Messrs. NEWINGTON & Co.	Mrs. GRIFFITHS
Messrs. F. & L. STONE	Mr. JOHN GRIFFITHS
Mr. E. C. MANN	Mr. C. COLBOURNE
Alderman A. TURNER	Mr. W. H. GODFREY
Mr. MAURICE INMAN	Mrs. A. H. WELLING
Mr. J. O. GERAGHTY	Alderman A. N. INNES

N.B.—Other signatures have come in since going to Press

National Savings Leaflet "Raid" May 1941   *Sx Arch Soc*

events that required dancers to be in evening dress or uniform. Despite all this the financial result was a huge success with the target being trebled at £317,659.

Officialdom could not turn a blind eye to an auction sale, arranged to support the week, which included two lots of controlled food. One lot of hothouse lemons that raised 24 shillings, the other a dozen eggs which sold at 12 shillings, both had been produced at home and were very scarce. The items could only be sold at the controlled prices and these had been exceeded at auction. A licence was required to sell foodstuffs and this would not have been forthcoming from the Food Control Committee. Later in the war despite having obtained a licence, a charity auction for The Red Cross nearly failed at Barcombe in May 1943 over eight bananas and some lemons brought back from Africa by an airman. The food office ruled that maximum prices would be exceeded so an auction would break the law. This time common sense prevailed by having donations instead. This somehow seemed to satisfy the food office.

HMS *Lewes* on East coast convoy duty   *IWM FL3260 Crown Copyright*

In 1942 it was the turn of the Navy when "Warship Weeks" were held. Lewes decided to try to raise the money to buy a Corvette, a small escort vessel for convoy protection, for which again the target would be £100,000. As added interest, if the campaign was successful the town could adopt the ship. The week was held from 28th February to 7th March and again the target was overshot reaching £210,000, that would be enough money to buy a Minesweeper. As there was a Town Class destroyer named HMS *Lewes* this was duly adopted. The savings weeks always featured a procession of Civil Defence, Fire Service, Home Guard, Land Army, Red Cross, St John, Land Army and Youth Organisations with either the Army Cadet or Air Training Corps bands. On this occasion a car was decorated as a model of HMS *Lewes* and driven in the procession.

HMS *Lewes* was an ex-American first World War One destroyer that had been moth-balled at Newport Virginia. In 1940 after losses of destroyers in the Norwegian Campaign and at Dunkirk and with the French fleet neutralised, Mr Churchill made a deal with the American President Mr Roosevelt, to lease 50 world war one destroyers in exchange for 99 year leases for the American Services to construct bases in the West Indies.

The ex-USS *Conway* became G 68 HMS *Lewes*. She was a four funnelled destroyer of 1,020 tons, length 315 feet, beam 30 feet, with 18,500 horsepower giving a speed of 30 knots. She mounted three three inch guns two forward and one aft and arrived at Devonport from America in November 1940 for refit. She was bombed while in dock and finally put to sea in February 1942 under the Rosyth Command. Ten months' convoy work followed then she was refitted as an aircraft target ship and left the Humber to join a trooping convoy to Capetown in 1943. In August 1944 HMS *Lewes* went on to Ceylon and in the following year she was sent to Sydney, New South Wales to act in her target role which she did until the end of the war. In 1946 she was scrapped, stripped of valuable metal and scuttled.

An exchange of plaques between the town and ship took place on Friday 2nd October 1942. The captain of HMS *Lewes* was prevented by duty from attending the ceremony in the Town Hall. Lieutenant Commander Harold Stephenson, flotilla commander, from Portsmouth came instead. The Ship's plaque was in gun metal on teak and bore the motto *Fides Tenex* (Proud and Tenacious Faith), now resides in the bar of the Lewes Arms.

The 1943 National Savings week was billed as "Wings for Victory Week" when efforts would be made to fund six bombers in the week commencing 22nd May. The sum needed would be £120,000. One of the highlights would be a "Wings for Victory Dance" at the Town Hall. To date the town had raised £1,473,000. By January the £2 million mark had been passed. The last of the "Weeks" took place in 1944 entitled "Salute the Soldier Week" with a target of £120,000 using the slogan "Sufficient to send a Division to Berlin", again the target was exceeded reaching £142,357. In February 1945 it was announced that between 1940 and 1944 the town had raised £2.5 million, by the end of the war this would have reached £2,563,000.

By January 1943 the need had been established for a National Savings Centre and this was opened by the Mayor Ald Crisp on the 11th January 1943 in the empty Singer Sewing Machine shop in the High Street opposite the Town Hall. Nine days later the "Hit and Run" air raid on the town shattered the windows but it continued to operate with the broken shop windows covered with corrugated iron and a "Business as Usual" sign. It functioned as a savings centre until closure on the 11th December 1946. As a mark of achievement, white plastic plaques two feet by one foot, bearing a different design for each year's savings week, would be presented to the town. These plaques would be hung in the Head Post Office and later in the Savings Centre.

Fuel Rationing

The Corn Exchange was taken over for use as offices for the Food Control Committee with the Town Clerk, Mr C W Stephenson as Controller. The Borough Treasurer Mr C T Butler acted as Fuel Overseer. The first items to be rationed were coal and petrol. The average monthly mileage by private motorists was cut from a pre-war 600 to 150 at the start of the war, to 125 in April 1941, in May 1942 down to 52 and finally in July of that year the petrol ration for private motoring was abolished for the rest of the war.

Coal deliveries were regulated at one hundredweight per week, in 1943 the maximum stock per home was 4 tons with not more than one ton per month to be delivered between June and October with part taken as coke. A year later the maximum stock allowed was down to one and a half tons. By March 1944 no coal would be delivered to a house that had more than two hundredweights, about two weeks' consumption, in stock. Railway overloading with war material for D-day was more of a problem than stocks of coal at the mines. The Lewes Gas Company's works in Foundry Lane were outdated and worn out before the war started but managed to keep supplies going. In July 1945 seventy-five feet of cladding of the purification plant fell into the river during a storm. The plant was unaffected but in the fuel shortage that followed victory, low gas pressure was frequently suffered in the distant parts of the town.

From January 1942 the first bus on a Sunday left Lewes for Eastbourne via Golden Cross at 1.10 pm and the last bus left the town at 9.00 pm every night. The long distance coach service from Seaford to London via Lewes established in 1931 was axed as an economy measure in 1942. The London train service that normally ran in two six-car sets of coaches lost the buffet car from one set and the Pullman car from the other in July 1942. Nearer to Lewes fuel restrictions in April 1942 curtailed retail deliveries to outlying districts only except coal, bread and milk that continued daily with no afternoon second deliveries of milk. In December Sunday milk deliveries ceased altogether and the practice of the eight dairymen delivering anywhere in the town at will was also stopped by the introduction of a zoning system. Each household was given a pink card informing them of their allocated milkman, this saved 20 gallons of petrol a week and the labour of two men.

Delivery restrictions meant the disappearance from the Lewes streets of one of the town's institutions, Mitchell's, Ironmongers and Oilmen of 22 Priory Street. They had toured the town twice weekly with an open sided van selling paraffin and housewares, but they were allowed to continue with country deliveries. Anomalies occurred, there were traders in greengrocery who relied on horse drawn rounds to supplement shop takings, the Lewes Co-operative Dairy used horse transport but they all fell victims to the economy cuts. Much to the annoyance of local traders an Ice Cream Van from Brighton traded in the town's streets in August 1942 and seemed to be exempt from petrol restrictions. It is likely that the newspaper report of the van's presence was sufficient to ensure that it came off the road.

Food, Sweets, Clothing and Furnishings Rationing

While rationing was regarded as a most vexatious matter, it did at least ensure that essential requirements were fairly available. The health of the nation had improved in the thirties and continued to improve despite the wartime diet and it was only increases in Tuberculosis and

Venereal Disease that gave cause for concern. A mass immunisation programme to protect school children from Diphtheria commenced in 1940. The welfare foods scheme for infants and children was operated through the Food Office who supplied Cod Liver Oil, Rose Hip Syrup and later concentrated orange juice. Infants under five had a green ration book which entitled them to extra milk, eggs and certain other foods. Expectant mothers had similar provisions.

The Food Executive Officer, Mr H Langridge, and his staff made the annual issue of ration books and issued licences to trade in foodstuffs to retailers and catering establishments. A less popular task was the prosecution of all those who knowingly or otherwise broke the regulations. Amendments to Identity Cards were also dealt with at the Food Office. Those residents lucky enough to go away from the town for a holiday would have to present their ration book at the Food Office where they could obtain an emergency docket for the week they were away against cancellation of the coupons in the holiday maker's book. These emergency ration dockets could be presented at any shop and would be honoured by the retailer. Servicemen home on leave would be given similar vouchers. In the early days of rationing a minor row erupted when a serviceman's ration card was refused at a local shop as the grocer was worried that he would not have sufficient supplies for his registered customers.

Householders would register with retailers of their choice and could change retailer at the commencement of each ration year. At other times the change could only be made by application to the Food Office. According to the commodity a retailer would either cancel the date space in the ration book or cut out the coupons for points foods or meat. These cut out portions had to be counted, enveloped and sealed. They were then placed in the shopkeeper's bank for safekeeping and returned to the Food Office for checking so that the retailer could order fresh supplies against a permit from the Food Office. Lewes had 13 Butchers shops, 46 Grocers including general stores, 9 Bakers, 21 Greengrocers, 10 Fishmongers, 8 Dairies, 20 Hotels, Tea Shops and Dining Rooms. These, whether selling rationed goods or not, were the subject of Food Office Control in respect of amounts they could sell, the type of goods sold and the prices charged. All would have required a licence.

Throughout the war, food prices were subsidised by the government. In 1940 a half price milk scheme started for pre-school children, without charge for low (twenty-seven shillings per week) income families. Rationing of meat by value at one shilling and ten pence later reduced to one shilling plus two pence in corned beef and four ounces of bacon per week started in March 1940. Sugar at twelve ounces per week and preserves at four ounces, in July of that year. Butter and margarine went on ration at the same time, six ounces of butter or margarine, the butter component usually two ounces per week, plus two ounces of lard or margarine and two ounces of tea per week. Eggs for adults were one per week if you were lucky. The original meat ration would provide about two pounds of stewing beef or three quarters of a pound of rump steak. A breast of lamb at four pence would be a popular choice. Soon after meat rationing started all the town's butchers closed on Monday, Wednesday and Friday afternoons to allow time for the butchers to deal with the ration coupons. Collectively they proposed to employ a bookkeeper to deal with the paperwork the rationing system had caused.

An announcement in June 1941 took the nation by surprise to the effect that clothes rationing would start immediately. A page of 66 spare coupons in the ration books would be used for this purpose. Trouser turnups and double breasted suits were banned. The coupons would provide about one complete outfit per year, shoes, underwear, suit and top coat, the materials being far less durable than today's man made fibres. Knitting wool was on ration but supplies were made available through Women's Organisations such as the WI and WVS to enable them to knit gloves, socks, pullovers and Balaclava helmets for the services. In July 1942 furnishing fabrics that had been exempt from coupons were put on ration as so many women were using them to make clothes. In 1942 the Utility scheme commenced which provided for clothing to be made to a standard specification of quality. All garments had a distinctive double cut cake symbol and "41". Later similar schemes would be introduced for furniture, household items and bedding, these goods being reserved for newly weds and those who had been bombed out.

Points rationing for tinned goods, cereals, dried fruit and eventually biscuits, commenced in November 1941. The following February soap went on the ration, three ounces of toilet soap, twelve ounces soap powder and four ounces of hard soap. Even a shaving stick required one soap coupon. In July 1942 personal points for sweets at two ounces per person a week were introduced, this had an immediate beneficial effect in that until now it had been almost impossible to get sweets, now at least one could get some. Product zoning was introduced to save transport which meant that confectionery from manufacturers distant from Lewes such as Rowntree's of York and Fry's of Bristol disappeared from the shelves for the duration of the war.

In 1943 the tea ration was withdrawn from the under fives but in January 1945 all those over 70 would receive an extra one ounce of tea per week, 1,787 Lewesians applied for it. The rationing system was flexible and values assigned to points goods varied according to supplies. Baked beans would require just a few points whereas a tin of red salmon would take nearly a month's points for one person. The weekly cheese ration varied from 1 to 8 ounces at different times. The milk ration for adults was set at two pints per week with more for infants and children who, with expectant and nursing mothers, received larger rations of eggs. Some workers, for example those in agriculture, were given larger cheese rations. Some foods were not rationed, offal, poultry, rabbits, sausages and made up meat pies became difficult to get and led to charges of favouritism from those who were unlucky in not obtaining them and charges that shopkeepers kept these items "Under the counter". Fish was free of ration but difficult to obtain, queues of customers would form at shops that had a supply of such foods which would be quickly sold out.

The queuing habit became a part of life. It was required by law when six or more people waited at a bus stop. A whisper was enough to start a queue forming at a shop which had off ration food in stock or items in short supply. Lewesians often joined a queue just because it was there and waited patiently to get into the shop in case it was something that they needed. Home-grown fruit and vegetables in season were never rationed but onions at times became scarce, un-rationed potatoes and bread became a staple part of the diet. Very little imported fresh fruit was available. Occasionally some oranges arrived which were reserved for children while bananas became but a memory.

Post-war bread rationing in 1946 was hard to take after having won the war. Memorable of those days will be the delights of American dried egg and Spam, both on points, and the unpleasantness of reconstituted National Dried Milk. Equally detested was the National loaf introduced in 1941 which had a grey look due to the 85% extraction of the flour compared with

73% for the pre-war white loaf. This hardship was compounded by the restriction on loaf types that bakers were allowed to make, from a pre-war possible 40 to just three, tin, sandwich and Hovis. Cottage, Cobourg, Farmhouse, French, Fruit, and Malt loaves disappeared for the duration of the war. Letters to the local papers in June 1943 illustrate some of the difficulties housewives faced. A correspondent asked what could be done when the one shell egg (as opposed to dried egg) you receive turns out to be bad? Another correspondent, a working mother, complained that by the time she left work and got to the shops well-to-do women, who did not work, were first in the queue. These women who had often waited over an hour had bought all the cakes so there was nothing left for working housewives.

The British Restaurant Battle

For many residents the most uncaring side of the Council manifested itself over the issue of a British Restaurant and its steadfast refusal to provide the facility both during and directly after the war. These restaurants were run on a non-profit making basis by councils and had their origins as emergency feeding centres for populations after heavy air raids during the winter of 1940-41. They were not needed for this purpose so they were adapted to providing a simple nourishing meal at a modest price and were much patronised by workers who did not have access to a canteen and by housewives. The opening shots in the controversy were fired when in October 1941 the Council affirmed that the Food Executive Committee would arrange to set up emergency feeding centres if they were required and that it did not favour British Restaurants. These restaurants would provide a sustaining two course meal and a cup of tea for eleven pence. Extra cups of tea were one penny and a slice of bread a halfpenny.

The following week it was observed that a Canteen for County Council employees functioned in the Forester's Hall and recently it had served hundreds of dinners at one shilling each. The Council was reminded that in the First War a successful Civic Restaurant had functioned in the Corn Exchange. Comparisons were made with Brighton, Haywards Heath and Eastbourne, where there were five such restaurants.

The Sussex Express headlines the burning issue of 1943

The Haywards Heath one was so well used that it made a weekly profit of £15 and would double its seating to 240. In February 1943 The Ministry of Food asked the Council to provide a restaurant and its reply was that there was no demand. In July workers petitioned the

Council, 150 workers from the Phoenix Iron works said they would use it Dr Eileen Nugent said it would meet a vital need among 300 women who came into the town to do war work.

The Ministry of Labour's local office said that there were 650 male heavy manual workers in the town. Many would spend nearly an hour trying to find somewhere to eat which had not sold out its menu within half an hour of opening. They had to make do with snacks being unable to afford two shillings for a restaurant meal. In September 1943 the Mayor and the local Food Office received a visit from the Regional Food Officer, Sir Eyre Garden, to discuss the question. Following the visit, Lord Woolton, Minister of Food, in response to a letter from Clr Penfold, expressed the hope that the matter would be settled soon. At the same time "John Bull" a popular national magazine commented on the Lewes Council's obstinacy, but the nationwide publicity had no effect. In November gas pressures became so low on the Nevill estate that it was impossible to cook Sunday dinners. The Gas Company apologised for the inadequate mains that could not be improved in wartime. The Sussex Express claimed that it supported the need for a British Restaurant.

In August 1943 the Sussex Express organised a ballot amongst its readers on the question of a British Restaurant, and 1,021 ballot papers were returned in favour. The Council still refused to budge. The Mayor reported that he had received unpleasant anonymous letters on the subject and stated the Council's reason for refusal was that the income being received for the use of the Corn Exchange, of £245 per annum from the Ministries of Power and Food would be lost. At this point Clr Dick Whittington resigned over the issue. Further suggestions were ignored, a proposal that a temporary building could be put on the slum clearance site on the north side of St John Street which after the war could be used as a war memorial building was turned down. An alternative request from Woolworth's for a snack bar licence to serve 23 railway workers who had supported the plan for the British Restaurant was refused.

Like most problems the answer is far from simple and lies in "Sussex Obduracy". The Council refusing to be driven, the economic consequence of the lost rent, a fairly strong catering lobby whose economic interests may have been threatened and more importantly the more catering licences issued the fewer supplies there might have been for existing caterers. Long after the war was over, in April 1947, a request from the Transport and General Workers Union was again turned down. The Council were almost equally divided on the issue, it being rejected by one vote. Although it might have been inconvenient the Town Hall Assembly room could well have been pressed into service with tables and chairs removed when the room was required in the evening.

Digging for Victory

Allotment gardening had long been a feature of life in the town but the war gave a great impetus to the hobby. Allotments were at Earwig Corner, The Coombe Malling Street, at Landport, Hill Road, Highdown Road, Valence Road, Bell Lane, Haredean and the Waterworks on the Kingston Road. In addition the lawns of The Grange were turned over to allotments, the Ringmer Building Works offered one acre of land at Ferrers Road for the duration of the war. In March 1943 the gardens of Lewes House were fenced off to provide yet more allotments. Railway employees had lineside plots near the station on what is now known as railway lands. Photographs of evacuees from Bermondsey digging plots at Landport were typical. Wherever there was access to ground, school children also tended plots. Encouragement of all kinds flowed. During the fruit season it was possible to obtain extra sugar for jam making, much of this being done under the auspices of the Women's Institute (WI) who were allowed to use the Town Hall kitchens at one shilling per session. Again both the WI and the WVS undertook each year to distribute seeds sent by well wishers in Canada and the United States. Householders, now that the Council had relaxed its rules on hen keeping, could if they chose take part in the scheme to surrender their shell egg ration for poultry feed. Rabbit keeping also thrived as did fur and feather clubs to foster this husbandry.

Salvage

Domestic refuse had, before the war, been collected by private contractors who tendered for the work. Messrs Carvill's, furniture removers of Bell Lane, were the contract holders in 1939. One Shelvoke and Drewery forward control tipper lorry, with a crew of three, sufficed to collect the town's rubbish. This unusual vehicle with three push up covers each side, was steered by a tiller and had a gearless transmission. The rubbish was taken to the Ham Lane outfall works and burnt. By 1940 salvage had become the watchword. Tins, glass containers, paper, rags and metal were all required in quantity for the war effort. The Council were pleased to accept the contractors' offer to collect salvage without extra cost. The Council provided additional storage at Ham Lane for the salvaged materials and then became aware that the contractors were making significant profits from the salvage which under the terms of the contract they were allowed to do. In the first six months of 1940 three tons of mixed metal, sundry rags and bones, 56 dozen jam jars and 130 dozen bottles were collected.

Moves by the Council to take over the refuse collection foundered because the only vehicle the Ministry of Supply would allow them to purchase was an electric battery powered lorry that would have been unsuitable. The Council also declined Carvill's offer of the existing refuse tipper. By 1941 Messrs Burchetts of Lancaster Street, secured the contract with the Council retaining the salvage profits, now running at £34 per month for 8 tons of material. Kitchen waste amounting to 16 tons per month was collected by three different firms of pig keepers for swill. In December 1942, house-to-house kitchen waste collections started with householders being issued with covered galvanised pails. This had its problems when in April 1945 two pig swill collectors were before the Court over a row that developed about unauthorised collections. They were bound over to keep the peace. The war caused a decline in consumerism to such an extent that it was possible to reduce the refuse collection from weekly to fortnightly in June 1942. By October 1943 the Council had been allowed to buy a petrol driven refuse freighter and salvage trailer and thereafter all salvage would be under their own control.

Iron railings from properties were removed for the war effort. Examples being Mountfield House, Nevill Estate, and South Place Flats all of which were Council properties. Private dwellings also contributed and were only exempted if the railings had a safety function such as protecting a basement. Householders had the right of appeal against removal of ironwork. Most appeals failed but an unusual case occurred where the railings were removed from the front of 203 High Street owned by Mr Walter Godfrey, the architect, and after a successful protest involving the antiquity of the railings they were actually replaced. The scrap value of the railings was twenty-five shillings per ton.

Another form of saving which had a mixed reception was the introduction of Double British Summer Time from 1941. From early April to the first week in August the clocks were advanced by two hours from Greenwich Mean Time and for the rest of the year they remained one hour ahead. These arrangements achieved significant savings in power and long summer evenings to enjoy, with darkness not falling until well past 10.30 pm. This meant that many workers travelled to work in the dark in the depths of winter.

The Burgess family at war, Civil Defence, Fireguard, Army Cadet, Junior Air Corps and Auxiliary Territorial. *F Burgess*

The Black Market

Controls both financial and by rationing or other controls always produce opportunities for circumvention. Most consumer items which had for so long been taken for granted became ever more difficult to obtain as the war progressed. Torches, so useful in the blackout, became useless without batteries which were often unobtainable. Bicycles, as essential as today's car, were difficult to get and spare parts were often of poor quality, wooden pedals, no chromed parts and tyres that seemed to wear out so quickly. Rubber pump connectors all but disappeared. Men found Brylcream hair dressing and razor blades hard to come by. Women's artificial silk stockings impossible to get. Elastic, an indispensable item, was frequently unobtainable. A grey market sprang up with clothing coupons. Large families with clothes to hand down and an extra entitlement for growing children would have coupons to spare. So might workers who received an "Industrial Ten" for overalls. The going rate for these coupons would be one shilling each. Food retailers as described elsewhere accidentally or knowingly broke the regulations and were caught. Petrol misuse was a frequent source of wrongdoing.

Controls on the production of non-essentials meant that most of these items were down to 25% of pre-war amounts. This included photographic materials for private use, so combined with security restrictions very little exists of wartime activity recorded by private photographers. Purchase Tax on non-essentials from 1941 and PAYE Income Tax from April 1944 damped down spending. One piece of fiscal legislation was the deduction of tax to be paid back after the war as "Post War Credits". The repayments were delayed, eventually until the creditor died or retired. The scheme ending not so many years ago.

The Media

Newspapers and magazines soon shrank in size down to eight sides to conserve newsprint and shipping space. The East Sussex News a broadsheet by Farncombe's amalgamated in July 1941 with the Sussex Express produced by F J Parsons that had earlier absorbed Beckett's Sussex County Herald. In 1938 these amalgamated titles eventually became the East Sussex Express and County Herald. The Southern Publishing Company's Sussex Daily News and Evening Argus, with the Lewes papers, served the town throughout the war and much of the material in this book has been gleaned from their files. The editorial column of the Sussex Express was entitled Lewes Rouser. Many of his comments struck home and produced change that otherwise might not have happened. His identity was the subject of speculation but the pseudonym cloaked Dudley Farncombe, former senior reporter, of the East Sussex News.

The newspapers featured official announcements on rationing, exhortations to save money and materials and to avoid unnecessary travel. Censorship restricted identification of places damaged by enemy air raids, pictures of bomb damaged buildings were captioned as a town or village in the south-east. That most English of topics, the weather and its forecasting was a banned subject as information of use to the enemy. National newspapers and magazines continued to be available but restricted in size and number of copies printed. To be sure of getting your copy a regular order to the newsagent was essential. The Blitz on London during the winter of 1940-1 meant that often the London newspapers were delayed in reaching Lewes due to difficulties in Fleet Street and on the railways.

A utility mains wireless for long and medium waves made its appearance. The pre-war radio programmes, the National on 1500 metres and the London Regional programme in the medium wave band were replaced by the Home service and the Forces programmes. Today's equivalent would be Radios Four and Two. Reception was poor and fading and loss of transmission occurred when the large German air raids took place in 1940-41. From 1940 Newsreaders would always identify themselves by name to guard against any possible enemy propaganda deception. Workers Playtime, Calling all Workers and Tommy Handley's ITMA will long be remembered. It was regarded as unpatriotic at the time but some Lewes residents would have listened, for amusement, to "Lord Haw-Haw" alias William Joyce a traitor who broadcast propaganda from Germany. Few would remember that he had appeared before Lewes Assizes in 1934 charged with unlawful assembly at Worthing. Along with fellow fascists the charges against him were dropped.

On 7th June 1944 a new transmission came on the air from Start Point in Devon on 285 metres medium wave, The Allied Expeditionary Forces programme begun at the express wish of General Eisenhower and was beamed to Normandy and southern England specifically for the troops after D-day and those waiting to go over the Channel. It was organised with the utmost secrecy so as not to reveal the locations of the landings. The material broadcast reflected the composition of the landing forces, 50% American, 35% British and 15% Canadian. At last the teenagers of Lewes could hear direct the number one American band, that of Captain Glenn Miller. The 45 strong orchestra split into a dance band with the title of the Swing Shift, a Jazz combo known as the Uptown Hall Gang and the Strings with Wings the twenty-piece string section of the orchestra. Between them they kept up a daily schedule of broadcasts over the next six months. The British band of the AEF was conducted by George Melachrino with Robert Farnon conducting the
Canadian band.

The one broadcast which most residents listened in to was the 9.00 pm news. From 1940 the Sunday transmission, broadcast the National Anthems of the allied nations. This practice ceased by the end of 1941, its patriotic uplift being diminished when a radio comic said " that it represented all the countries overrun by Hitler and if he invaded any more there would be little time left for the news".

RCHME Crown Copyright
Windows taped, Lewes painted out, but still open

16. Victory

In April 1942 morale was at its lowest ebb, while defeat no longer seemed a possibility the road to peace seemed long and hard. The Japanese forces had achieved lightning victories in the Far East at great cost to the allies. The war at sea was still much in the balance. Successes in East Africa, the Middle East and Madagascar had to be set against the latest reverses in the Western Desert with the loss of Tobruk that had brought the British Eighth army back to El Alamein by July. In August a further German attack was repulsed by General Auchinleck. This paved the way for General Montgomery's success on 23rd October. This, six months, later led to the German and Italian forces being cleared from North Africa. Simultaneously between August 1942 and January 1943 Russian forces had encircled the German sixth army at Stalingrad and forced its surrender. In October, in common with the rest of the nation, Lewes could hear church bells ringing in celebration of the victory at El Alamein. Since 1940 they had been silenced, to be rung only if the Germans had invaded. From May 1943 The Control of Noise Order was lifted and church bells could thenceforth be rung on all occasions.

The blackout was the first wartime irritation that the townsfolk were glad to see go. The Council in October 1943 arranged with the two lighting companies that served the town to quote for putting the street lamps in working order and replacing 64 lamps accidentally destroyed by passing military traffic. Reduced street lighting with low powered bulbs was allowed from 27th September 1944. The switch-on took place one month later from 10.00 pm until midnight. Reinstatement had cost the Council eleven shillings for each lamp renovated. "Moonlighting" as it was known was allowed on 116 lamps on classified roads and 64 lamps in side roads of the town, this represented only one third of the total. There was an element of risk in the arrangement as there was no master switch to turn off the lights should an air raid occur. In April 1945 street lighting would be installed in Railway Lane, Walwers Lane and in the Bradford Road to Prince Edward's Road path, to "Obviate Nuisances". Full street lighting was resumed from 5th July 1945 but for fuel economy the lamps would remain unlit during Double British Summertime that ended in August.

In August 1944 a fund was established to give the town's servicemen and women a welcome back. It soon reached £400 and the total climbed slowly but steadily to reach nearly £2,000. It was helped on its way by a Concert in the Town Hall in which Max Miller and other artists appeared. The music was provided by the NFS Dance Band from Brighton, the evening raised £51. Mr Sains the Chief ARP Officer was appointed the Honorary Secretary of the fund and although the fund raising might have been a hard task it was nothing compared to the difficulties experienced when it came to apply the fund. In May 1945 it was reported to a town meeting that support for the fund was meagre. Many suggestions were made including the gift of an engraved cigarette case, which floundered because it was realised that not all the ex-service men would have been smokers, a wallet was another suggestion so too was a welcome home dinner. Finally the wisdom of Solomon prevailed and each man or woman on return was asked to present themselves at the Council Treasurer's office to sign for their share, 25 shillings! Each member of the services also received a scroll of appreciation signed by the Mayor Ald Crisp. There was some doubt as to the exact number that had enlisted. The figure of 1,500 was quoted for the welcome back fund distribution, but in 1946 at the Victory celebrations it was recorded that 600 had accepted the invitation to participate and this was thought to be half the number possible.

Victory in Europe

By late spring of 1945 the allied forces were advancing in Italy and into Austria. The Russians also were making huge gains in the east and the Anglo-American forces advanced rapidly from the west, it seemed that the war in Europe would soon be over. On 29th April fighting ceased on the Italian front and on 5th May in Western Europe the war was over. A Home Office circular arrived on the 4th May detailing the arrangements for "VE" Day. It said that The Prime Minister, Mr Winston Churchill, would broadcast to the nation at 3.00 pm on 8th May. HM the King would speak on the Radio in the evening of the same day. The 9th May would also be a public holiday. Church bells would be rung on Sunday which would be a special day of thanksgiving for victory.

Gabriel in the Market Tower was tolled and church bells in the town were rung. A Southover ringer remembered ringing for the Armistice in 1918. Flags and bunting were strung across the High Street from the Town Hall. At 9.30 am the Mayor, Ald Crisp, addressed the crowd that had gathered outside. Three cheers were given by the throng, thankful that at least part of the war was over, but mindful of the conflict continuing in the Far East where Lewes men were still fighting or in captivity. A party of Canadian Soldiers on leave from the fighting in Europe paraded a captured Nazi flag in the High Street. In Fisher Street an electrical shop displayed a "V" in coloured lights in its window. Coastal dim out regulations prevented hill top beacons but a large bonfire was lit in Firle Park.

In the evening crowds gathered near the War Memorial singing and dancing. Later they moved

L Davey Sussex Express
Grange opening 16-5-1945 Ald Crisp with returned prisoners. Flt Sgt Hall back row 3rd rt. (p159)

on to the County Hall in the High Street, where, at the junction with Station Street, a large bonfire was lit in the roadway fuelled by blackout shutters that had once protected the windows of Woolmore's tobacconist's shop. The celebrations were punctuated by the occasional discharge of thunderflashes and fireworks. Fires blazed on Cliffe Hill where some members of the Home Guard, now officially stood down, disposed of some surplus anti-tank Fougasse drums of mixed paraffin and engine oil. The NFS was called to the bonfire in the High Street but wisely confined their firefighting to preventive spraying of nearby buildings. Most of the town's Police Force including the Special Constables were on duty and with commendable restraint allowed the celebrations to continue without incident. The crowds finally dispersed homewards at 2.00 am and as a final spectacular act, an explosion took place in the steel emergency water tank Number 3 that stood in the roadway outside Boots the Chemists. The force was sufficient to rupture the sides which sent 5,000 gallons of evil smelling water running down Station Street in a torrent. No one was hurt in the incident that has become a much recounted local story. There were many names put forward as to the possible identity of the saboteur but one that crops more than others, is that of Mr Frank Martin of Allington Farm East Chiltington, an ex-Home Guard, but this has never been proven. The remains of the water tank, damaged by plastic explosive was removed in May. Later a £25 War Damage claim was met to repair the roadway.

"VE" party Waterloo Place 11-5-1945 *Sussex Express*

For eighteen months a combined committee of the Lewes Bonfire Societies had been meeting under the chairmanship of Clr Bill Penfold to plan the resumption of Guy Fawkes night festivities. This committee were called upon to make arrangements for a torchlight procession on the night

Wednesday 9th May. Two thousand torches were made and dipped and a combined procession set off at 9.15 pm from the *Swan Inn* Southover, led by the band of the Lewes Squadron of The Air Training Corps. The procession marched in fancy dress, around a circuit of public houses, to the *Red White and Blue* public house in Friars Walk at the corner of Pinwell Lane, then to the *Snowdrop* in South Street, next to Malling Street turning at Soap Factory Lane. It continued along Cliffe High Street to the War Memorial where a Guard of Honour was mounted. The marchers then turned into Fisher Street to the *Elephant and Castle*, from there via the Avenue, Bradford Road, Irelands Lane, St Anne's Hill to the *Brewers Arms*. The procession returned to and circled the War Memorial then went on to the County Hall where Clr Penfold read a patriotic address and an effigy of Hitler was burnt. At each stop torches were replenished and no doubt thirsts were quenched as well. That evening the Town Hall was crowded for a public dance to the music of Bert Munt's Band.

A United Civic Service took place in the Dripping Pan at 3.00 pm on Sunday 14th May. The Mayor, Corporation, Home Guard, Civil Defence and Youth Organisation attended. In the weeks that followed, the community spirit fostered by the war, continued to show itself with residents organising street parties for the children of the town. North Way fêted 150 youngsters, tables and chairs were borrowed from the YMCA, Dr C G Sinclair distributed the prizes won in the sports and games. Brook Street and Spring Gardens excelled with bunting and flags for their party illuminated by NFS floodlights and music from the ARP loudspeaker van. St Anne's Crescent held a party outside the Library with each child receiving a shilling. West Street held a party on the site of the bombed houses opposite the Co-op Stores. Sun Street entertained 70 boys and girls with music provided by a piano pushed into the street. Talbot Terrace had a sing song at their party led by Harold Emery on an accordion and then marched in procession round the neighbourhood. Everywhere the story was of housewives raiding store cupboards to produce the jellies, blancmange, trifles, sandwiches of jam and paste, buns and cakes. A Victory Supper was held in St John's Parish Room where 70 residents partook of sausage rolls and joined in singing and dancing. Parties continued until 25th June in various parts of the town and surrounding district.

The 1945 General Election

On 18th May the Prime Minister invited the leaders of the other parties in the wartime coalition government to continue in partnership until the defeat of Japan. The Labour party declined to do so and a General Election had to follow. Mr Churchill headed a caretaker administration, after 1,902 days in office as Prime Minister, of the fourth longest Parliament in history of nine years and six months. Nominations closed on 25th June and polling took place Thursday 7th July. In Lewes, the candidates were Major Tufton Beamish MC of Chelwood Gate, Conservative, son of the retiring member, Mr Albert Oram of Patcham, Labour, Mr Peter Cadogan, Liberal and Mr E Verner, Independent. The poll lasted from 8.00 am to 9.00 pm with Mrs A S Blaker, the 96 year old widow of a former Town Clerk, claiming to be the oldest voter going to the poll. In some areas of the country polling took place later in the month and the declaration of results was delayed until 26th July to allow time for the overseas service vote to arrive for the count. Nationally it was a sweeping victory for Labour. In Lewes the Conservatives retained the seat. Mr Churchill returned from the Potsdam Conference of the victorious allies for the declaration and was replaced immediately at the conference by the new Prime Minister, Mr C R Attlee. Major Tufton Beamish chose for his maiden speech the subject of "Realism and the United Nations Charter" which he expounded must represent more than just a "Paper Security".

Victory over Japan

The newspapers of 7th August 1945 gave details of a new type of bomb, of unprecedented power. This had been dropped on the Japanese city of Hiroshima. Two days later another Japanese city, Nagasaki, was destroyed by a similar but more powerful bomb of this type. On 10th August the Japanese government indicated that they would accept the Potsdam unconditional surrender terms and on the 14th the fighting ceased. Mr Attlee announced the news at midnight on the 14th saying that Wednesday 15th and Thursday 16th would be public holidays.

On "V J" Day a small crowd assembled at the War Memorial and sang and danced for a short while after Mr Attlee's broadcast. At 9.15 am on Wednesday 15th Ald Crisp formally announced from the Town Hall entrance to a crowd, which had waited in the rain, that the war was over. Bunting and flags were again in evidence and short Thanksgiving services were held in the town's churches. The atmosphere was one of deliverance and thankfulness rather than jollification. Three cheers were given, for the Mayor Ald Crisp and the official party then retired to the Mayor's Parlour where he thanked all those who had unstintedly supported him during the war years. Ald Hoyle paid tribute to Mrs Turquand the Mayor's daughter who had given up her home in Brighton

T Dumbrell Sussex Express
"VJ" night 15-8-1945 Town Hall dance Flt Sgt J Dwyer on embarkation leave centre front

to support her father throughout the war. The occasion was tinged with sadness as Ald Crisp would be leaving the office of Mayor after seven continuous years in office.

During the morning a queue of 100 people assembled outside Clr Penfold's shop in Lansdown place with over 50 bicycles propped up everywhere showing that the news had travelled widely that he was selling fireworks. A loudspeaker van toured the town giving details of events during the next two days. Council recreational facilities would be free of charge. Dances would be held both nights in the Town Hall, these proved to be so popular that the overflows were accommodated in Holloway's Restaurant. Flight Sergeant J Dwyer recalls the Victory night dance as he was home in Lewes on embarkation leave for the Far East, a pleasurable evening enhanced by the knowledge that his long distance travel arrangements would be cancelled.

"VJ" Day children's party Talbot Terrace August 1945   *T J Dumbrell Sussex Express*

On Wednesday morning a procession of children in fancy dress led by Britannia journeyed from Talbot Terrace to the steps of County Hall where three cheers were given. At the Town Hall the Mayor took the salute as the procession passed. On returning to St John's Parish Room the Rector, the Rev H J Langhorne, gave a stirring address and this was followed by patriotic songs. Celebrations continued until October with a round of street and other parties celebrating final victory. Landport, Malling, Waterloo Place and the Alpha Cement Works at Rodmell were typical party locations. New Road and Paddock Road combined to hold their party in St John's Parish Room with a top table of elderly ladies each of whom was given a shilling. A minute's silence was observed for the fallen. Afterwards a procession formed up outside Day's shop in New Road and marched to the Paddock where a bonfire was lit and fireworks set off, concluding at 10.30 pm with the burning of an effigy of General Tojo, the Japanese Prime Minister, who was later executed as a war criminal in 1948. St John's Women's Institute held a Victory Supper attended by 69 members. Ringmer had a party for 150 children on the Green while Kingston entertained 25 younger members of the village. Bonfires were lit in Lancaster Street on waste ground near the Naval Prison. Commandos billeted in the town joined in the Sun Street celebrations, which ended with a torchlight fancy dress parade and fireworks.

Two Lewesians were moved to compose poems, one in remembrance of the 14th British-Indian Army that had turned defeat into Victory under General Slim in Burma, and regarded itself as forgotten at home by the nation. The other was of thanksgiving by the Sussex Express columnist Lewes Rouser. A combined torchlight procession of the Bonfire Societies took place on the Thursday night when 3,000 were used. The procession started at the *Kings Head* in Southover and marched to the *Thatched House* in Malling Street returning to the *Brewer's Arms*. Next it called at the *Black Horse* and the *Elephant and Castle* before finally marching to the bonfire at the junction of Hill Road and Offham Road. This had unfortunately been pre-ignited. The NFS attended and this literally put a dampener on this part of the proceedings. The South Street Juvenile Bonfire Society had its own impromptu fire on the West Street bomb site.

A United Drumhead Service was arranged in the Dripping Pan conducted by the Rev D G Matthews, Rector of Southover, and the Rev Allwright of Eastgate Baptist Church. Music was provided by the Salvation Army Band and the football area was filled by the public. The Rev Langhorne preached a thought-provoking sermon at the St John sub-Castro's victory service, that the war could be seen as a punishment for the Nation's apathy, between the wars, to events in the world. He warned that World War Three was possible if the defeated nations sought revenge.

Least we Forget

The flag of peace thank God has been unfurled
and flutters proudly over our troubled world

Brings fresh hope to those who knew, ere long
That right must triumph over wrong

The long night ends, once more the sunshine gleams
No longer must we suffer nightmare dreams

But as we waken, let us not forget
the hidden hand behind the tears and sweat.

by Lewes Rouser

Forgotten Fourteenth

No doubt you've heard of Libya's sands
and Italy's Terra Firma
But have you heard of real bad lands
of Assam and North Burma?

These are the lands of Jungle deep
of swamp and blood sucking leeches
Of everything that God made creep
where only experience teaches

This where the fittest survive
and the weak just fall by the way;
where only tablets keep you alive
and the sweat drips off you every day

Where a sniper lurks in every tree
and each hilltop shelters a gun
as you scramble along on hands and knees
Killing Japs of the rising sun

Where the roads are only Jungle tracks
where mules are known to falter;
But men carry on with loaded packs
Through mud and stagnant water

Where there are no towns to liberate
No civvies to cheer you on
Just millions of insects to irritate
and the jungle rolling on

So when you read of Britain's might
On Europe's plains and beaches
just spare a thought for those who fought
mid jungle swamps and leeches

By ex-Cpl G L Hayler formerly of 41 The Cliffe, later of 14 Fisher Street

BOROUGH OF LEWES

VICTORY CELEBRATIONS
8th JUNE, 1946

HIS MAJESTY'S GOVERNMENT HAVE APPOINTED THIS DAY OF PUBLIC CELEBRATION OF THE SUCCESSFUL ISSUE OF THE COMBINED ARMED AND CIVIL FORCES OF THE CROWN, AND OF THEIR DOMINIONS AND ALLIES, FROM A LONG PERIOD OF HARD STRUGGLE COMMENCING ON THE 3rd SEPTEMBER, 1939, AND ENDING ON THE 15th AUGUST, 1945

PROGRAMME
OF
FANCY DRESS PARADE : SIDE SHOWS : SPORTS
ENTERTAINMENTS : TORCHLIGHT PROCESSION
OLD FOLKS' TOUR ——— REFRESHMENTS

The Official Celebrations aim, primarily, to provide pleasure to Children resident in the Borough of Lewes, and every young Citizen will have a pass to the free enjoyment of Refreshment—limited, unfortunately, by National circumstance—and every Child of School age a free voucher for a round of the Side-Shows with a prospect of a Prize for his or her skill.

Observing, however, that a Child derives encouragement from the presence of his elders, grown-ups are invited to participate in the enjoyment of the Day—in the case of Side-Shows by purchasing the necessary Voucher—and, generally, by attending in force and assisting, in the spirit, the aim of the Organizers to make the Eighth of June a day to be remembered by the Children.

PUT OUT YOUR FLAGS

FREE REFRESHMENT TICKETS—CHILDREN UNDER SCHOOL AGE. Applications for Free Tickets should be made in person by the Parent or Guardian who will accompany the Child on the day, at the Borough Treasurer's Office, Council Offices, Fisher Street.
——— APPLICATION MUST BE MADE BEFORE 6th JUNE. ———

CHILDREN ATTENDING SCHOOLS IN LEWES WILL RECEIVE FREE REFRESHMENT AND SIDE-SHOW TICKETS THROUGH THEIR SCHOOLS. THOSE ATTENDING SCHOOL OUT OF LEWES SHOULD MAKE PERSONAL APPLICATION AS ABOVE

[FOR DETAILS OF ARRANGEMENTS OF OLD FOLKS'
TOUR AND TEA, SEE BACK OF PROGRAMME]

November 1945 produced two events that the town had forgone during the war years. Local Council Elections took place for the first time since 1938. 4,723 Lewesians turned out from an electorate of 9,000 to vote. Despite all the Ratepayers' Party candidates being elected, the control of the Council remained in Conservative hands. More importantly for some, the Bonfire Celebrations were resumed in earnest for the first time for six years. Again not without the help of the NFS which was called to deal with a fire in a storeroom at the rear of the Dorset Arms in Malling Street where 600 torches, which had been prepared for the Uckfield Celebrations, caught alight. It required twenty minutes' pumping to bring the blaze under control and prevent it spreading to inflammables stored in the adjacent County Council Yard.

Victory Day 1946

A National Victory Day was arranged for Saturday 8th June, the Borough of Lewes producing a programme of events of which to be proud. A printed programme in red white and blue with the seal of the Borough surmounted by the flags of the Commonwealth informed residents of the day's events, a fancy dress parade, side shows, sports, entertainments, torchlight procession, and open air dancing. The old folks would have an outing and a tea. Every child of school age would have a voucher for free refreshments and entry to the side shows. Adults and parents were invited to attend to encourage the younger ones. A request was made to put out flags and bunting. Ten classes were organised for the fancy dress competition with entrants assembling at Castle Banks at 1.30 pm. Rain however forced a move into the Town Hall. At 1.55 pm the contestants mostly rain coated, against the chilly breeze, marched to the Dripping Pan via School Hill, Friars Walk and Station Approach where they were met by the Mayor, Ald W E Witcher, and 1,000 spectators. From 2.30 pm until 7.00 pm 25 different sideshows, including a treasure hunt, bowling for a pig, a rifle range and greasy pole, could be enjoyed. The children had twelve free attempts, after that they had to pay two shillings for twelve entries. The fancy dress competition was then judged by the notables including Mrs R Turquand, Mrs M Holman, Miss N Stacey, Sir George Boughey Bart, H W Walton and Martin R Heriot. Music for the event was provided by the Town Band. Surprise field events were arranged and Punch and Judy made four appearances. Teas were served in a running buffet in a marquee in the Convent Field from 3.45 pm until 5.30 pm. At 7.00 pm the Mayor presented the prizes. This was followed by dancing on the green in the Dripping Pan to Ernie Took and his Melody Makers. Over 3,000 people attended the event many coming in from the villages and from Newhaven and Seaford which did not have celebrations on the same scale.

The cinemas were full and many stayed in town to watch the torchlight procession. The combined Bonfire Societies arranged the procession which commenced at 10.00 pm. The procession which used 1,000 torches was led by the Seaford British Legion Band. After assembling at Cliffe Corner it marched through the High Street to St Anne's Church Room returning via Western Road to the County Hall, ending with the burning of an effigy of Hitler. This ceremonial destruction went with difficulty owing to the dampness. Floodlighting of public buildings had been organised free by the Lewes and District Electric Supply Company but somehow the County Hall was in a pool of darkness. This dark spot was enlivened by some sailors who led the singing, dancing and revelry of those waiting for the procession. The merrymaking ended at midnight.

> To
>
> *Raymond George Hallett.*
> *Corpl: 14680354. R.A.O.C.*
>
> The Mayor, Aldermen, Councillors and Burgesses of the Borough of Lewes desire to perpetuate, through the medium of this Scroll, their great appreciation of the services rendered by you in the Armed Forces of the Crown during the Great War of 1939-1945, to convey to you their congratulations on a safe return home, and to express the hope that you may be spared for many years to enjoy the blessings of peace.
>
> *Chas D. Crisp*
> Mayor

Each returning serviceman and woman received a scroll and twenty-five shillings   R Hallett

Each school child was presented with a special Victory Message from HM King George VI printed in blue on card commending them for their wartime fortitude. Victory was also marked by the issue of two commemorative stamps, 2½d blue and 3d mauve, which when used were franked by post mark depicting victory bells. During the war two more sets of stamps appeared, the six definitives from a ½d to 3d in 1941/2 printed with less dye as a war economy measure and the Postal Centenary 1840-1940 when six commemoratives were issued, which brought forth local adverse comments that the stamps themselves did not refer to the reason for the issue.

On the Friday before, the old folk of the town were taken on a tour and to tea, starting at 2.30 pm from the County Hall where they were seen off by the Mayor Ald Witcher. The party journeyed via Westmeston, Hassocks, Poynings, Steyning and Arundel to Littlehampton for tea where the Mayor and Mayoress waited to greet them. The return journey was made via Worthing and Brighton arriving back in Lewes at 7.00 pm dropping the party goers at points near their homes. Much of the cost of the Victory day's arrangements (£585) had been met by sponsors and by donations with £300 from Clr Stacey leaving a bill for the ratepayers of just £60. This did not stop the Rev Langhorne of St John-sub-Castro commenting on the morality and expense of the victory celebrations nationally.

17. The Aftermath

The Town Plan and Housing

Just as the preparations for war began in 1937, before hostilities commenced, so the plans for peace began in 1943 anticipating the end of the war by two years. Lewes Council, in March of that year set up a special subcommittee to consider the effects of the Beveridge plan for social reform and the post war housing needs of the town. Landport would be developed with two sites, totalling 25 acres, north and south of the existing estate to take 50 and 80 houses respectively while a further 3 acres at Mill Fields Malling would hold another 30 homes.

In August 1944 the Council considered purchasing Southover Grange that it had so far leased. A swimming bath was proposed for the south-east corner of the grounds. Another feature of the Grange would be the building of a Health Centre. A solution to the traffic problem at the bottleneck was a suggestion to build a new road behind St Michaels Church. This would leave the Church and other adjacent properties as an island and would create a one way system rejoining the High Street at Castlegate. Better bus services, a new Head Post Office and an automatic telephone exchange were also listed for the "New Lewes". The total cost of a ten-year plan for the town was estimated at £604,000.

A further 76 houses were planned for the Wallands Estate the first to be completed would be in Valence Road where foundations laid in 1939 had been abandoned because of the war. Provision of a Maternity Unit would be referred to the Victoria Hospital. The Cattle Market would be moved to *Leighside*, south of Friars Walk with an abattoir on the same site. Road improvements were listed for Westgate Street, New Road, Hill Road, Bell Lane, Rotten Row and Winterbourne Hollow. Landport was to have a community centre and the town was stated to need more car parks, better refuse disposal, outfall arrangements and a water softening plant. On 18th August a map of the bottleneck proposals showed a road line from *Shelleys* Hotel to Castlegate. It was felt these proposals would need careful consideration, fortunately they did not survive.

Demolition of surface shelter Morris Road May 1947 *F Burgess*

Council house building before the war had progressed at a rate of 30 per year. A rate of 70 per year would be needed to meet the demand. Pre-war private building had produced 61 houses per annum. To complete the picture Lewes would have to attract light industry and not rely on rural based employment. In March 1945 plans were approved to place 30 prefabricated houses, at the Landport and Winterbourne Estates, these were of the Arcon type made by Taylor Woodrow.

The sites were ready by the time the first six arrived in November, the first one being completed and occupied by March 1946. The houses came complete with enamel work surfaces, a refrigerator, cooker, ducted air heating and cost £1,000 each. They comprised two bedrooms, kitchen, living room and bathroom. They were all electric, much to the annoyance of the Lewes Gas Company who were excluded from competing as they had done in past Council Housing projects.

1994 Westgate Street shelter converted into garages   *R A Elliston*

Other housing changes were afoot. The war had led to many properties becoming empty while more people required homes. War workers and those bombed out from London and Eastbourne came to live in the town. By 1944 the council had requisitioned 114 empty properties for housing needs and had accommodated 453 persons. These properties were in addition to those taken over by the military. In April 1945 a start was made on the drainage and roadways for the new estate at Landport. German prisoners of war, of whom there were several hundred at the Prison and in camps outside the town, were employed on the work. In June it was decided to allow interchange of council house tenancies to make better use of housing stock. Rents would be increased and a charge would be made if lodgers lived in the house. The first council houses were ready by Christmas 1946. The post-war housing shortage was so acute that the council refused an application by the Red Cross to use 31 The Avenue as a headquarters. By May 1947 there were 750 applicants waiting for council houses and a points scheme was introduced to accord priorities. Such was the demand for housing that a report appeared in the Sussex Express of 13th September describing the arrival of a moving van after midnight at the National Fire Service Nissen huts next to the Fire Station in North Street. The huts had been unused for some time and Clr Bill Penfold was noted as being present. After official protests the family was allowed to stay. Squatters also moved into the two wooden army huts next to the Offham filling station. These had been earmarked for farm workers by the War Agricultural Executive, but the squatters were allowed to stay.

Back to Normal

Road direction signs removed in 1940, to hinder any invading German troops, were replaced in February 1944. It was generally agreed that their removal had caused more confusion among the British and Canadian forces and civilians than the security their removal achieved. In May 1946 the demolition of the 1,475 civilian wartime structures got under way. It was estimated that there were 300 Anderson shelters to be dismantled and collected. A further 200 had already dismantled and awaited collection. Public shelters in York Street, Malling Street and elsewhere awaited removal. The above ground control centre, built in 1942, behind Barclays Bank, for £700, cost a further £205 to demolish. In Westgate Street a 6,000-gallon water tank had to go. The Gas Decontamination centre had a temporary reprieve while the possibility of converting it to public baths or toilets was considered. The idea was abandoned.

1994 Anderson Shelters rust in retirement, Haredean Allotments   *RA Elliston*

In May 1947 the Council honoured its pledge to the site owner in Westgate Street on which a brick surface shelter had been built and allowed its conversion to a pair of garages. These remain to this day and are easily identified between the YMCA and the Women's Institute Federation buildings. Surface and semi-surface shelters on private property waiting to be removed totalled 70, at Landport 24 brick surface shelters would be retained as allotment sheds, at Winterbourne 6 out of 29 brick shelters would be left for storage. The static water tank on Castle Green with 14 others in various parts of the town would be cleared, the brick rubble would be taken to the outfall works and it was estimated that 14 men and the bulldozer required to do the work would cost £2,753. The anti-tank pillbox on School Hill was demolished in September 1944 and the static water tank on the east side of the War Memorial was removed in November 1945.

Dilapidations

By 1945 road maintenance had fallen behind and heavy military traffic made the state of the roads worse, 75,000 yards of roads would require tar and chipping dressing. The road to the Golf Course had been damaged by army lorries and the War Office was to be asked for restitution. By December 1947 the Council had purchased the Golf Course pavilion for £1,607 which included £894 worth of repairs. The army had at last relinquished the 19th hole of the course. In October it was hoped the Racecourse that had been requisitioned would soon be released. In March 1946 it was reported that the Racecourse was in a poor state because of wartime occupation. Rusty barbed wire abounded, the winning post and jockeys' number board were badly damaged, the Totalisator was in need of major repairs, the stand and stewards' room had been severely damaged in the fire of February 1941. Much rotten wood needed replacing and repainting would be required. The first post-war meeting took place in July 1946. *Heath House* and *School Hill House* were released by the military on 9th April 1945. A year later *Astley House, Albion House* and *Mountfield House* were still under requisition. The Golf Course was released by the army on 24th May 1946 and the Grange on 6th August. By April 1946, the youthful evacuees having left, Glyndebourne had been refurbished.

The Stanmer Estate, taken over by the army in April 1941, was released in August 1946. It presented a scene of dilapidation. Concreted hard stands for tanks, Nissen huts used as wash houses, cook houses and dormitories abounded under the trees. Stanmer House had been home recently to 80 members of the Royal Engineers, cranes and bulldozers were parked amid the trees, brambles and nettles covered once trim lawns. Junk, scrap metal, and old tyres were everywhere. The village had been used as a "Town Fighting Area". Not a piece of glass remained, doors were wrenched off internal partitions and ceilings were down in all the cottages. The churchyard was overgrown but the church, with windows boarded up, was intact. In April 1944 the churchyard had become the burial place of the last of the male Chichesters, the 8th Earl, a Captain in The Scots Guards, who had been killed in a road accident near Doncaster. Some alarm was felt in Lewes Council circles when, in November 1946, Brighton Council commenced negotiations to acquire the Chichester Estate at Stanmer. Lewes regarded it as encroachment on the town by its large neighbour Brighton.

Clearing the Downs

In April 1946 it was felt necessary to issue a warning about the dangerous state of the South Downs, used as wartime training areas by the army. From north of the Lewes-Brighton road to Blackcap and Ditchling Beacon as far as Clayton and to the south of the Brighton road to Telscombe village, Newmarket Hill, Kingston Village, Iford and Rodmell the Downlands were all in a highly dangerous condition owing to the presence of live ammunition. By August 18,000 of the 30,000 acres of Downland had been cleared of ordnance, warning notice boards and barbed wire fences. Elsewhere the closure order under Defence Regulation 31(2)b remained in force.

1994 Empty Fireguard watchtower at the Council Offices surveys the town   *R A Elliston*

That same month gelignite, gun cotton primers, detonators, mortar bombs and hand grenades disappeared from a barn in the training area used by the army as a store. Following a visit to local schools by the police, six boys aged 13 to 16 years came before the magistrates and were each fined from £3 to £5. The materials had been taken from an unlocked barn and some had been exploded by the boys in rabbit holes. In August three youths stole three rifles and 4,000 rounds of ammunition from the Mountfield Road Drill Hall, they then toured the local countryside in a stolen car shooting up road signs. They were apprehended and dealt with by the courts.

Ordnance accidents continued to happen. In March 1945 a boy and girl playing behind the pillbox opposite Spital Road found a box of phosphorous grenades. Both were burned in an explosion and required hospital treatment. In February 1946 another box of glass phosphorus anti-tank grenades was found in the garden of School Hill House. A live No 6 grenade was found amid scrap metal in Every's Ironworks yard in June 1948. A garden shed at No15 St Swithun's Terrace was the home of a live Mills hand grenade until removed by the army.

The Lewes Division of the Sussex Police arranged a firearms amnesty in March 1946. It yielded 2,741 weapons and 77,400 rounds of ammunition. Included within the totals were 74 machine guns, 1,900 handguns, 478 rifles, 84 shells, mortars and grenades. Some of this would be souvenirs brought home by returning servicemen and much of the rest would have been materials abandoned by service units and the Home Guard. The latter may have had hidden caches that were forgotten at "Stand Down" in December 1944.

The initial clearance of the training areas during the winter of 1945-6 was visual only, this would leave live ammunition in grass and scrub. In May 1946 during ploughing at Preston Court Farm

Beddingham a 25lb artillery shell was turned up with a 2-inch mortar bomb. It was the practice to have a boy on the tractor as a lookout for shells turning up in this way. In 1952 following the death of a boy from Haywards Heath due to wartime explosives it was decided that the Downs should be swept by the army. The Royal Engineers would undertake the task, which would take a year to complete. Most of the work would be done by Ukranian displaced persons living at Newhaven Fort. A year later after the clearance a prison warder on his way to work across the Downs picked up a pipe like object. When he arrived at the Prison it was found to be a mortar bomb. The police were called and removed the item for disposal. This underlines the fact that a clearance may not be complete.

Ammunition continued to be found. In July 1957 a 25-pounder shell was recovered from the Pells, later a rusty machine gun was also found in the water. In March 1958 schoolboys found a quantity of ammunition on the Downs near the Racecourse. Wisely they called the police, the bomb disposal squad found that they were two-inch smoke mortar bombs. Paul Williams aged 13 found a live three-inch mortar shell near the two-mile start of the Racecourse in April 1962. This was removed by the bomb disposal squad to a rubbish tip at the west end of Christie Road and detonated with a smoke bomb that had also been found.

Other military relics continued to turn up. In January 1970 the army combed Place Farm at Firle and collected a significant quantity of shells that had fallen short of Blackcap to which they had been fired from Caburn. In June 1973 a suspected bomb in the Ouse at Isfield turned out to be a wartime drop tank from a British aircraft. In June 1980 the army was called in to deal with six bombs kept in a Lewes house since the previous Christmas. The location where the items were found on the Downs was not revealed and the Police toured the schools to warn children of the dangers of old ordnance. Soon after the Fougasse installation was found in Ashcombe Lane in the spring of 1994, two people using Metal detectors found a live mortar bomb on the Downs nearby. It should be emphasised that metal detecting should only be carried out with the landowner's permission. A live two inch mortar was found at Housedean Farm in August 1998 Searching for military relics in former training areas is a highly dangerous pastime.

Return to An Uneasy Peace

Municipal progress was made when it was decided to proceed with the purchase of Southover Grange from Clr Harry Stacey in December 1944. It had been leased from 1943 for £400 per annum for the house and £10 for the garden. The purchase would go ahead, when The Grange was released by the army, at the option price of £9,500. In November 1944, £400 was set aside to re-seed the old wartime allotments in the gardens. The official opening took place in May 1945. An opening ceremony was arranged which included music provided by the band of the Royal East Surrey Regiment. Some expenditure was necessary to refresh the band and distinguished guests. This proposal caused some acrimony in Council with the Ratepayers' representatives. The row subsided very quickly when it became known that returned prisoners of war were to be invited. The guests were photographed with the official party and at least one of the figures in khaki battledress had an empty sleeve. In October 1945 the Priory Ruins were bought for the town for £850 from the Kenward family for the price offered in 1925.

In March 1945 after delays due to road improvements on the Landport estate the first town bus service commenced. A half hourly service from the Nevill Estate to Landport with pay-as-you

1994 Wardens' post No 8, door and reinforced roof visible in the wall in Western Road   *R A Elliston*

enter buses. In the same month it was announced that Mr and Mrs J C Robinson of Isfield had donated £4,000 to build a new Scout and Guide headquarters in the town. This was constructed on a slum clearance site in St John Street. In June the Council decided to open the town's pleasure gardens from 2.15 pm on Sundays. Objections were raised by the Free Church Council but in the end the new arrangements went ahead but team games would not be allowed. The same body objected to Sunday Concerts in the Town Hall where admission fees were charged. Under the Butler Education Act of 1944 the Council accepted that the Town's Education Committee would cease with education becoming a County Council function. Wartime rationing and trading restrictions had affected the profitability of the Lewes Co-operative Society in West Street. For the first time in its eighty-year history it failed to declare a dividend.

Peace had returned to Lewes, a further nine years of rationing followed, victory had exacted a price, the town was much shabbier and families mourned their lost ones. The "Cold War" and the Berlin airlift heralded a return to an "Uneasy Peace". International tensions have continued to this day. Leaders who ignore the lessons of history make the same mistakes that have been made in the past. It is to be hoped that the lessons from the thirties have been well learnt by the decision makers. With an effective United Nations it is possible that no writer in the future will have to record the history of Lewes in another war.

18. Roll of Honour

The War Memorial at the top of School Hill, dedicated to the fallen of World War One on 6th September 1922, was deemed to be the appropriate place to record the names of those from the town who gave their lives in World War Two. Accordingly the Borough Council, following the practice of 1918, invited residents to send in names for inscription on the memorial. By 21st July 1950 only 42 names had been received. The Council were certain that this hardly represented the full number lost. In the circumstances a small plaque, costing £37, approval for the expenditure of Council monies having been obtained from the Ministry of Health, was added dedicating the memorial to the Second World War fallen. Inscriptions from the Prime Minister, Mr Winston Churchill's "Finest Hour" speech, were also added to the shaft.

In 1977 the Town Council again considered the matter and the Mayor, The Rev John G Hapgood MA and Clr Dr Graham Mayhew JP agreed to undertake the research to identify the remainder of the town's war dead. This was a particularly difficult task after such a passage of time but investigations in old newspapers and publicity enabled a list of 126 names to be inscribed on two panels on the north and south faces of the plinth. This memorial was dedicated on Sunday 1st March 1981 in the presence of over 100 relatives and representatives of the armed forces' associations.

Key to references in the Roll of Honour.

* Indicates an inscription on St John-sub-Castro memorial
** Indicates an inscription on St John the Baptist Southover memorial
Four servicemen are inscribed on both the above memorials and are indicated thus (*)(**)
(Presumptive) matches information held by Commonwealth War Graves and Registrar General's Department in most respects.
No further information currently available indicates that a reliable match cannot be made after reference to the Commonwealth War Graves, the Registrar General St Catherine's House, the Public Record Office Kew, the Imperial War Museum or the appropriate Service or Regimental Museum.

THE MEMORIAL

Abrey, Private, 2092107, William Thomas, Royal Army Ordnance Corps, 13 South Street died Hurlingham Hospital Middlesex leaving a widow on 7th May 1944. He is buried in Lewes Cemetery.

Ainsworth, Lance Corporal, 2027186, Frederick, 210 Field Company Royal Engineers aged 19, of Green Wall House, Green Wall, killed on active service 19th May 1940 and is interred in Oudenarde Communal Cemetery west of Brussels, Belgium.

Arnold, Sapper, 2067377, George, 210th Field Company Royal Engineers, aged 35, of Cliffe Square, killed in Egypt as a result of an explosion, 14th November 1942 and buried at the El Alamein Cemetery in a collective grave along with comrades killed in the same incident. He was a Pells scholar and a footballer for the Swifts team who worked on Mr T H Rea's farm at Kingston. He is listed on the memorial under his stepfather's name of **Brown**.

Avis, Corporal, T/7904128, Bernard, Royal Army Service Corps, aged 33, of Barons Down Lodge died on Active Service North West Europe 2nd September 1944 and is buried in St Pierre Cemetery Amiens France.

Axtel, Leading Stoker, P/KX85771, Royal Navy, Leonard George of 2 Pump Cottages Beddingham and 14 The Course, HMS *Fleur de Lys*, a Corvette of 925 tons built in 1940, missing presumed killed 14th October 1941, when the ship was sunk by a U boat west of Gibraltar. His loss is commemorated on the Portsmouth Naval Memorial. **

Baker, Sergeant Air Gunner Wireless Operator, 751839, John, RAF 49 Squadron, aged 20, of 122 St Anne's Hill, missing in action 25th August 1940 while flying with a group of 14 Hampden bombers from Scampton Lincolnshire on a mission to Berlin. A Central schoolboy who became a draughtsman in Brighton, enlisting just before the war. His loss is commemorated on the Runnymede Memorial.

Baldwin, Corporal, Albert Ernest, Royal Engineers. Of 36 North Street, returned home at the end of the war having suffered severe injuries and loss of sight while on active service as a result of a land mine explosion. He died shortly after the end of the war.

Ball, J. The Commonwealth War Graves Commission lists 14 servicemen of this name, a positive match has not been made. No other Lewes information discovered. The only family of this name lived at 10 Toronto Terrace but is not known to have had a son. The name is not on the St John-sub-Castro memorial. There may be confusion with J. Bell.

Barnes, Second Lieutenant, 190696, John Archibald, Royal Artillery attached Royal Indian Army Service Corps, aged 26, died of fever on the North West Frontier India January 1943 and is buried in Karachi War Cemetery Pakistan. A Lewes County Schoolboy 1932-5. Until he joined up he worked in a bank. Twin brother of Robert Walter (see below).

Barnes, Second Lieutenant 167164 Robert Walter, aged 26, MA (Cantab) Army Pioneer Corps drowned in Iran 28th March 1943. Member of Lewes Rugby Club, a Lewes County Schoolboy 1932-6. He is buried in Tehran War Cemetery. Twin brother of John Archibald (see above).

Barnett, Sapper, 2113349, Frank Edwin, Royal Engineers 3 Castle Terrace, New Road, married the previous year, died of wounds in Oxford Road Military Hospital Reading 28th October 1940, aged 28. He is buried in Lewes Cemetery. *

Beale, Leading Seaman, 113014, Edward Arthur, Royal Navy, aged 31, married of 2 Spital Road, killed on 25th February 1941 when HMS *Exmoor* a Destoyer of 1,000 tons built in 1940 was sunk by German "E" Boats, off Lowestoft, while on convoy protection duties. He had been in the navy for 15 years and had served in the destroyer *Ivanhoe* during the Altmark Incident and at Dunkirk, he survived the torpedoing of HMS *Ivanhoe*. Before enlisting he attended Western Road School. His loss is commemorated on the Chatham Memorial.

Beck, Able Seaman gunner, P/SD/X1442, Walter Raymond, Royal Naval Volunteer Reserve, HMS *Excellent*, a shore establishment, Whale Island Gunnery School Portsmouth aged 23, of 2 Windover Crescent, a Lewes County schoolboy 1930-4, died from exposure in a ship's boat after the SS *Britannia* 8,700 tons built in 1927, was sunk in the Atlantic Ocean 350 miles west of Freetown. Of the 483 passengers and crew on the vessel bound for India, 249 were lost when she was attacked on the 7th April 1941 by the German commerce raider *Thor*. Before the war A/S Beck worked in the County Medical Officer's Department. His loss is commemorated on the Portsmouth Naval Memorial. **

Bell John, Company Sergeant Major, 6391060, 7th Battalion Royal Sussex Regiment, aged 43, of 29 Meridian Road a married man with four children. A Bisley Prizewinner injured at the Battle of Amiens May 1940 who died of wounds 8th October 1940. A first World War veteran and as part of the honour guard played "The Last Post" at the unveiling ceremony of the Lewes War Memorial in 1922. A member of Cliffe Bonfire Society. He is buried Viroflay New Communal Cemetery near Versailles France. *

Beney Sergeant Air Gunner, 1277051, Eric T, Royal Air Force 7 Squadron killed in action 8th March 1943 while flying a mission in a Lancaster bomber from Waddington, he is buried Les Soudesmes Cemetery France. *

CSM John Bell

Beney Ronald John, Gunner, 1605137, Royal Artillery, aged 30, died 14th February 1942. His loss is commemorated on the Singapore Memorial.*

Bennett, Sergeant 6403462, Frank E, 4th Battalion Royal West Kent Regiment, aged 26, killed in action at Kohima Burma 6th April 1944. His loss is commemorated on the Rangoon Memorial. The only son of the landlord of the *Lewes Arms*, who enlisted in 1942. Former postal worker. *

Blythe, Flying Officer Navigator, 133459, Ronald, Royal Air Force 49 Squadron, aged 20, of 5 Manor Terrace Southover, missing on operations in a Lancaster bomber flying from Scampton Lincolnshire over Cologne after being attacked by German nightfighters, June 1943. Found in the North Sea and buried at Vlissingen Northern Cemetery Flushing, Holland. An Accountant at Holland, Frank and Co, in the High Street, a sportsman and member of the operatic society and Rugby club, educated at the County School for Boys 1934-41. **

Bolton, misspelt should read **Boulton** Flying Officer, 40362, J E, Royal Air Force 310 (Czech) Squadron, Czech Military Cross (Post), aged 22, an only son, formerly of Prince Edward's Road. Shot down while leading Czech squadron in Hurricane fighters from Duxford, 9th September 1940. Educated at the County School for Boys 1930-32. He is interred at Bandon Hill Cemetery Beddington Surrey.

Boughey, Second Lieutenant, 124549, John Fletcher, Coldstream Guards, son of Sir George Monteith and Lady Boughey 9th Baronet, of the Coombe, Glynde and Malling House, aged 21, killed in action 31st August 1940, and buried in South Malling Churchyard. He played for the Sussex County Cricket Club.

FO J E Boulton

Breeds, Private, 6403035, Ronald Clifford, 4th Battalion Royal Sussex Regiment, aged 24, of 45 St John Street, died of wounds in the Middle East, 27th October 1942, enlisted January 1940. Dairyman for Uridges Southover, his brother also served in the forces. Pte Breeds is commemorated on the Alamein Memorial. *

Brown, Sapper, George Arnold see under entry for **Arnold** George.

Brown, Sapper, 2063756, Raymond, 210 Field Company Royal Engineers, of Offham Terrace formerly of 17 Thomas Street killed in action Belgium 1940. He was married the previous year. He was a Territorial and worked at the Phoenix Ironworks. He was also a member of Cliffe Bonfire Society.

Button, Sapper, 1986286, Alfred, Royal Engineers, No 9 Movement Control Group, aged 27, married ten months, of 22 Leicester Road, died in the 24th (London) hospital Belfast after an operation, 3rd August 1942 and is buried in Lewes Cemetery. A railway worker and holder of Boy Scouts Gilt Cross for gallantry.

Caplin Able Seaman Richard Merchant Navy, aged 58, of 1 Swallow Street Poplar London born in Lewes. Lost with SS *Mallard* 352 tons built in 1936, while carrying a cargo of stone in convoy from Newlyn to London 10th July 1940. The convoy was attacked by a German "E" boat. *Mallard* had a crew of eight plus a gunner, five crew and the gunner were lost, the rest were taken prisoner.

Card Colour Sergeant, 6395628, Wallace Syril, aged 30, 7th Battalion Royal Sussex Regiment 20th May 1940 buried at Abbeville Communal Cemetery extension France (presumptive). *

Carpenter, Corporal, 775542, Francis Charles, 210 Field Company Royal Engineers, aged 30, of 5 York Street, killed in action 13th May 1940 and buried in the Oudenarde Cemetery west of Brussels, Belgium. *

Casselden, Petty Officer Telegraphist, P/WX666, George Albert, Royal Navy, aged 26, of 47 New Road missing on operations, when *HMLC(H) 185* of 384 tons was mined during operation Neptune (Normandy landings) 25th June 1944. This type of Landing craft was designed to hold 200 men for up to 48 hours and land them in the follow up to an assault. The designation (H) stands for headquarters craft which would be fitted with additional communication equipment. This explains PO Casselden's presence on board. His loss is commemorated on the Head Post Office memorial and the Portsmouth Naval Memorial. He left a widow and three daughters. Before the war he was a Post Office sorter and counter clerk. *

Chadwick, Sergeant, 3655324, Frank, 13th Battalion Parachute Regiment, The Airborne Division, aged 25, of the *Snowdrop Inn* South Street killed in action in North West Europe 3rd January 1945 and buried Hotton War Cemetery south east of Namur Belgium. He had served throughout the war and had taken part in the D-day landings. Notification of his death was received on the day his second daughter was born.

Chapman, Sapper, 2030565, Joseph Patrick Anthony, aged 28, 35th Fortress Company, Royal Engineers youngest son of the family, of Keere Street, missing later reported killed at Singapore.

A time serving soldier who spent four years in the Far East, previously employed at Baxter's The Printers. A sportsman, his original home at New Street was destroyed in the bombing 20th January 1943. It is known that subsequent to being captured he died in Thailand on 2nd December 1943 and is buried in the Kanchanaburi Cemetery on the Mekong River 70 miles from Bankok.

Comyns, Major, 57052, William Francis, 9th Field Regiment Royal Artillery, aged 33, killed in action 22nd April 1945, and buried in Becklingen War Cemetery Soltau north of Hanover Germany.

Cook, Flight Sergeant, 1158471, Donald Herbert William, 97 Squadron Royal Air Force, aged 24, of 31 New Road. Killed in action 14th January 1944 whilst flying a Lancaster from Bourn in Cambridgeshire. His loss is commemorated on the Runnymede Memorial. *

Cork, Able Seaman, P/SD/X 1502, Eric Wallace, Royal Navy, aged 24, of 7 The Fosse. He was engaged and due to be married on his next leave. Died 21st December 1941 whilst a member of the crew of HMS *Celandine* a Corvette of 925 tons. Built in 1941, it sank U 556 in the Atlantic and later served on D-day, finally going to the breakers yard in 1948. A/S Cork is buried in St John Anglican Cemetery Newfoundland Canada. At the outbreak of war he was mobilized from the RNVR and served for two years in HMS *Ark Royal*. He was employed by J Sainsbury's of Brighton. *

Cox, Stoker (1st Class) C/SS 124641 Maurice Jack, aged 39, Royal Navy, an elder son living at 60 North Way killed when HMS *Kelly* a Destroyer Flotilla Leader of 1,760 tons was sunk off Crete by aircraft on 23rd May 1942. Survivors were rescued and taken to Alexandria by another destroyer HMS *Kipling* the adopted ship of Brighton. Stoker Cox was employed at Eastwood's Cement Works, was a scholar of Malling School and is commemorated on the Chatham Naval Memorial.

Cramer, Sapper, 2072276, Arthur, 211 Field Park Company Royal Engineers, of 16 Dale Road last seen by fellow soldiers on the beach at Dunkirk on 31st May 1940. His loss is commemorated on the Dunkirk Memorial. He had three brothers and a sister in the armed forces.

Crock, Gunner, 2046428, Patrick Amos, 4th Regiment Royal Horse Artillery, aged 24, eldest son of the family of 5 Mount Place killed in action in the Middle East at El Alamein 30th October 1942, and is buried in the El Alamein War Cemetery Egypt. Enlisted 1938, a Pells scholar, a member of St John's-sub-Castro Choir, a Commercial Square Bonfire Boy. *

Cruttenden, Private, 6104043, Frederick, 1st/7th Queens Royal West Surrey Regiment, aged 34, of 6 De Montfort Flats. Killed in action 21st July 1944 and buried in Ranville War Cemetery near Ouistreham, France. He enlisted in 1941. Before the the war he was employed as a building worker.

Cunnington. Corporal, 2042346, Cedric Augustus, 279 Field Company Royal Engineers, a married man, aged 26, of 3 South Place Flats died of wounds in action, North-west Europe 3rd December 1944 and interred in Nederweert War Cemetery Holland, west of Roermond. A Central School boy who had worked as a butcher for Mr C Colbourne. **

Davis, Marine, PO/X100583, Albert Richard, Royal Marines, aged 30, of 5 Talbot Terrace, died at Portsmouth while on active service February 1944 and is buried in Lewes Cemetery. *

Donovan, Private, 14989655, Francis Edward, 1st Battalion The Queens Royal West Surrey Regiment, aged 19, killed in action in Burma 10th June 1945. His loss is commemorated on the Rangoon Memorial

Dunk, Boy 1st class, P/JX157915, Walter William, Royal Navy, aged 17 of 51 Priory Street died when HMS *Royal Oak* a Battleship of 29,000 tons built in 1916, was torpedoed by a German submarine U-47 at a supposedly safe anchorage at Scapa Flow with the loss of 810 men on 14th October 1939. An only child, a scholar of St Pancras School, he belonged to the YMCA, and was a keen footballer. He enlisted two years previously as a wireless telegrapher and was the first Lewesian to become a casualty of the war. His loss is commemorated on the Portsmouth Memorial. **

Dunne, Lance Corporal, 7903863, Frederick Francis, Trooper, Tank Delivery Regiment Royal Armoured Corps, aged 36, a married man of 45 Priory Street died of wounds while in the Middle East 15th November 1942 after two years' service. He is buried in Halfaya Sollum War Cemetery. **

L/Cpl F Dunne

Edwards, Second Lieutenant, 86445, Frank Bernard, 5th Medium Regiment Royal Artillery, of The *Crown Hotel* a County school boy missing in action 29th May 1940. His loss is commemorated on the Dunkirk Memorial. *

Edwards, Lance Sergeant, 5575484, Leslie Arthur, 2nd Battalion Wiltshire Regiment, aged 30, of 7 Toronto Terrace wounded in Italy October 1943, died 21st February 1944 and is buried in Minturno War Cemetery.

Ensell, Midshipman, Maurice Austin Standish, Royal Navy, aged 18, lost while serving in HMS *Neptune*, a Cruiser of 7,000 tons built in 1934. In action at Calabria 1940, the sinking of the Bismark 1941, the Malta Convoy Force "K" 1941, finally sunk by a mine off Tripoli 19th December 1941. Midshipman Ensell had been a Cadet at Dartmouth Naval College becoming Chief Cadet and receiving the King's Dirk. He was the son of the Rev Ensell of St Anne's Rectory. His loss is commemorated on the Plymouth Naval Memorial.

Fairweather, Leading Aircraftman, 1808349, R W, Royal Air Force (Volunteer Reserve), aged 22, of 13 Malling Down, son of the Lewes Stationmaster, posted missing on active flying operations, subsequently buried 7th February 1947 in Lewes Cemetery.

Fellows Leading Seaman, C/JX129405, Frederick, Royal Navy, aged 32, lost in Destroyer HMS *Blean* 1,050 tons built in 1942 sunk by a U boat west of Oran Algeria while on Convoy Duties to North Africa, 11th December 1942. A Pells Scholar, formerly of Edward Street. His loss is commemorated on the Chatham Naval Memorial.

Funnell, Private, 14422615, Edward John (Jack), 6th Battalion Kings Own Scottish Borderers aged 19, younger son of the family, formerly of 3 Lee Road died of wounds 2nd August 1944 in Normandy. Before the war he was employed at Novington Manor Plumpton by Mr W D Rodgers. He is burried in Hottot-Le-Bagues cemetery Calvados.

Funnell, Private, 5346233, Leslie Alfred, 4th Battalion Wiltshire Regiment, British Liberation Army, aged 31, of 109 South Street killed 24th November 1944 in Holland, he left a widow and two daughters. He volunteered for the army in 1940, and landed on D-day. A scholar of Central Boys' School, he worked for Yorkshire Bakery and the Ringmer Building Works, he was a member of South Street Bonfire Society. He is commemorated on Groesbeek Memorial Opende, Holland.

Gale, Corporal, George, 1869504, 11 Field Coy Royal Engineers, aged 29, of 2 De La Warr Green a regular soldier one of three brothers serving in the army, died of wounds June 1940 and buried in Lewes Cemetery. Formerly a bricklayer, he was a keen boxer and Boy Scout. He left a widow and four children. *

Geraghty, Captain, 267455, John Oliver, Royal Army Service Corps, Mentioned in Dispatches, aged 39. Buried Lewes Cemetery 31st March 1946.

Gibbs Private, 23553, Charles, Royal Army Ordnance Corps, aged 55, of 24 Station Street died in a military hospital in Hertfordshire after a major operation, and was buried in Lewes Cemetery. For many years manager of Hepworths and later owned his own outfitting business in Station Street. A World War One veteran volunteering for the National Defence Force in September 1939 transferring to the Royal Sussex Regiment. An active member of the British Legion.

Gibson, Captain, 143584, Ian Grant, 4th Battalion The Welch Regiment stationed at Faversham Kent, aged 22, a student whose home was Barnes London SW13, born 1921 at Bucklow Knutsford Cheshire died 12th August 1943 following a grenade accident at Ashcombe near Lewes. He is buried in Lewes Cemetery. No other Lewes connection has been found. (See Misadventure)

Gilham, Able Seaman, LT/JX202140, Stanley, Royal Naval Patrol Service, aged 31, died on active service in HM Yacht *Dunlin*. The vessel was a private yacht the *Amazone* of 229 tons hired in 1940 as an examination vessel. She survived the war to be returned to her owners in 1945. A/S Gilham died on 24th March 1942 leaving a wife and daughter. Before the war he managed the Lansdown Place Fisheries. He lived at Brighton and is buried in the Brighton and Preston Cemetery.

Glover H misspelt should be **Grover,** Bombardier, G/4268, Harold Russell, 6th Field Regiment Royal Canadian Artillery, killed in action 19th April 1945. He was married to a Lewesian. He is buried in Holten Canadian War Cemetery Edeventer Holland. **

Grayson, Flight Lieutenant, 46769, Charles, 228 squadron Royal Air Force, aged 32, eldest son of the family of 29 Leicester Road killed July 1945 in a flying accident in Wales. He attended St Anne's School and Uckfield Grammar School. Joined RAF in 1932 at Halton and flew Hurricanes from Tangmere in the Battle of Britain parachuting to safety so qualifying for Caterpillar Club membership. Served for two years in Canada at Medicine Hat training pilots, on return flew Sunderlands and Liberators for Coastal Command. He is buried in Lewes Cemetery.

Green, Second Lieutenant, 314915, Anthony Charles, 13th Battalion Queens Royal Regiment, aged 23, only son of the family of 3 Fitzroy Road died of wounds in Holland 27th September 1944. Educated at Pells School, a member of St John's Church. He was a member of the editorial staff of the East Sussex Express and County Herald. He is buried in the Arnhem War Cemetery Holland. *

Haines, Sub-Lieutenant, Pilot, Peter, Fleet Air Arm, HMS *Jackdaw* a shore base at Crail at the easternmost tip of Fife, Scotland of *"Trevose"* Gundreda Road, killed 20th December 1941. Youngest son of Percy Haines, Outfitter of School Hill. He is buried in Guildford Cemetery Surrey.

Hadley, Provost Lance Corporal,7690083, Arthur E, aged 33, of 32 Caburn Crescent died while a Prison of War in Thailand on 16th August 1943. Before the war he was employed by the Prudential Insurance Company. A keen club motorcyclist, he was called up in 1940. Earlier news of his capture came in May on the second birthday of his daughter who was the only child born in Warship Week the previous year. He is buried in Thanbyuzayat Cemetery Thailand.

Haldey A E Reported in the Sussex Express March 1981 that this name was an incorrect inscription of the preceding name Arthur Hadley.

Hall, Flight Sergeant Wireless operator/Air Gunner 908443, Charles Frank, Royal Air Force (Volunteer Reserve) aged 25, posted missing while on an operational flight 7th September 1941. A Lewes County Schoolboy who is listed on the memorial section "missing believed killed". Some time elapsed before the family learnt that he had been captured. In 1995 he was living in retirement in the West country.

Hankins Sergeant Wireless Operator/Air Gunner, 1353269, Philip, Royal Air Force Volunteer Reserve, aged 24, of 8 Nevill Crescent, enlisted in 1940. A member of 102 (Ceylon) Squadron was killed in action on the night of 25/26th June 1942. His plane a mark II Halifax bomber flying from Topcliffe Yorkshire was on a raid to Bremen when it was lost without trace. A King's Scout of the 1st Lewes Troop he was also an assistant Cubmaster. Formerly an employee of the Ringmer Building Works. His death is commemorated on the Runnymede Memorial.

Hansford, Boy Telegraphist, P/JX171869, Peter Colin, Royal Navy, of 39 North Way eldest son of the family missing believed killed in HMS *Cornwall* built in 1928, a 6-inch gun cruiser of 10,000 tons, one of four ships, the others being a sister ship HMS *Dorsetshire*, the aircraft carrier HMS *Hermes* and a destroyer HMS *Vampire*, sunk by Japanese dive bombers off Trincomalee Ceylon 5th April 1942. Educated in Lewes enlisted November 1939 and passed out as a wireless operator October 1941. His loss is commemorated on Portsmouth Naval Memorial.

Telegraphist P C Hansford

Hathaway, Aircraftman, 1437229, Albert, Royal Air Force, of 17 Paddock Road, aged 22, drowned at Haifa while on active service in the Middle East in 1942. He was a Pells schoolboy and a member of St John's-sub-Castro choir. He worked for Mr George Poole's racing stables. A/C Hathaway is buried in Haifa Cemetery. *

Hathaway, Flight Sergeant/Air Gunner, 1330482, Stanley, 83 Squadron Royal Air Force (Volunteer Reserve), aged 21, of 17 Paddock Road missing on an operational flight in a Lancaster bomber from Wyton Lincolnshire, 13th May 1943. A Pells schoolboy and member of St John's-sub-Castro choir. Before volunteering in 1939 he had worked at the Lewes Co-operative Society. He is buried in Amersfoot Central Cemetery Holland. * Brother of Albert (see above).

Hayward, Private, 5389366, Thomas Alfred, 1st Battalion Oxfordshire and Buckinghamshire Light Infantry, aged 29, of 66 Malling Street killed in North West Europe when the unit's headquarters came under enemy shellfire 8th February 1945, educated at Uckfield Grammar and the County School for Boys'. His widow was serving in the ATS. Before joining up he was employed by the East Sussex County Council in the Public Health and Taxation Offices. He is buried in Jonkerbos War Cemetery Nijmegen Holland.

Herriot, Corporal, 2030738, George, 210 Field Company Royal Engineers of 14 Dale Road, aged 24, last seen in an ambulance in France May 1940, died of wounds between the 27th May and 2nd June 1940. He had been a member of the Territorial Army for nine years and worked for Baxter's the Printers and the Ringmer Building Works before the war. He played football, cricket and was a member of the Lewes Darts' League. His brother was in the Royal Engineers. Cpl Herriot is buried in Longuenesse Souvenir Cemetery St Omer France.

Private T A Hayward

Holford Petty Officer Writer, P/MX61048, Ronald Franklin aged 20, RN Lost when the cruiser HMS *Dunedin* of 4,850 tons built 1919 was sunk 24th November 1941 by a U-boat in the Atlantic, on passage between West Africa and Brazil. A pupil at the County Boys' School 1931-6. Before enlisting he worked in the County Clerk's Department. He is commemorated on the Portsmouth Naval Memorial. *

Horton, Driver, 1946137, Ronald Frank, aged 22, Royal Engineers 140th Mechanical Equipment Workshop and Park Company, of 9 Chapel Hill, Captured by the Italians in October 1942. Drowned some time between 26th October and 14th November when a ship carrying prisoners of war to Italy was torpedoed by a British Submarine. He was one of five brothers and worked for Boot's the Chemist before joining up. His loss is commemorated on the El Alamein Memorial.

Mclean-Inglis, Piper, 2766032, Kenneth Michael, 1st Battalion The Black Watch, of 45 Cliffe High Street killed 17th March 1943 while serving in Tunisia. Before he joined up in November 1941 he was a member of "A" Company 16th Sussex Home Guard. He was a member of Cliffe Church choir, and a server. He was also a keen Boy Scout and educated at Mountfield Road School. He is buried in Sfax War Cemetery Tunisia.

Jacobs, Private, 14388135, James Ernest, 2nd/6th Battalion Queens Royal West Surrey Regiment, aged 20, of 1a Castle Banks killed in action 3rd August 1944. He was an ARP Messenger and Warden, and had been employed at Marsh the Butcher and the Lewes Co-operative Society, he was a member of St John-sub-Castro Church choir and he had attended the Pells School. His loss is commemorated on the Bayeux Memorial France. *

James, Miss Betty, Women's Land Army, aged 27, of Southdown Avenue, died in February 1942 in Uckfield Hospital a week after a machinery accident while on duty at Shenlands Farm, Blackboys. She was a scholar at the County School for Girls'. The funeral and interment took place St John-sub-Castro church. One of the two Lewes women to give their lives on War Service. *

Jenner, Aircraftwoman 1, 2004609, Ena, Women's Auxiliary Air Force, aged 26, of 24 Eastport Lane died 26th June 1942 in the RAF General Hospital Cowbridge near Bridgend South Wales, following an operation, after an illness that lasted two weeks. She had been in the service for one year, her husband was in the Royal Armoured Corps. Mrs Jenner is the second woman commemorated on the memorial and she is buried in Lewes Cemetery.

Johnson, Leading Writer, P/MX58762, Stanley Frederick, Royal Navy, aged 23, of 12 Mountfield Road among 1,755 lost when HMS *Hood*, a Battle cruiser of 42,000 tons built in 1916, was blown up by gunfire from the German battleship *Bismark* 24th May 1941 in the Denmark Straits. He attended the Pells School and for five years worked for the solicitors Blaker Son and Young. He joined the navy in January 1939 as a career entrant, he had passed his Petty Officer's examination and was undergoing training for a commission. He is commemorated on the Portsmouth Memorial. **

ACW1 Ena Jenner

Kemp, Flight Sergeant Engineer, 1801055, Robert William, Royal Air Force 626 Squadron, aged 22, of 45 Priory Street missing while on operations over Belgium, 22nd May 1944 while flying a Lancaster bomber from Wickenby Lincolnshire, he left a widow and two sons. Before the war he was employed at the Ringmer Building Works. He is buried in Schoonselhot Cemetery Antwerp Belgium. **

Ketchell, Sergeant Pilot, 1155502, Brian John, Royal Air Force 102 Squadron, aged 23, of 71 Park Street Falmer, missing in action 8th December 1942 while piloting a Halifax bomber flying from Dalton Yorkshire to Turin, Italy. A pupil of the County School for Boys' 1930-8, School Captain in 1938. He entered the Civil Service as an executive officer in the Board of Trade's Marine Department. Member of the school and Falmer Scout Troops. Joined the RAF in 1940 and spent a year in Canada under the Air Training Scheme. His loss is commemorated on the Runnymede Memorial.

Lawrence, Gunner, 835018, G, 346th Battery 87th Field Regiment Royal Artillery, of Bristol died 1st September 1941 at Glynde buried in Lewes Cemetery. (See Misadventure chapter) No Lewes connection has been found.

Leaney, Boy (1st Class), P/JX171791, Robert Thomas, Royal Navy, aged 17, an elder son living at 10 Lansdown Place lost in HMS *Hood* 24th May 1941, three days after joining the ship. Attended Malling and Western Road Schools. At fifteen years of age he entered the training ship HMS *Ganges* and then HMS *George* another training ship. HMS *Hood* was his first sea-going ship. He is commemorated on the Porstmouth Memorial.

Lumb Flying Officer, 61284, Theodore A, Royal Air Force 83 Squadron killed on operations flying a Manchester bomber from Wyton Lincolnshire 23rd September 1942. Member of Lewes Rugby Club. He is buried Kiel War Cemetery.

Martin, Sergeant, 990898, Arthur Richard, Parachute Regiment, of 66 Western Road missing at Arnhem 1944. He had served in the African campaign and in Sicily. He joined the army in 1940 before this he had worked in footwear shops, Milwards and Huggetts of School Hill. His younger brother was also in the army. Sergeant Martin was captured at Arnhem and sent to Fallingbostel POW camp. His name, listed on the memorial section missing believed killed, is not included in any list of casualties other than the Red Cross list of prisoners of war. It is assumed that he survived the war.

Martin Leading Airman Telegraphist/Air Gunner FX/96799, George Henry 772 Squadron Fleet Air Arm based at HMS *Landrail* Scotland. Crashed in the sea at Iron Rock, South West of the Isle of Arran whilst a crew member of a Miles Martinet Aircraft, a two-seater wooden plane used for towing targets, on the 17th of February 1944. His death is commemorated on the Lee-on-Solent Memorial.

Millot, Sergeant, 14352895, J, Royal Army Medical Corps attached to 9th Parachute Regiment, aged 35, killed in action 24th March 1945. He is buried in the Reichswald Forest War Cemetery south-west of Cleve Germany.

Mills, Lance Corporal, 6094018, Patrick Arthur, 2nd/7th Battalion Queens Royal West Surrey Regiment, aged 27, younger son of the family of 28 Nevill Road was wounded while serving in the Central Mediterranean Theatre, died in a prisoner of war hospital in Badmunder Germany 18th March 1945, following an enforced march westward from a prison camp, buried in the Central Cemetery, Hanover. He served for four years and was at Dunkirk. He attended Western Road School and had worked for Mence Smiths in the High Street.

Monday, Gunner, 1098609, Joseph James, 4th Medium Regiment Royal Artillery, of 13 Market Street, aged 22, died while on active service in North Africa 28th February 1943. Before enlistment he worked as a gardener in Lewes. He is buried in Medjez-El-Bab War Cemetery Tunisa.

Moore, Sapper, 20143520, Frederick Martin, 270 Field Company Royal Engineers, aged 27, third son of the family formerly of Dale Road who died of wounds received while on active service in Italy on 2nd October 1943. He served overseas for two years with the 1st Army in Tunisia then at the Salerno landings. A County Grammar School Boy

Gnr J Monday

and assistant Scout Master of the 1st Lewes troop, he also worked at W H Smith's station bookstall. He is buried in Coriano Ridge War Cemetery near Rimini Italy **

Moppett, Leading Aircraftman, 1281149, Dennis George, Royal Air Force (Volunteer Reserve), aged 24, only son of the family of 6 Abinger Place (now renumbered 25). Died on Moena Island South Celebes on 6th January 1945 after three years a prisoner of the Japanese. A repatriated fellow prisoner brought the news in October 1945. The bearer of the news also brought with him a diary kept by Dennis Moppett on odd scraps of paper, written in homemade ink. The diary was hidden in a bamboo cane and referred to the writer continuing to follow his pre-war hobby, which had been radio. It was his way of saying that he had been in touch with the progress of the war but sadly he died in the camp hospital before the war ended. A County Grammar School boy who was employed in the Sussex Rural Workers' Insurance Society, he was a member of the Lewes branch of the Crusaders' Union and volunteered a few months after war broke out. He was captured at Singapore and was first held on Java. He is buried in Ambon War Cemetery Indonesia. (*)(**)

Newham, Lieutenant, 133017, Hugh Malpas, Royal Army Service Corps, aged 42, died of wounds in the Middle East, leaving a widow, on 3rd March 1942. Manager of Mansfield's Motor Engineers, member of the South Saxon Lodge, a first war veteran on the officers' reserve, he volunteered for overseas service at the outbreak of war. A keen yachtsman he took a small boat to Dunkirk and later to St Valèry-en-Caux where he rescued 16 injured French sailors. He is buried at Tel-el-Keber War Cemetery Egypt.

Newman, Flight Sergeant Air Gunner, 925797, Hubert Ernest, Royal Air Force 90 Squadron, aged 24, lost on operations over Russelheim Germany, 26th August 1944. He is buried in Dornbach War Cemetery south of Munich, Germany.

Newnham, Able Seaman, P/SSX24399, William Harold, Royal Navy, aged 20, of *Weald View* The Avenue, drowned when the destroyer HMS *Glowworm* built in 1936 of 1,345 tons was sunk off Norway April 8th 1940 by gunfire from the 10,000-ton German cruiser *Hipper*. He had served in the navy for eighteen months. He is commemorated on the Porstmouth Memorial. *

Olliver, Private, 6411955, Ronald, Queens Own Royal West Kent Regiment, aged 19, of 6 Priory Place was killed in 9th January 1944 while serving in Burma, before enlisting he was employed in London. He is buried in Taukkyan War Cemetery Rangoon Burma. **

Olliver, Driver, T/279703, Stanley G, Royal Army Service Corps, aged 35, of 24 Horsfield Road. Died in Cambridge Military Hospital Aldershot November 1941 leaving a widow and a son. He had been employed by the Lewes Co-operative Society for 21 years and was in charge of the provisions' department when he was called up in July 1940. He is buried in Lewes Cemetery. (*)(**)

Pte R Olliver

Olliver, Aircraftman (1st class), 1295038, William James, Royal Air Force, aged 22, of 24 Nevill Road. Died following an operation after a flying accident. He had served for twenty months. Before enlisting he was employed at Wyborns the Chemist and he was a Pells scholar. He is buried in Lewes Cemetery.

Opie, Private, William, Royal Sussex Regiment, of 102 Western Road missing on active service in the Middle East November 1942. He has served in the army for two and a half years and before enlistment was employed by Mr Relf, Grocer, of High Street Southover. His name is included in the group on the memorial as missing believed killed. There is no record at the Commonwealth War Graves Commission of his death, nor is his name on the Army Roll of Honour at the Public Record Office Kew. The service register of deaths of soldiers overseas at St Catherine's House does not show his name. The Lewes Electoral Roll for November 1945 lists W H Opie who was not listed before the war or there again afterwards. It is presumed that the missing report proved ultimately to be incorrect.

Ormerod, Captain, 113691, George Wareing Drewry, 232 Battery, 67 Medium Regiment, Honourable Artillery Company, aged 33, one of the three sons of a former Chief Constable of East Sussex Colonel G H Ormerod of King Henry's Road. A married man, killed in action in Normandy 11th July 1944. A lawyer, a graduate of Queen's College BA (Oxon) who lived in London and became a Covent Garden jeweller. A member of the Lewes Rugby Club. He is buried in St Manvieu Cemetery Cheux France. *

Parsons, Sapper, 2066518, George Charles, 582 Field Company Royal Engineers, aged 24, of 62 Priory Street, a Territorial, landed on D-day and fought through France, Belgium and Germany. He was with a comrade when both were run down and fatally injured by a train on 8th February 1946 near Homsburg Germany. They were travelling in a Jeep and were held up by floods, and decided to cross a railway bridge on foot but did not hear the approaching train. He attended the Pells School. He is buried in the Reichswald Forest War Cemetery Cleve, Germany.

Pasquale, Lance Corporal, 7359503, Joseph, aged 25, Royal Army Medical Corps Medical Section No 4 Commando, killed in action 6th June 1944 leaving a widow and an infant son. He is buried in Hermanville War Cemetery Courseilles France. *

Piper, Private, 14416980, Kenneth Arthur, Royal Army Ordnance Corps, aged 19, of 21 Dale Road died while on active service in the Central Hospital Birmingham following a road accident on 18th November 1943. He had two brothers, one in the army. He volunteered nine months earlier. Beforehand he worked for the Belgrave Supply Depot (Motor Accessories) Lansdown Place, a member of St Michael's Church, the Lewes ATC and ARP Messenger. A former pupil at Pells School. He is buried in Lewes Cemetery. **

Pollard, Rifleman, 6403842, Albert Edward, 12th Battalion Kings Royal Rifle Corps, aged 22, youngest son of the family, a brother and sister were serving with the forces, of 18 Landport Road killed in action in Normandy 1st August 1944. Before his call up in 1940 he had worked for the Home and Colonial stores and the Ringmer Building Works, he attended Western Road School. He is buried in Holtot-les-Bagues War Cemetery Tilly-sur-Seuelles Caen, France. (*)(**)

Pollard, Private, 14663626, Frederick Arthur, 2nd Battalion Kings Shropshire Light Infantry, aged

32, of 11 Horsfield Road killed in action in 17th October 1944 in North West Europe. He left a widow and a young baby. He was called up in March 1940. Before enlistment he was a lorry driver for the East Sussex War Agricultural Executive. He was a scholar of Central School. He is buried in Mierlo War Cemetery near Eindhoven, Holland. (*)(**)

Pollard, Trooper, 6405142, Stanley William, 5th Battalion Royal Inniskilling Dragoon Guards, Royal Armoured Corps, aged 23, of 17 St Peter's Place killed in action whilst advancing into a German town, 30th March 1945, as a Wireless Operator/Gunner in the leading tank of a troop. A Central Schoolboy who worked as a painter and decorator joining The Royal Sussex Regiment in 1940 when he was 18, later transferring to the Royal Armoured Corps. He is buried in the Reichswald Forest War Cemetery Cleve, Germany.

Pugh, Lance Corporal, 1870777, Albert William, 629 Field Squadron Royal Engineers, aged 27, of Birmingham, son-in-law of Mr and Mrs Day of North Street. Killed in action on D-day 6th June 1944. He was married at Eastgate Baptist Church in March 1944, but never saw his son born in October 1944. He is buried in Hermannville War Cemetery Courseilles, France. *

Redman, Corporal, 610728, Douglas George, Royal Air Force, killed in flying operations over Italy 3rd April 1945, aged 24, of *Green Bank* Rotten Row. Joined RAF in 1938 from Roborough School Eastbourne, second son of the family, his father was head of the Auctioneers J R Thornton and Co of Lewes Cattle Market. Before enlisting was employed as a Surveyor. He is buried in Naples Military Cemetery. **

Redman, Sergeant, Royal Artillery, Geoffrey Henry, seriously injured at Anzio in January 1944, died as a result of war injuries in King's College Hospital London on 22nd December 1950 after spells in Catterick and Roehampton Military Hospitals. Educated at Roborough School, Eastbourne, worked in Thornton's Auctioneers, a member of the Rugby Club and brother of Douglas George. (see above) He is buried in the family grave in Lewes Cemetery.

Richards, Corporal, 14429728, St Jean Marvin, aged 19, 12th (10th Battalion The Green Howards [Yorkshire Regiment]) Parachute Regiment Army Air Corps, born in Dorset and domiciled in Kent but formerly of 10 Paddock Road, killed in action North West Europe April 1945. He landed in Normandy on D-day. He was a keen sportsman excelling at boxing, football and cross-country running. Two brothers also served, one in the Navy the other in the army, a prisoner of war in the Far East who survived torpedoing while being transferred to Japan. Corporal Richards is buried in the Reichwald Forest War Cemetery Cleve Germany.

Ridley Wing Commander, 03036, Claude Alward DSO MC aged 45 of *Bleak House* 6 De Warrenne Road. As a Second Lieutenant in Royal Fusiliers was awarded the MC in 1915 and mentioned in dispatches five times. Royal Aero Club pilot's certificate 1915, transferred to Royal Flying Corps. Awarded DSO, 14th November 1916 for his part in bringing down Zeppelin L15 during the defence of London. Retired from RAF in 1928, married the daughter of Sir Robert McAlpine. Recalled to service in 1939 died in London from natural causes 27th June 1942. He is buried in Saints Mary and Margaret Churchyard Stow Maries Essex. *

Rogers Company Sergeant Major, 6341763, Ronald, 1st Battalion Queens Own Royal West Kent Regiment, aged 30, of 22 Leicester Road. Killed in action in Italy 28th July 1944. He joined the army at the aged of 17 and was a reservist when the war started. Buried in Florence War Cemetery Italy.

Ruck, Driver, T/117102, Albert Edward, aged 32, Royal Army Service Corps, a married man formerly of 6 Timber Yard Cottages was killed in action at Dunkirk on 12th June 1940. The notification was received by the family after the war in September 1945. Before enlistment he was employed by the Home and Colonial Stores and Hooper the Butchers and lived at 9 Mill Path Ringmer. His name is inscribed on the Ringmer Memorial and with no known grave he is also commemorated on the Dunkirk War Memorial.

Scoates, Gunner, 892398, Ronald E, 98th Field Regiment Royal Artillery of 3 Firle Crescent, killed in action 25th May 1940, buried in Steenwerck Communal Cemetery France.

Scrase, Leading Aircraftman, 1446658, Raymond, Royal Air Force, aged 22, of 22 Valley Road died 18th September 1943 while on active service in Assam India from an acute illness. Before joining the RAF in August in 1941 he was a member of the Home Guard. He attended Central School, was a choir boy at Southover Church and was employed at Beard's Brewery. He is buried in Gauhati War Cemetery Shillong, India. **

Shipp, Sergeant Flight Engineer, 1197149, William Henry, 44 Squadron Royal Air Force, aged 34, a married man with five children, formerly of 57 South Street missing on operations over Berlin 30th March 1943 while flying in a Lancaster bomber from Waddington Lincolnshire. He is buried in the Berlin Central Cemetery. He had served for three years. Before enlistment he was employed by Messrs Elphick and Son.

Simmons Stoker, Charles Royal Navy of 16 Talbot Terrace lost on 7th April 1945 from HM *Torpedo Boat 494*, a wooden launch of 85 tons and a top speed of 20 knots built in 1942 and surviving the war. His loss is commemorated on the Portsmouth Memorial. * (Presumptive)

Smith, Sergeant Navigator/Bomb Aimer, 1331800, Frederick Jasper, Royal Air Force 100 Squadron, aged 28, of 3 St Pancras Gardens killed in action in the Middle East 17th November 1943. He was educated at Central School and Brighton Grammar School. He was employed at the Lewes Post Office. He is buried at Ramleh War Cemetery Israel. **

Souter, Driver, 2584300, Harold W, Royal Corps of Signals, 44th Divisional Signals, aged 22, second son of the family, living at 48 Western Road. Died in hospital in the Middle East from wounds received in action on 9th September 1942. The service records list the name as **Sowter** although pre-war Lewes directories and electoral rolls give the former spelling which the family used in connection with a shoe repairing business.

Steer, Sergeant Flight Engineer, 922222, George, 51 Squadron Royal Air Force (Volunteer Reserve), aged 23, of 139 High Street failed to return from an operational flight in a Halifax bomber from Snaith Yorkshire 15th May 1943. He joined the RAF as a fitter rigger in April 1940 and subsequently volunteered for flying duties. His sister was in the WAAF. On leaving school he was employed at Baxter's Printing works as an engineer's assistant later working in Brighton as a toolmaker, he is buried at Wierden General Cemetery Overijessel Holland.

Stiles Sergeant, 772577, Alfred James Wade, 1st Lothians and Border Horse, aged 35, second son of the family of 28 Southover High Street killed in action in Normandy 14th August 1944. He had served in the army from 17 years of age in the Royal Scots Greys and was recalled to the colours as a reservist in 1939. He is buried Bonneville-La-Campagne War Cemetery Troarn France. **

Taylor, Flight Sergeant Wireless Operator Air Gunner, 624640, Henry Charles, Royal Air Force 138 Squadron, aged 24, of 7 Cross Way missing after a raid over Germany on 23rd December 1942 in a Halifax based at Tempsford Lincolnshire. He had been employed at Every's Ironworks and was mobilized with the Territorial Royal Garrison Artillery in 1939 and transferred to the RAF in October 1939 and had been on many operational flights over Germany. He left a widow and a son. Sgt Taylor is buried in Staphorst General Cemetery Holland.

Taylor, Gunner, 938125, Ronald Arthur, 68th Medium Regiment Royal Artillery, aged 21, of 73 Highdown Road. Captured at Benghazi Libya 1941. Volunteered in 1939. Died after the ship that was taking him to Italy, as a prisoner, was torpedoed by a British Submarine 14th November 1942. A painter and decorator by trade a former scholar at Pells School and is commemorated on the El Alamein Memorial.

Gnr R A Taylor

Tindale, Cadet, R A (Bruce), Merchant Navy age 18, A County School for Boys' pupil, lost when the MV *Empire Stanley* built in 1942 of 6,900 tons, was torpedoed by *U197* on 17th August 1943 while on a voyage between Lourenco Marques and Aden. He was last seen helping to launch the ship's boats. Of 56 on board, 18 crew members, one passenger and six naval gunners were lost. The vessel was unusual in that it was equipped with a catapult launched Seafire fighter plane which after engagement if not able to reach land ditched in the sea, the pilot and aircraft often being lost. **

Tomley, Sergeant-Pilot, 924204, Maurice John, aged 21, Royal Air Force 201 Squadron, County School for Boys' pupil 1932-8, killed accidentally 31st July 1942 while on patrol in a Coastal Command Hudson from North Coates. A married man before enlistment he worked for Dr Woodhead the County Analyst. His loss is commemorated on the Runnymede Memorial.

Towner, Flying Officer Observer, 119476, Jack, Royal Air Force 150 Squadron, aged 23, of 9 Grange Road killed on active service during a daylight raid on Essen, Germany 31st October 1942 when his Wellington bomber flying from Kirmington Lincolnshire was shot down. A County School boy 1930-5 who had passed his Civil Service entrance examination and was a keen rugby player for Lewes. He is buried in Gerdringen Roman Catholic Cemetery Groningen, Holland.

Truman, (CWGC record spelt **Trueman**) Lance Corporal, Signalman, 4969595, Harry Marshall, 3rd Division Signals Royal Corps of Signals, son-in-law of Mr and Mrs H Windless of *The Forge* Southover reported killed in action 4th June 1940 and is buried in the Canadian War Cemetery Adegem Belgium.

Turner, Flight Sergeant Wireless operator/Air Gunner, 751657, Leslie, Royal Air Force 226 Squadron, aged 21, of 15 Talbot Terrace missing on an operational flight in a Fairey Battle light bomber flying from Faux-Villcerf France 13th June 1940 at Melun 38 miles from Paris. He was a

Pells schooboy who afterwards was employed as a mechanic at J C H Martin's garage at Cliffe Bridge. He is buried in the Communal Cemetery at Chapelle Vallon with his Pilot. *

Unsted Driver, T/166840, Eric, Royal Army Service Corps died 7th January 1943, of St John's Parish, and buried in Brookwood Military Cemetery. *

Wares, Private, 6094013, Richard Albert, 1st/5th Queens Royal West Surrey Regiment, aged 26, of 1 Meridian Road killed in action while serving in Italy on 20th October 1943. Before enlisting he had been employed by the East Sussex County Council and latterly the Southern Railway. His brother was a prisoner of war. Pte Wares is buried in Minturno War Cemetery. *

Way, Stanley William Alfred, Pilot Officer, 116133 RAFVR, aged 21, of 49 Squadron flying Hampden bombers from Scampton Lincolnshire, missing whilst taking part in a bomber action on 12/13th February 1942 against the German battleships *Scharnhorst, Gneisenau and Prinz Eugen* which escaped up the Channel from Brest. He lived at 1 Nevill Crescent and is listed on the memorial as M Way. He was born at Parkhurst IOW where his father was in the prison service, the family moved to Lewes after 1931 when the prison reopened. Stanley attended Western Road School followed by Clark's College Brighton. He joined the Post Office and volunteered for service in 1940. He is commemorated on the Runnymede memorial.

Webb, Guardsman, 2660221, Albert Edward, 3rd Battalion Coldstream Guards, of 5 St. Pancras Gardens died as a prisoner of war 7th June 1941, he is buried at Benghazi Libya. **

Weir, Sergeant Observer, 926306, Hugh, Royal Air Force (Volunteer Reserve), aged 25, married the previous year, of 28 Mountfield Road killed 24th October 1941 when his plane crashed while on an operational flight at Ploughley Upper Heyford. A scholar of Pells and Brighton Grammar Schools. He commenced work as a cost accountant at the Ringmer Building Works. He was a keen sportsman and had been in the service for 18 months. He is buried in Lewes Cemetery. *

Wharmby Flight Lieutenant, 104524, Roy Bernard. Royal Air Force 7 Squadron, Pathfinders, killed with his crew on operations 14th January 1944 over Wilhemshaven flying a Lancaster from Bardeny Lincolnshire, a native of Cheshire married to a Lewesian from Abinger Place. Before enlistment worked for Bibby and Co Feed Merchants in East Sussex. He is buried in Hanover Central War Cemetery. *

Names not inscribed on the War Memorial

Brown Private, 5573415, Arthur George, aged 22, 2nd Battalion Royal Sussex Regiment killed in action 28th October 1942 buried in the El Alamein Cemetery, a native of Bournemouth but with parents as next-of-kin living in Lewes.

Brown Ronald, aged 27, of 7 Friars Walk died on 12th August 1942, he is buried in Lewes Cemetery. Described in the cemetery register as an ex-soldier and is buried in a private grave.

Booth, Private, 6407665, Clifford George Royal Sussex Regiment, aged 28, of 2 Priory Place Flats Priory Street, milk roundsman, died at home of an infectious illness 28th September 1944 and buried in Lewes Cemetery.

Cranmer, Sapper, 207267, Arthur, 211 Field Park Company Royal Engineers, aged 24, of 16 Dale Road missing at Dunkirk between 31st May and 2nd June 1940, he is commemorated on the Dunkirk Memorial.

Funnell, Able Seaman Gunner, James, Merchant Navy, of Dale Road, missing when his ship the MV *Warwickshire Castle* built in 1930 of 20,400 tons was sunk on 12th November 1942. The ship was a trooper and after landing troops in North Africa was returning empty to the United Kingdom when it was torpedoed by U 413 off the coast of Portugal. The U-boat had lain under the convoy and torpedoed the last ship as it passed. He had served for two years and before the war attended the Pells School. His two brothers served in the forces.

Green, Private, 634818, Ronald Hubert, 2nd Battalion The Queen's Own Royal West Kent Regiment, aged 28, of 37 South Way. Six years in the army, four of which were in Malta. Captured in the Dodecanese Islands released as a POW in May 1945. A Lewes County schoolboy, School Captain. Worked for Lewes Motors and Baxter's the Printers before joining the army. Died after illness, buried in Lewes Cemetery 14th March 1946. Husband of Mrs Joan Irene Green of Lewes.

Harvey, Gunner, 11266294, Thomas Frederick, Royal Artillery, aged 25, buried in Lewes Cemetery 7th February 1947 son of Mr and Mrs A Harvey of Lewes.

Potter, Craftsman, 6392193, Samuel, Royal Electrical and Mechanical Engineers, aged 46, buried in St John-sub-Castro Churchyard 6th April 1946.

Roser, Lance Corporal, 2072748, Roger, Royal Engineers, aged 25, 18th December 1943 following an infectious illness, son of Mrs Ethel Roser of Lewes. He is buried in Lewes Cemetery.

Shifner, Major, 14502, Sir Henry Burrows (Bart), OBE 51st Field Regiment Royal Artillery, Coombe Place Offham on active service in the Middle East 22nd November 1941. He is commemorated on the Alamein Memorial.

Wingrove, Able Seaman, PJ/X318946, Robert, Royal Navy, HM Submarine *Thorough*, age 20, recorded in the War Graves Register as buried in Hamsey (St Peter) Churchyard 19th October 1944 son of Mr and Mrs H J Wingrove of Lewes. A/B Wingrove was flown home seriously ill from India and died in Haslar Naval hospital. Before the war he worked in the Maypole Dairy Co Lewes. The Wingrove family came from Wokingham in the mid-thirties and lived at Offham not in Lewes.

War Memorials cannot be taken to be definitive statements of the fatal casualties suffered by the population of the areas in which they are located, the Lewes Memorial is no exception. It is customary to invite the next-of-kin and relatives to submit names for inclusion on a memorial. Depending on the lapse of time between the end of a war and the call for names the response will vary reflecting the movement of families away from the town and on occasion the deaths of the next-of-kin themselves. Those arranging the collection of the names for the Lewes memorial may also have faced difficulties over the criteria to use.

The Lewes Memorial inscriptions are perhaps a model of tact and respect, the names include those killed in action, missing in action believed killed, those lost at sea, those lost in air operations, died of wounds, died of disease, died in captivity or died because of an accident. The names include those who died later as the result of injury received or illness contracted on active service outside the customary dates of the 25th August 1939, the date of mobilisation and the Victory Celebration of 8th June 1946. The names include residents born in Lewes who had enlisted from the town, those who through the war had married into local families, those who worked in the town but who lived elsewhere. Similarly those men born in the town and had moved away, many with relatives still in the town, and those who died in or near the town either through accident or enemy action were included. The memorial includes a section of eight names headed missing believed killed. Three of the eight survived the war, Sergeants Martin and Hall and Private Opie. It is possible that other Lewes men's names may still need to be commemorated. There is one common factor, all those who died gave their lives for their country.

Numerically the sacrifice represents about 10 per cent of those Lewes men and women who enlisted. All the Commonwealth War Grave burials in Lewes cemeteries of the town's servicemen have now been listed in the rolls of honour above. Memorials have been erected in the town's churches, St John's-sub-Castro has a memorial to 35 parishioners who died, one quarter of the total loss of the town, this is to be expected as the parish is the largest. St John the Baptist Southover has on its north wall inscriptions to 22 members of the parish who gave their lives between 1939 and 1945.

County Boys' School Memorial Chapel

The former County School for Boys Chapel is now incorporated with the adjacent Priory School. This is a fine memorial to 55 boys, 14 of whom are known to have come from Lewes, who gave their lives in 1939-45. The inscriptions include those who came to the school from outside the town. The idea for a memorial chapel came to the headmaster Mr N R J Bradshaw as he lay in a hospital bed in 1942. There was land available at the school and once the proposal became known to parents, donations started to come in. It was estimated that the cost would amount to £10,000, by the end of the war £1,292 had been raised. A major fund raising effort in November 1945 produced another £1,750 after that a long hard run of conventional fund raising followed.

In 1953 through the good offices of local organ builders William Hill, Norman and Beard, an organ was obtained from a theological college near Oxford and placed in store. The Education Committee could not help with the building costs of the chapel but could and did meet the cost of refurbishing the organ. There followed a saga of frustration, a suggestion of a shared funded combined assembly hall and chapel came and went. In 1957 through one of the Governors, the aid of Sir Edward Maufe, who had designed the Runnymede RAF Memorial was enlisted to help with a new design. In 1958 a tender of £26,612 was accepted for a building in cast Portland Stone. The bell from the demolished Naval Prison in North Street was obtained from a local builders' yard. Furnishing, hangings, and items of construction were also given. The figure of St George over the west door was carved by Alan Collins. Construction commenced in January 1959 and finished in June 1960, the dedication by the Bishop of Chichester took place on 10th July 1960.

The Head Post Office has a memorial to its employees who were lost. The pavilion at the Stanley Turner Ground records the names of 10 members of the Lewes Rugby Club who fell. One of the club members, Flying Officer A A Green RAF, was a Tooting Bec evacuee schoolboy who lost his life in a flying accident while at the 35th Service Flying Training School at North Battlefield Saskatchewan Canada. A private memorial is inscribed on a child's grave in the Lewes Cemetery recording the loss of a brother, Leading Writer Stanley Johnson RN at sea in HMS *Hood*. St Anne's and Cliffe Churches each contain an individual memorial. A private grave in St John-sub-Castro churchyard of the former Chief Constable, Colonel George Ormerod, had a memorial added to his son Captain George Waring Ormerod, Honourable Artillery Company, killed in Normandy 1944.

Until World War One burial of British war dead was a matter of chance. If battle conditions permitted interment would be undertaken by comrades. Sometimes markers or memorials would be erected. Otherwise it would be done by the local inhabitants. Formal identification of British War dead and the recording of the place of burial was first undertaken by the British Red Cross Society ambulance units on a voluntary basis. Officers of these ambulance units behind the western front in France in 1914 became concerned that men were being buried in the cemeteries of the French Communes close to where they had fallen and little record was being kept. The War Office then asked the Society to act as its agent for war graves' registration until 1917 when the Imperial War Graves Commission was set up to carry out the work, later its Imperial title changed to Commonwealth. The organization is responsible for the care and maintenance of graves in the wake of war, in large military cemeteries and isolated plots in cemeteries throughout the world. It has been a tradition that British servicemen should be buried where they fall, officers and enlisted men together. Repatriation was forbidden after 1915. An exception was made after the Falkland's Campaign.

Those with no known grave are commemorated on memorials. Soldiers are listed throughout the world on memorials close to the battlefields where they fell. Airmen's names are recorded at Runnymede for those lost on operations from England, Malta for the Western Mediterranean, Tunis and El Alamein for North Africa and Singapore for the Far East. The Home Ports of Chatham, Portsmouth, Plymouth, Lee-on-Solent, Liverpool and Lowestoft each has a memorial to men of the Royal Navy lost at sea. The losses from the Merchant Navy are recorded on the memorial at Tower Hill London. In the Sailors' Chapel at Chichester Cathedral a book of remembrance is kept of Sussex men and women lost at sea with no known grave during 1939-45. The beautifully inscribed book was prepared in 1958 for the Chichester Branch of the Royal Naval Association but in common with other memorials is incomplete in not having the names of seven of the lost Lewes seafarers.

The Town Council in October 1941 agreed to set aside a suitable plot in the cemetery for war graves, section F contains 13 graves with the remaining nine graves being located in sections B, J, G and K one of these being in the eastern section. Of the 22 graves, 17 have a stated connection with Lewes, three are burials relating to the victims of ordnance accidents, two of which were men from Derbyshire and three gave no home address but these are identified in the text. Also buried in Lewes Cemetery is a Belgian Martin Paul H------ interred on the 1st May 1942 from Lewes Prison, Michelle Beccafico aged 42 an Italian prisoner of war, a Roman Catholic Chaplain from the Newick Hostel was buried on 1st December 1945. A German war prisoner Hugo Steck from the Billinghurst Hostel was buried on the 3rd March 1946.

The Member of Parliament for Lewes Admiral Tufton Beamish was to lose his youngest son Captain John Otway Hamilton Beamish, Royal Artillery, in Burma in January 1945.

The Commonwealth War Graves Commission, 2 Marlow Road, Maidenhead, Berkshire SL6 7DX, 01628-34221 will provide free of charge details of burials or memorials to the relatives of servicemen wherever they are buried or commemorated. The records are now on a card index to which public access is not granted. The dates of death for inclusion are September 3rd 1939 to December 31st 1947. Death should be due to injury, accident or disease. By 1999 the records were computerised and available on the Internet. It may now be possible to ask about the names of all the war dead who enlisted from or who were residents of Lewes. Spouses take next of kin priority, Lewesians marrying away from the town may not have been included on the memorial.

Until World War Two it was the practice to commemorate the Armistice at the eleventh hour, on the eleventh day of the eleventh month with a period of two minutes' silence, all traffic coming to a standstill and men standing bareheaded to attention in the streets or workplace. Ceremonies of remembrance would be held at memorials, Lewes being no exception. Every's Ironworks hooter would sound the commencement and ending of the period of silence and army trumpeters would sound the Last Post and the Reveille. Throughout the war years 1939-45 a simple ceremony took place at the memorial without the traditional two minutes' silence. After the war from 1946 a National day known as Remembrance Sunday was instituted on the nearest appropriate date in November. A time-honoured tradition of wreath-laying and homage is also observed by the Lewes Bonfire Societies at the Memorial during the annual celebrations of the 5th November.

Unveiling plaques of the dead of World War Two 1st March 1981　　　　　　　　　　*East Sussex News*

****

Bibliography

Action Warning Red, History of The Royal Observer Corps, David Wood, Macdonald & Janes
British Vessels Lost at Sea 1939-45, HMSO 1947, reprinted Patrick Stephens
British Prisoners of War in German Hands, Red Cross List, IWM
The British Army in World War II, Brian L Davis, Greenhill
The Canadian Army, An Official Summary, Col C P Stacey, Kings Printer Ottawa
The Half Million, The Canadians in Britain, Stacey CP and Wilson Barbara R
University of Toronto Press
Designed to Kill, Major Arthur Hogben, Patrick Stephens
The Dieppe Operation, Brigadier General Dennis Wheeler
Formation Badges of World War 2, Howard Cole
Last Ditch, David Lampe, Cassel and Co
Pillboxes, Henry Wills
Sussex Airfields in The Second World War, Robin J Brooks, Countryside Books
Sussex Sappers, Col L F Morling, Christians W J Offord and Son Ltd.

Sources

History of the Lewes Fire Brigade, L Davey, East Sussex Record Office
History of the East Sussex Police Force, RV Kyrke, Sussex Arch Soc
Ringmer in World War Two Albert Jenkins, Lewes Library

The underlisted from the East Sussex Record Office The Maltings Lewes
Dr Graham Mayhew's War Memorial papers

Sussex Police Authority SPA 1 and SPA 2

1/1	Air raid incidents	1/10/7	W Wells air raid diary
2/21	4,5 & 6 Air raid incidents	2/21	7 & 8 Bomb incidents
2/21	9 Flying Bomb incidents	2/21	10/31 Air raids supplementary
2/21	38 Personal injuries training	2/21	39 Misdirected fire
2/21	41 Crashed Aircraft cards	2/21	45 Crashed aircraft files
23	1 Home Office instructions	23	3 Air raid warnings
23	4 Objects dropped from the air	23	6 Photos of bombs and explosives
23	7 War zone courts	23	8 Plans of nodal points
23	9 Southdowns regulations	23	10 Training areas
23	13 Regulated areas		

Home Guard enrolment HGD 4

Borough of Lewes BLE

A3/10	Fin & G P 1935/42	A3/11	Fin & G P 1942/45
A3/12	Fin & G P 1946/49	A3/62	Allotments
A3/24	High & Wks 1934/38	A3/49	High & Wks 1936/46
A370a	High & Wks 1935/42	A370b	High & Wks 1943/46
A3/65	ARP	A/66	Civil Defence
A/76	CD Accounts	A77	Miscellaneous papers
DLB1	Cemetery Registers by dates		

Civil Defence Papers (CD)

8/108/9	ARP Organisation Lewes	9/130/3	Counter invasion measures
10	Civil defence schools	38/1/2	Shelters & strutting
11	Warnings and wardens	12	Fire raids & decontamination
14	Transport	15	65/1 Lewes control
16	176/1 Military liaison	16	176/2 HG Formation
16	176/3 Female auxiliaries	17/18	Counter invasion/War book

Appendix

These pages of air raid shelter details have been transcribed from the Lewes War Book with the contemporary typing layout used. Extra wording has been italicised. Brackets indicates spare places in school shelters.

Part A Shelters

(a) The existing shelter accommodation in use in the Borough is provided in the following classes of shelter :-

     (i) Public Shelters
     (ii) School Shelters
     (iii) B.C.F. Type Concrete Shelters
     (iv) Brick Communal Surface Shelters
     (v) Brick Individual Shelters
     (vi) Strutted Basements
     (vii) Anderson Shelters
     (viii) Private Shelters

Under the Nodal Point Shelter Scheme provision has been made for 100% of the population.
(b) In view of the fact that the existing shelter accommodation caters for the whole of the population, no arrangement has been made for slit trenches or other improvised shelter.

A plan showing the location of the larger shelters accompanies these notes.

The following lists give the addresses and accommodation figures for the different classes of shelters mentioned under (a) above

(i) Public shelters

Bell Lane	Concrete lined	50
Castle Bowling Green	Concrete lined	100
Church Lane	Timber lined	50
Bradford Road	Concrete lined	50
Grange Road	Timber lined	50
Lancaster Street	Steel lined	50
Mount Harry Road (Quadrangle)	Timber lined	24
Nevill Crescent	Concrete lined	50
Pinwell Road (rear of)	Concrete lined	24
Winterbourne Hollow	Concrete lined	50
White Hill	Concrete lined	24
South Street	Timber lined	24
Malling Street	Timber lined	24
Cliffe Corner	Steel lined	50
Ruggs Garage	Basement	75
		total 695

(ii) School shelters

Mountfield Road	Concrete lined	500 (200)
Western Road	do.	132
St. Pancras	do.	132
South Malling	do.	140
St. Annes	do	72 (36)
Pells (1) (2 shelters)	do	100

Pells (2) (3 shelters)	Arched steel	150
Southover (St. James St.)	do	150
Girl's County School	Surface Shelter	350
Boy's County School	Surface and Concrete	
Tubular	550	
	total 2,276	

(iii) B.C.F. Communal Shelters

Road or District	Detail of site	Seating accommodation
Malling	Front of Mill House Mill Road	50
	Top of Mill Road	50
	End of road to Malling Down	50
	Rear of Malling Villas	50
Winterbourne	5 Shelters along boundary fence	250
Garden Street	2 at corner with Priory Street	100
Prince Edwards Road	2 in verge near Ferrers Road	100
Grange Road	On island site Junction St. Pancras Road	50
East Street	In garden South side	50
Union Place	Rear of "Thatch" Public House (2 Shelters)	100
Ferrers Road	At end of	50
Gundreda Road	At end of	50
South Street	At rear of No. 57	50
	At rear of No. 27	50
	At side of Wille Cottages	25
Malling Street	Cliffe Old Rectory	50
	Rear of Nos. 94-96	50
	Rear of No 5 access from Chapel Hill	50
	In Coombe	50
Chapel Hill	On site of demolished house	50
Southdown Avenue	In garden of "Locarno"	50
Houndean Rise	In garden of "Foasdyke"	50
	In access road top end	45
Valence Road	Corner of Leicester Road	50
	Bottom of Guys Road	50
Westgate Street	At rear of Y.M.C.A. garages	50
Paddock Road	At rear of Sports Pavilion	50
New Road	Front of 79	50
The Avenue	Rear of Avenue House (Children's Home)	50
Bradford Road	Rear of "Treetops"	50
Park Road	Rear of Paddock House Prince Edwards Road	50
De Montford Road	4/50 Shelters in Grounds (De Montford Flats)	200
St. Annes Crescent	Rear of County Library	50
St. Peters Place	At end of	50
Juggs Road	At rear of Swan Inn	50
St. Martins Lane	Access through walls	45
Nevill Crescent	2/50 person shelters on the Green	100
Mount Harry Road	On quadrangle	50

Highdown Road	3/50 on Downs at rear	150
	At rear of Church	50
	At side of No. 29	50
	2/50 near shops	100
Firle Crescent	2/50 on Downs at rear	100
East Way	2/50 on Downs at rear	100
South Way	3/50 on Downs at the rear	150
Cross Way	2/50 in Verge	100
Middle Way	In gardens of No 29 (Cul de sac)	50
	total	3,265

Note :- All B.C.F. Shelters are suitable for use under Nodal Point conditions

(iv) BRICK COMMUNAL SURFACE SHELTERS

Road or District	Detail of site	Seating accommodation
South Street	Odeon Car Park	120
	Rear of No.30 (3/12)	36
Cliffe High Street	Harveys Brewery (4/12)	48
	End of Povey's Passage	36
	End of Greens Passage	48
	At rear of No. 19 access off North Court	48
Malling Street	At rear of Jireh Chapel	24
	At rear of Caffyns (in yard)	96
	At rear of Wharf House	96
Morris Road	At end of	48
York Street	At end of	24
North Street	Near Petrol Station	72
Brook Street	In Jubilee recreation Ground	48
Broomans Lane	Through hole in wall	36
Westgate Street	Between Y.M.C.A. Gymnasium and Garages	24
Friars Walk	Rear of Friends' Meeting House	24
Landport Estate	Passageways (Protected)	478
Nevill Estate	Protected passageways	60
Meridian Road	3 Shelters between houses	60
Evelyn Road	7 Shelters between the houses	166
Baxter Road	2 Shelters between the houses	20
Fitzroy Road	2 Shelters between the houses	21
Lee Road	4 Shelters between the houses	53
Landport Road	4 Shelters between the houses	38
Horsfield Road	4 Shelters between the houses	55
Eridge Road	3 Shelters between the houses	27
De La Warr Green	Shelter on Green	36
Arundel Green	Shelter on Green	24
Pellbrook Road	At side of Electricity sub-station	12
	total	1,868

(v) BRICK INDIVIDUAL SURFACE SHELTERS

Vale Road	At rear of Nos. 7-8, 15 & 16, 19 & 20	
		3 x 12

Vale Road	At rear of No. 9, 10, 11 & 12, 13 & 14	4 x 9
	At rear of Of Nos, 17-18	9
	At rear of Nos. 19-20, 23 & 24	2 x 12
	At rear of Nos. 21	6
Stansfield Road	At rear of No. 14	12
	At rear of Nos.6-8	6
Arundel Green	At side of No. 2 Arundel & No. 2 Lee Roads	12
Landport Road	At rear of No. 16 Landport Road and No. 1 Eridge Green	15
	At rear of of No.17	9
Horsfield Road	Ar rear of No. 29	9
Baxter Road	At rear of No.1 Baxter and No. 5 Stansfield Rds	24
Eridge Green	At rear of No. 20	9
Pellbrook Road	At side of No. 5	9
Lee Road	At rear of No. 34, 32 & 1 Evelyn Road	2 x 9
North Street	At rear of Corporation Villas	12
Malling Street	At rear of Dorset Arms (P.H.)	12
		total 240

Note :- All Brick Communal and Individual Surface shelters are suitable for use under Nodal Point conditions.

Persons Index

Adkin Miss -	124	Chiasson Mr J	130
Allwright Rev J	183	Chichester Earl the 8th	191
Appleby Mr A W	29	Christie Mr John	32
		Clements Mrs Anne	143
Baines Mr J H	32	Collins Mr Alan	213
Baker Mr Herbert	108	Collins Miss Kate	152
Baker Lt	41	Cook Mr George	108
Baker S Clr	26	Cooke Lt W E	41
Barsby Mr W	15,16,89	Coote Mr F H	100
Barton Mr P G	35,37	Coote Sgt R B	50
Barwell de B Maj	101	Cosworth Capt C	101
Beamish Ad Tufton	14	Cotter Mr D E	35
Beamish Maj Tufton	180	Courtenay Mr -	35
Beard Maj G B	100	Courthope Sir George	21
Beeforth Mrs A	35	Crisp Ald C D	22,24,25
Bell Bishop	11,213		26,32,37
Bell Mr C	97,128,141		53,62,75
Bennett Mr George	44		83,88,118
Bentley Miss A	35		125,126,159
Bing Mr Rudolf	32		167,177,178
Birch Mr Charles	78		181
Birch Mr & Mrs J S	48		
Bishop L/Cpl	46	**D**algety Mr A W	104,136
Blaker Mrs A S	180	Davies Mr J A	67
Boughey Miss Camilla	129	Day Mr Ken	108
Boughey Sir George	129,185	Demetriades Sir Stephen	138
Boughey Lady	124	Denman Lady	161,163
Bowley Mr H J	35,38	Dicker Clr Hamilton	30
Braddock Maj G	101	Dolden Mr -	35
Bradshaw Mr N R J	40,213	Downey Capt L	102
Brefitt Mr R E	65	Dunk Boy Seaman William	25
Brickell Mr Eric	108	Dunstan Dr W R	22
Brickell Mr Richard	39	Dusart Mr F H	137
Bridgman Mr Kenneth	160	Dwyer Sgt J	182
Bridgman Mr Percy	108		
Briggs Mr R	127	**E**dgerton Lady Rachael	94,125
Bristow Mr B	35	Edwards Col Powell	11,23,101
Broadbent Mr A C	67		102
Buckwell Mrs Annie	144	Emery Mr Harold	180
Burgess Family The	174	Ensell Rev C	11,104
Burgess Mr F	52	Every Mr John	29,164
Burtt Mr G F	84		
Butler Mr C T	88,168	**F**ergusson Major John	66
		Flight Miss E	23
Carter Ch Off George	74,75,77	Fooks Colonel	14
	78	Ford Mr Thomas Edward	143
Carter P Cons John	71	Fowler-Tutt Miss	11,28
Cawston Dr A E	120,122	Frank Mr C	29
Cecil Capt The Hon T	101	Fuller Mr Roy	39
Channon A C Clr	26,67,108	Fuller Warden	137
Cheale Mrs	16	Furmidge Mr Cyril	145
Cheale Mr R P	75		

Galbraith Dr D	120	Johnson Stanley Master	25,58
Gander Miss Edith	149	Johnston W R S	17,20,89
Gard P Cons	70		
Geal Mr W C	102	**K**elly Lt J W	41
Gearing Mr C	108	Kenward Clr	11
Gebbie Mr T H	100	Kenyon Pte Clifford	39
Geering Mr C	75	Kidgell Mr A	100
Geering Mr Elgar	145	King Mrs E	42
Geering Stn Officer G F	62,86	Knight Mr William	142
Geering Mrs M	62,119,124 125	Kraushaar Mr C G	67
Geering LAC T	130	**L**amberth Insp W	71
Geering Mr Wm	82,83,90	Landgridge Mr H	169
Gibson Mr S R	32	Langford Dr L	137
Giles Mr Richard	108	Langhorne Rev H E	25,182,183 185,186
Glass Capt D	101		
Godfrey Mr Walter H	98	Lee Miss (WI)	161
Goode L/Cpl Raymond	107	Lipscombe Miss Molly	149
Green Lt J	41	Lister Mrs M	124
Griffiths Flt/Lt Alan	165	Lusted Miss Joan	159
Griffiths Mr D S	35		
Griffiths Canon E	23,165	**M**ann S Cons	71
Gwynne Col Roland	136	Markham Clr C F	30
		Martin-Cramp Mr Robert	160
Hale Col Churchill	75,137	Martin Mr Jack	179
Hall Mr A R	100	Masson Mr T	104
Hall Sgt F E	159,160,178	Masson Mrs T	124
Hall Ald T E	17,18,19	Masters Mr W W	89
Hapgood Rev John	195	Matthews Rev D G	183
Harmer Mr Jack	108	Mayhew Dr Graham	195
Harmer Mr Gerald	160	Mellers Mr J T	29
Hayler Cpl G L	184	Miller (WRP Cons) John	71
Heavens LAC Ronald	130	Miller Mr Max	127
Heriot Mr M	76,77,100 185	Mills Police Sgt	72
		Mitchell Mr W	102
Higgins Sgt RAF	45	Moorey Mr A W	93
Hills Master Stanley	152	Morris Lt J	74
Hoare Dr E F	142,153	Morris Capt M	30
Holford Mr F	100	Munday WR Cons	72,73
Holman Mrs M	185	Munt Mr Bert	180
Hope Mr Henry	143		
Horrocks Pte P	130	**N**ewling Clr.	30
Hoyle Clr W J	88,100,118 181	Newson Capt R B	19,30
		Noel Pte	51
Hullock P Sgt	71	Norris Police Cons	72
Hullock L/Firewoman	86	North Mr S V	29
Humphreys Mr Edward	144,145	Nugent Dr E	120,144,171
Ingram Mr -	72	**O**ldfield Police Sgt	73
Innes Ald A N	26	Oram Mr Albert	180
Irvine Dr M L	120	Oram Mr Stanley	53
		Ovenden Engineer E	74
James Miss Betty	146	Owen Mr William	108
Janson Capt G	102		
Jennings Driver	159	**P**age Mr -	35

Pallen LAC Henry George	59	Sutton Ald T	26
Palmer Pte C	130	Sutton Major T	13
Palmer Mr Jack	44		
Parsons Mr Stanley	160	Tappenden Mr George	150
Parrish Mr Eric	160	Tappenden G F Clr	30
Pelham Mr W G	101	Temple Miss Beatrice	108,109
Penfold Clr W	30,172,179 180,181,189	Tillstone Mr John	39
		Took Mr Ernie	185
Pennington Clr H	29	Tooth Dr R S	120
Perrot Miss Agnes	130	Trigwell Master John	153
Pett Mr -	35	Turner Mr L A	35
Pike Col E J W	101	Turquand Mrs H J	155,181,185
Piper Mr William Arthur	147		
Pollard Mr Albert	160	Valentine Mr H	35
Ralli Mrs S	138	Waghorne Miss Emma	152
Rawlings Rev K	11,20,23 127	Walker Miss Margaret	147
		Walton Mr H W	165,185
Reading Lady	94	Walton Miss	52
Rees Mr F	104	Webber Mr Bill	108
Reeves Mr Edward	43	Wells S Cons 233 W	52
Rice Dr H	120	Whickham Pte H W	159
Ridley P (WR) Cons	72,137	Whiteman Lt Col B	101
Robinson Mr & Mrs J C	193	Whittington Clr D	30,172
Rodgers Police Cons	71	Whittington Mr Tony	39
Rundle Mr E C	29	Williams Master Paul	193
Russell Brig Gen The Hon A F V	101	Wilson Sqd L H J	45
Russell Mr E C	25,89	Wilson Capt J C	45
		Witcher W E Clr	26,185,186
Sains Mr G C	49,53,83 88,89,91 98,177	Woolard Mr H	75
		Woolmore Clr H C	83
		Worman Lt J	41
Sanderson Sir Frank & Lady	30	Wycherley I	103,104
Sandles Miss H	15		
Sclater Sir Henry	9		
Selby-Bigge Sir Amherst	138		
Shepherd Rev D	11		
Sinclair Dr C G	120,180		
Smith Mr -	35		
Smith Mr L	29		
Smith Mr H Mellard	89		
Smith Mr Tom	108		
Snaith Mr Harold	137		
Stacey Clr Harry	26,186,193		
Stacey Miss N	185		
Stephenson Mr C W	28,168		
Stephenson Lt Cdr	167		
Stevens Mr -	35		
Stewart Lt Col P O	14		
Stoors Dr W	120		
Stripe Mr -	35		
Sturgis Capt J	101		
Styles Capt H W	101,102,104 110,118		
Sudell Mrs -	119		

Subject and Place Index

AA gun sites	64	Chailey	31,32,43
AFS	24,76		46,47,64
Aggression	10,28		79,101,103
Agriculture	161		116,119,140
Aircraft Incidents total	43		147,150
Aircraft incidents British	47	Cinema de Luxe	9,26,30
Halifax Landport	48,49		127
Aircraft Incidents German	46	Cooksbridge	69,101,103
Gotha at the Gallops	44		105,108
Me 109 at Houndean	45,46	Co-operative Society	14,168,194
Aircraft incident US Dakota	49	County Schools	40,41
Airfields, Chailey, Deanland, Friston		Courtain & Warner	154
Kenley and Wilmington	43	Culverwell's	154
Air Raid alerts	45,54		
Air Raid Cliffe & Southover	55	**D**-day	139
Air Raid New Rd & Elm Grove	59	Defences	
Air Raid North St & West St	56-59	Fougasses	114
Air Raid The Wallands	62	Pillboxes	112,113
Air Raid shelters	95-98	Pipemines	114
Air Raid warning system	52	Road blocks	111
Air Training Corps	41,90		
Alfriston	12,137,149	Digging for Victory	32,35,36
Army (Royal Sussex) Cadets	41		40,172
ARP tests	20,23,91	Dornier Raid on Kenley	48
		Dunford's Garage	53
Barcombe	31,46,47	Dutch Children	42
	57,64,74		
	115,116,140	**E**astwood's Cement works	154
	146,166	Election General 1945	180
Battle of Britain	38,45	Election Local 1945	185
Baxters Printers	14	Employment protection	164
Beddingham	47,54,64	Entertainments	123
	101,108,140	Erry & Son	97
	193	Evacuees	17,30
Bevin Boys	160	Evacuees Chailey RDC	31
Bishopstone	47,137,139	Evacuees Glyndebourne	31,32,40
	140		139
Black market	174	Evacuees Haberdashers	33
Blackout infringements	28	Evacuees list of schools	34
Blackout test	22,23	Evacuees Raines School	33
Bombs on Lewes	54	Evacuees Tooting Bec	32,44
Bridges	115	Every's Ironworks	17,53,56
British National School	19,86		82,120,116
British Red Cross	92,124,159		154,164
	189,214British		
Restaurant	164,171	**F**almer	36,46,47
Burchetts Contractors	173,97		101,135,138
Burfoot & Sons	97	Fire action stations	77
Butterfly Bombs	53,63	Fire Brigades	
		Barcombe	74
Canteens' Services	124,125,126	Chailey	74
Carvills Messrs	173	Lewes	75
Casualty Stations	92	Fires Civil Defence Store	86
		E Sx Steam Laundry	75
		Kingston	75

Lewes Outfall Wks	75
Race Stand	75
Fire Service AFS	24,76
Fire Service NFS	78
Emergency water	79,80,81
Fireguard	82,83,84
Trailer pumps	17,37,76
	77
Fire Stations	19,62,78
Firewatching	82
Firewatching & women	85
Firle	31,43,47
	64,68,101
	103,108,133
	135,140,148
	151,152,178
First aid posts	16,88,92
First aid service	92
Food control	27,69
Forward HMS	119
Friendly fire	136
Gas masks	15,16
Gas decontamination	17,93
Girls' Training Corps	41
Glynde	71,101,103
	133,145,146
Glyndebourne	40,108,139
Gotha at the Gallops	44
Halifax at Landport	48,49
Hamsey	31,55,57
	69,79,115
Harveys Brewery	77
Haywards G J Builders	97
Home Guard	
Aux Units	107
C D Platoon	91
Cossacks	104
11th Post Office	105
12th Southdown	105
25th S Rly	105,106
Defence posts	106
Women's Aux	104,108
Hunt Jesse Coal Merch	77
Iford	36,39,46
	47,101,191
Incendiary bombs	21
Invasion German	116
Garrison of Lewes	120
Nodal defence point	118
War Book	119
Isfield	46,47

Jackson's shop	60,61
Jeep in Keere St	128
Kemp B W Builder	97
Kingston	12,19,36
	64,75,94
	101,137,140
	142,191
LDV	100,101,102
Lewes H M S	166,167
Lewes Territorials	156
Royal Art 159th Batt	12,13,158
Royal Engs 210 Fd Coy	12,157
Royal Engs 264 Fd Coy	157
Royal Sussex Regt 5th CP	12,156
Lowdell's & Cooper	64
Martin's Garage	92,154
Media newspapers & radio	175
Memorial Chapel Co Sch	213
Messerschmitt at Houndean	45
Military exercises	138
Military traffic	138
Mitchell's Oilmen	168
Mountfield Road Schools	9,35-38
Muddell C L Builder	97
National Anthems	176
National Savings	38,165
Spitfire Fund	165
War Weapons	165
Warship week	166
Lewes HMS	166,167
Wings for Victory	167
Salute Soldier	167
National Service	155
Newmarket	47,50,136
	138,191
Newhaven explosion	138
Newhaven	13,68,101
	105,115,139
	140,161
Newick	31,64,101,
	103,116,140
North St Fire Stn	19
Observer Corps	9,66.67
Odeon Cinema	9,26,30
	56,127
Offham	54,101,103
	108,116,150
Official Photographs	98
Old British School	19

225

Peace Movement	11,28	Southover House	141
Philcox Bros Builders	97	Southover Manor School	26
Plumpton	40,47,69	Southover Old Rectory	29
	101,116,136	Sports facilities	128
	138,148,149	Spot It competition	24
Plumpton Ag College	136,162	Stanley Turner ground	128,141
Poem Least We Forget	183	Stanmer Village	131,191
Poem Forgotten Fourteenth	184	Street lighting	177
Police Auxiliary Messengers	65		
Records	68	Tank accident Cliffe	144
Defence regulations	68	Teachers	35
Motoring offences	69	Town Plan post war	188
Reinforcements D-day	66	Trenches	17,35
Womens' Auxiliary Police	65		
Post war dilapidations	191	Uneasy Peace return to	194
Clearing the Downs	191		
Firearms amnesty	192	V1 "Doodlebugs"	33,63,64
Prison civil	27	Victoria Hospital	89,92,140
Prison mutiny	73		142-152,186
Prisoners of war	158	Victory Day 1946	185
Prisoner's Tale Sgt F E Hall	159	Victory in Europe	178
		Victory over Japan	181
Radio	175		
Rationing		War Agricultural Exec Ctte	162
Fuel, Food, Sweets,		Wardens Post list	89
Clothing and Furniture	168	War Graves Commission	214,215
Registration National	27	War Memorials	214
Rescue & Repair	93	Weddings	129
Restricted areas	70	Canadian brides	129,130
Ringmer	12,26,40	Wicks P R Builders	97
	47,57,64	Women at war	160
	75,101,103	Women's Institute	161,172
	116,131,133	Women's Land Army	161
	142,152,153	WVS	21,22,33
Ringmer Building Works	97		94,129
Rodmell	31,36,47	Wycherly A R Builders	97
	101,138,140		
	191	Youth Service	39
Roistering servicemen	70,71,72		
St John Ambulance	13,92		
Salvage	173		
Sandbags	21,24,89		
Sandbag accident	143		
School Health & Safety	37		
School shelters	23,35		
School welfare	36		
Seaford	57,101,105		
	107,132,142		
	150		
Services welcome home fund	177,186		
Southease	48,115		
South Heighton	46,47,115		
Southern Railway	29,105,106		
	154		

Military Index-British Army

6th Airborne Div	140
1st Armoured Div	132
38th Welsh Div	132
45th Division	132
46th Division	148
55th West Lancs Div	132,146
1st Army Tank Bde	132
44th Royal Tank Regt	144
43rd Reece Regt	136
59th Reece Regt	149
55th Reece Sqd	150
44th Royal Tank Regt	143
No 1 Commando	134
No 4 Commando	126,130
Argyll and Suth H	132,143
4th Devons	138
8th Devons	132
5th Duke of Cornwalls L I	102
10th & 11th Durham L I	140
Hallamshire Regt	140
2/4 Hampshires	148
23rd Hussars	148
Kings Own YLI	140
4th Lincolnshire Regt	140
2nd Lothian & Border Y	143
5th Manchester Regt	138
8th Middlesex Regt	138
2nd Queens Royal Regt	124,122
2/5 Sherwood Foresters	148
1st/4th South Lancs	39,122,123
	130,132,145
	146
Suffolk Regt	72
1st Tyneside Scottish	140
1/5 Welch Regt	16
4th Welch Regt	150
6th Welch Fusilliers	152
4th Welsh Guards	136
Royal Artillery 87 th Fd Regt	146
94 th Fd Regt	149
96th Fd Reg	137
43rd Div Artillery	137
69th Anti-tank Regt	142
70th Sussex Searchlight	133
338th Searchlight unit	133
450th Searchlight unit	133
46th Heavy AA Bty	133
Royal Corps of Signals	109
53rd Div Engineers	115
RAMC 181st Fd Amb	124,127
81st General Hospital	140
Royal Engineers	108
86th General Hospital	140
185 Coy Military Police	140
50th Pioneers	140
204th Pioneers	140
23rd Kinema section	134
9th Mobile bath unit	134

Canadian Army

1st Can Corps	131
1st Canadian Div	104,123,124
	132
2nd Canadian Div	132,133
Ammn Coy	147
3rd Canadian Div	147
4th Canadian Div	133
1st Can Inf Bde	133
3rd Can Inf Bde	132
4th Armoured Bde	152
RCA 1st Can Field regt	133
2nd Can Field reg	133
3rd Can Field regt	131
3rd Can LAA	49
5th Can LAA	137
8th Can LAA	138,152
Canadian Artillery School	135
Argyle and S H of Canada	137
Black Watch of Canada	133
14th Calgary Tanks	132
Carleton & York Regt	133
Fusilliers Mont Royal	132
Lake Superior Regt	133
North Nova Scotia H	149
Princess Patricia's CLI	134,149
Royal Deuxieme Regt	139
Royal Can Arm Cps	152
RCASC	152
Ryl Winnipeg Rlfs	148
12th Manitoba Dgns	152
Regina Rifles	147
Seaforths of Canada	134,146
South Alberta Regt	150
South Saskatchewan Regt	132,147
Toronto Scottish	138
West Nova Scotia Regt	60,139,146
45th Gen Trans Coy	150
69th Gen Trans Coy	151